Twayne's English Authors Series

Sylvia E. Bowman, *Editor*
INDIANA UNIVERSITY

George Farquhar

TEAS 58

George Farquhar

By ERIC ROTHSTEIN
University of Wisconsin

Twayne Publishers, Inc. :: New York

Library of Congress Catalog Card Number: 67-19355

MANUFACTURED IN THE UNITED STATES OF AMERICA

to my wife
for sentence and solas

Preface

WHILE critics have written graciously and even perceptively about George Farquhar's plays, no one has as yet looked at them all closely. This book does exactly that. It also, for the first time, discusses his non-dramatic work, and indicates the development of his techniques and interests through his comedies, his poems, and his prose. This is originality by default; I can only hope that it encourages further studies. With these goals in mind, I have examined all Farquhar's work, except for a few minor letters and poems, in chapters 2–7. Chapter 1 presents most of the scanty biographical material that has drifted down to us, so as to provide the analyses with program notes of a sort. Chapter 8 tries to bring together the salient points of the analyses, so as to provide a view of the woods as well as of the trees.

For the sake of clarity and balance, I have avoided going into great detail in discussing background material. The book speculates on the dramatic antecedents of Farquhar's characters or plots only when knowledge of such antecedents directly affects a reader's understanding of the plays. Regretfully, I have abandoned the idea of describing at length Farquhar's theater and his stage company. Furthermore, in order to throw Farquhar's achievement into sharp relief, I have at times simplified dramatic history by using terms like "Restoration comedy." The implication that everyone from the blandly amoral Etherege through the humane Vanbrugh fits into the same writers' union, with a single cynical spokesman, is false. Nonetheless, it is true enough from Farquhar's historical perspective to be useful, once one is aware of the rhetorical and intellectual traps of such calculated imprecision. I hope that by the end of the book my intentional sins of omission and simplification will seem justified; for any others, I can only beg indulence.

Although some of the plays and the "Discourse upon Comedy" are at present readily available, Farquhar's complete works have been collected only in a costly limited edition, that of Charles Stonehill (London, 1930). I have used Stonehill's edition throughout my text, unless there is a note to the contrary. I have also accepted the corpus that he presents, with two exceptions: he includes certain letters that Farquhar probably did not write,[1] and he omits two prologues that Farquhar almost certainly did write.[2] For the convenience of the reader, I have inserted references to Stonehill's edition into my text without identifying tags. To avoid confusing volume numbers with act designations, I have adopted the convention of giving page references to Volume I in Roman type and to Volume II in italics. Thus "(*235*)" means "Volume II, p. *235*," and "(V.i, 139)" means "Act V, scene i, p. 139 of Volume I."

Quotations in the text, whatever language they were written in, have been given in English. The only exceptions are some short French phrases and the passages from De la Chapelle's *Les Carosses d'Orléans* (Chapter 4). In this case, reproducing the French text seemed mandatory if the nature of my stylistic comparisons with Farquhar's *Stage-Coach* was to be clear. Unless otherwise indicated, translations are mine.

The Modern Language Association has graciously granted permission to publish as Chapter 3 a revised version of an article that appeared in *PMLA*, LXXIX (1964). Support for my research has come in part through the generosity of the University of Wisconsin Graduate School.

To the staffs of the British Museum and the University of Wisconsin Memorial Library, where I did research for this book, I owe thanks. Miss Patricia Boyce was most helpful with typing the manuscript. For invaluable stylistic suggestions, I am grateful to Miss Karen Rubin; and for editorial advice, to Professor Sylvia Bowman. My greatest debts are to the dedicatee.

ERIC ROTHSTEIN

University of Wisconsin

Contents

Chronology

1677? George Farquhar born in Londonderry, Ireland, son of a clergyman, William [?] Farquhar.

1694–1696 Student, Trinity College, Dublin.

1696–1697 Actor in Smock Alley Theatre, Dublin; driven from the stage through an accident, leaves for London, perhaps with plans for his first comedy, *Love and a Bottle.*

1698 Drury Lane production of *Love and a Bottle* and publication of novella *Adventures of Covent-Garden,* both in December. (*Love and a Bottle* published 1699.)

1699 Drury Lane production, in November, of *The Constant Couple, or A Trip to the Jubilee.* (Published 1700.)

1701 Drury Lane production, in April, and publication, in May, of *Sir Harry Wildair.*

1702 Drury Lane production of *The Inconstant* and *The Twin-Rivals,* in February and December, respectively. Publication at the beginning of the year of *Love and Business,* Farquhar's miscellany of verse and letters, and (March) of *The Inconstant.* (*The Twin-Rivals* published 1703.)

1703 Marriage to Margaret Pemell. Lincoln's-Inn-Fields production of *The Stage-Coach* (published 1704) may have come during the fall season.

1704–1706 Recruiting service in the army, as a lieutenant.

1706 Drury Lane production of *The Recruiting Officer* in April, and publication of that play. Farquhar becomes gravely ill.

1707 Queen's Theatre production of *The Beaux' Stratagem* (March), and publication of that play.
Farquhar's death during the third week in May, burial May 23.

1710 Posthumous publication of Farquhar's heroic poem "Barcellona."

CHAPTER 1

Farquhar: The External Facts

IT has often been said, perhaps truly, that the greatest English playwright, the greatest English novelist, and the greatest English poet of the twentieth century have all been Irishmen. The student of Augustan literature can be amused in a similar vein, particularly if he interests himself in the first generation of writers born in the reign of Charles II. Richard Steele was Dublin-born; William Congreve, Dublin-taught; George Berkeley, Jonathan Swift, and George Farquhar were Irish in birth and education. All five men were Protestants, since Irish Catholics were kept too poor and ignorant to cut much of a figure in cultural life. All five had to go to England in order to swell their reputations and pocketbooks. Steele went on to pass a long political and theatrical career, ending in penurious drunkenness. Congreve became a gentleman, and spent his life in gormandizing leisure. Bishop Berkeley and Dean Swift returned to Ireland as clerical men of letters. And Farquhar, tossed by a fickle public, died young in a poet's garret or its equivalent, like the pale hero of a flushed melodrama, while his greatest success enraptured audiences a half-dozen blocks away. Not very much is known about what happened to him before then, but with some winnowing of unreliable biographers and unsure anecdotes, we may arrive at enough significant facts to illuminate his literary career and accomplishment.

George Farquhar was born in Londonderry, near the northernmost tip of Ireland, in 1677 or 1678. His father William, we are told, was "an Eminent Divine of ye Church of England," who tried to support seven children on £150 a year.[1] Unfortunately, the "Bloodless" Revolution had particularly brutal side-effects in Northern Ireland; and, as a Protestant clergyman, William Farquhar was a special target for the Catholic supporters of James II. He "was plundred and burnt out of all that he had, and not long after dy'd with greif." His adolescent son must have been given a stomachful of war at this time, for young George not only lived through the appalling siege of Londonderry, as I note in Chapter 5; but he also is supposed to have fought in some capacity at the Battle of the Boyne (1690). From these experiences may have come George Farquhar's military fervor and anti-Catholic zeal; or rather, the experiences may have strengthened such feelings, common to a great many middle-class English and Irish Protestants. Popular psychology would no doubt see Farquhar's inheritance from his father as his rebellious predilection for the fleshpots and the stage—never very clearly separated in the minds of many seventeenth-century men—coupled with his habit of looking at all situations morally. How accurate this assessment may be, I do not know.

Farquhar's first tutor was a classicist named Ellis Walker, who was competent enough to have produced a verse translation of Epicurus' *Enchiridion* that went through at least seven editions in the next fifty years. Under Walker's guidance, Farquhar is reputed to have written his first extant poem at the age of ten. The exact mixture of precocity, reëditing, and biographers' gullibility behind this assertion will never be known, but the poem itself is pleasant and sententious:

> The pliant Soul of erring Youth
> Is, like soft Wax, or moisten'd clay,
> Apt to receive all heav'nly Truth,
> Or yield to Tyrant ill the Sway.
> Shun Evil in your early Years,
> And Manhood may to Virtue rise;
> But he who, in his Youth, appears
> A Fool, in Age will ne'er be wise.[2] (357)

With such minor accomplishments in his past, Farquhar entered Trinity College, Dublin, in 1694 as a sizar. That is, he received a small allowance—"size" actually referred to a portion of bread and ale—in return for which he had some small menial duties like cleaning and serving. He may have felt the job humiliating, especially as a reminder of his family's poverty, and he exerted himself to win a fixed scholarship (known as an "exhibition") in the next year.

This burst of academic success was unusual for Farquhar. The heavily classical curriculum of Trinity bored him: "the modes of study in that place being calculated rather for making deep than polite scholars, and Mr. Farquhar being totally averse to serious pursuits, he was reckoned by all his fellow-students one of the dullest young men in the university, and even as a companion he was thought extremely heavy [i.e., tedious] and disagreeable." [3] Their wit was not his; his was not theirs. Two anecdotes, whether they are apocryphal or not, support the college view of Farquhar as a flippant and "disagreeable" young man, as well as a wit. In the one case, Farquhar "sent to a Gentleman to borrow *Burnet's History of the Reformation;* but the Gentleman sent him Word he never lent any Book out of his Chamber; but if he would come there, he should make use of it as long as he pleas'd. A little While after, the Owner of the Book sent to borrow Mr. *Farquhar's* Bellows; he return'd him the Compliment."

The other story concerns an essay assigned Farquhar upon the miracle of Christ's walking on the waters. When he appeared in the examination hall, the essay had not been done, and he offered to mollify his tutor by an extemporary disquisition. After mulling over the subject for a while, he brightly suggested that the miracle might be explained by the proverb "He that is born to be hanged needs fear no drowning." To jest after failure to do the work was bad enough, but to jest impiously before such a grave, pious man as the tutor, Owen Lloyd, was insufferable. At least, so Lloyd is reported to have thought, although Farquhar's antic speech was not, so far as we know, formally punished. It was not until he got into a brawl at a fair that he was suspended from his exhibition, and forced to revert to sizarship.

Farquhar's plays on a number of occasions scorn pedants and pedantry, and one may well believe that this scorn was one conventional stage attitude about which the playwright was quite sincere. He ended his unpleasant college days in 1696, but remained in Dublin to take up the stage, probably not much to the surprise of Owen Lloyd. The theater in Smock Alley was managed by Joseph Ashbury, about whom actors united in praise: "Mr. *Ashbury* was not only the principal *Actor* in his Time, but the best *Teacher* of the Rudiments of that Science in the three Kingdoms. I speak not only from my own Judgment, but that of many others, as Mr.

Wilks, Mr. *Booth*, Mr. *Keene*, &c." [4] Such a testimonial is a strong one. The writer, W. R. Chetwood, was himself an important teacher and a man of the theater (prompter, manager, author) for many years; Theophilus Keene was an actor of some note; and Wilks and Booth were the two leading actors on the London stage for twenty years. Farquhar, then, enjoyed an excellent initiation into the theater, placed as he was in close contact with the members of the company and taught practically and theoretically by a man of great skill. This training shows up in his comedies, which are less literary and more thoroughly conceived in terms of production than those of most of his predecessors and contemporaries.

Not all the talents of Ashbury could make Farquhar a good actor. The highest praise that any of his early biographers give him is that he was "extremely beloved in *Ireland*" and "never met with the least Repulse from the Audience in any of his Performances." This source goes on to say that he "had indeed the Advantage of a very good Person, though his Voice was weak." Another credits him with a "ready memory, proper gesture, and just elocution" as well as good looks, but objects to his weak voice and his being "defective in point of assurance." These evaluations are as charitable as any. A blunter author says that Farquhar "attempted several Parts, but was very unfortunate in performing each of them." [5] But however adequate or inadequate he was, an accident cut short his stage career, probably in early 1697. After Farquhar's debut as Othello, he had been assigned a series of noble-spirited innocent young men; and on the day of the accident, he was playing Guyomar, Montezuma's pure-hearted son in Dryden's *Indian-Emperour*. In Act V, Guyomar duels with, and kills, the Spaniard Vasquez, who has been responsible for the death of Guyomar's brother. Farquhar threw off his lines with as much *brio* as stage fright and a weak voice allowed, crying out to his beloved, who came to help him, "Rather then by thy aid I'le Conquest gain,/ Without defence I poorly will be slain." At this, he assaulted Vasquez, the actor Price, and ran him through, for he had forgotten to use a blunted foil. Despite Price's recovery after some weeks, Farquhar was too affected to continue on the stage, and after a benefit performance generously allowed him by Ashbury, he left for London.

While still in Dublin, Farquhar had made his most valuable friend, the actor Robert Wilks. Some dozen years Farquhar's senior, Wilks was a man of good heart and some good taste; he was also an actor of talents so brilliant, both in comedy and in tragedy, that he was soon at the head of his profession. According to one plausible account, it was he who "advised [Farquhar] to relinquish that Method of Life [i.e., acting], and think of writing for the Stage; he told him at the same time that he would not meet with Encouragement in *Ireland,* adequate to his Merit, and therefore counselled him to go to *London.* . . . By this time Mr. *F[a]rquhar* had prepared the *Drama* of his Comedy, call'd *Love and a Bottle,* which he shewed to Mr. *Wilks,* who approving of it, advised him to set out for *London* before the Tide was too far spent, meaning while he had any Money left to support him; he took his Counsel, and bid him adieu, and the next Day went on board a Ship bound for *West-Chester.*" [6] Wilks was a number of times to prove the man whose counsel, generosity, and talents were to keep Farquhar from disaster. He eventually proved insufficient, but no one could have done more. In the matter of Farquhar's leaving Ireland, I should be inclined to accept the account above, that Wilks had seen a plot sketch of *Love and a Bottle* ("the *Drama* of [the] Comedy") before urging the unproved twenty-year-old boy to risk the expensive rigors of London. Such a story jibes with Farquhar's timidity and Wilks's good sense.

In 1698, near the end of the year, *Love and a Bottle* was produced at Drury Lane with moderate, not rousing, success. Since the pair of summer performances in July, 1712, could be advertised as "Not Acted these Twelve Years," it can hardly have been in great demand despite Farquhar's general popularity; when *Love and a Bottle* reappeared, after another dozen years, it had been "Carefully revis'd." [7] But in the winter of 1698, it won enough favor for a nine-day run, or so an unreliable source tells us.[8] To understand what this means, we must know that Restoration playwrights were not paid like modern ones. "The [modern] dramatist gets a minimum of five percent of the first $5,000 per week, seven and a half percent of the next $2,000 and ten percent of receipts above $7,000. Prominent playwrights may negotiate better terms than these, up to twelve and a half percent." [9] The Restoration playwright was paid with the receipts from the third and sixth nights' performances, and sometimes the ninth. "Six performances in an initial run constituted a success, warming the dramatist's heart and lining his pockets." [10] If *Love and a Bottle* ran for nine nights, Farquhar would surely have made enough money to live decently for a year, and the money from publishing the play would have come as a delightful bonus.

Somewhat earlier in December, 1698, the publishers of *Love and a Bottle* also undertook a pamphlet called *The Adventures of Covent Garden.* No name was on the title page, but it seems certain that Farquhar's should have been. There are several pieces of evidence for such an assumption: "in [Farquhar's] *Love and Business* we find the poem *The Lover's Night* lifted entire from *The Adventures* and reprinted with the addition of six lines. Why should we accuse Farquhar of theft, and particularly why should we brand him for the theft of a piece of such obviously inferior quality? . . . Moreover two lines from the same poem occur in *The Constant Couple* (Act iii, end of sc. 1)." [11] These exact repetitions make the use of incidents from *The Adventures* in *The Constant Couple* into evidence for authorship rather than plagiarism. Finally, the discussion of Collier (see Chapter 3) and the rules of the drama, and the quotation from Guyomar's part in *The Indian-Emperour,* might be expected in Farquhar's work. Less to be expected was the choice of the names "Peregrine" and "Lord C—" for the amorous antagonists: *Love and a Bottle* is respectfully dedicated to Peregrine, Lord Carmarthen, a powerful if incompetent British admiral. Lord Carmarthen would not have been pleased with either of the roles in *The Adventures.* One can suppose that unconscious recollection, or, better, conscious mischievousness urged Farquhar to hint at Carmarthen in an anonymous work while paying solemn respect to him in a signed dedication. Here again is the young man who expounded wittily on Christ's walking on the waters.

However playful Farquhar was, he rapidly became respected at the theater, as is suggested by the circumstance of his discovery of Anne Oldfield, who was a principal ornament of the London stage for many years. While dining at the Mitre Tavern in St. James's Market, owned by Mrs. Oldfield's aunt, Farquhar "heard Miss Nanny reading a play behind the Bar with so proper an Emphasis, and such agreeable Turns suitable to each Character, that he swore the Girl was cut out for the Stage, to which she had before always expressed an inclination." [12] (The play was Beaumont and Fletcher's *The Scornful Lady,* one of those in which Farquhar himself had acted with Ashbury in Dublin, so that he must have had a keen sense of the possible treatments of the lines.) Through his influence, Mrs. Oldfield was given a trial and hired. Such an instance of Farquhar's connoisseurship again provides evidence of his thorough knowledge of the working theater. He was a man who could make recommendations of this sort and expect to have them heeded; who knew the needs and powers of the company, and was alert to improvements; who was a personal friend of the actors, among whom Wilks had by now arrived, and therefore understood what the public responded to and by what means the company could give them what they wanted.

Out of this knowledge came *The Constant Couple,* better known as *The Trip to the Jubilee,* in November, 1699. It was one of the most enthusiastically received plays in the history of English drama. Farquhar later boasted that he had "*brought the Playhouse some fifty Audiences in five Months,*" and an enemy wrote sourly that "never any thing did such wonders." "The *Owl* was never more esteem'd at *Athens* than the *Trip to the Jubilee* was here." [13] One of the actors, Henry Norris, was nicknamed "Jubilee Dicky" to the end of his career; and even the dashing Wilks typed himself by being so masterful as Sir Harry Wildair that "whatever Wilks is acting, . . . the vulgar spectators turn their thoughts upon Sir Harry Wildair." [14] Nor did this popularity soon abate: in 1703, *The Constant Couple* was chosen "For the Entertainment of their Highnesses the Prince and Princess Landgrave of Hesse," and more grimly in 1708 "For the Benefit of the Author's Widow and Children," at least the sixth time since the fall opening of the 1701 season that it had been chosen for a benefit night. At twenty-two, Farquhar had suddenly become the most popular dramatist in London, even an exclusively popular dramatist, because the *Jubilee* craze was such as to prevent the success of possible competitors. The playwright Abel Boyer wrote that his *Achilles* (1700) labored under the difficulty of "being acted at a time when the whole Town was so much, and so justly diverted by the *Trip to the Jubilee*," while John Cory bemoaned the failure of his *Cure for Jealousie* while "we find an Audience crowding to a JUBILEE-FARCE, and Sweating to see DICKY play his Tricks."[15]

Such fame has almost inevitably two results, courtiers and enemies. Provided one trusts neither, both are to the good, particularly if they are impotent. One such enemy was John Oldmixon, a playwright and pamphleteer to whose dramatic opera *The Grove* Farquhar contributed an epilogue. Subsequent events provide some idea of the intensely personal nature of London literary activities at the time. After hoots and whistles from the Drury Lane audience had defoliated *The Grove*, Oldmixon took his next play to the other theater, Lincoln's-Inn-Fields, where he charged that the successful Drury Lane fare was claptrap and *The Trip to the Jubilee* mere farce. This conduct brought him a cheerful rebuke in the form of a new prologue to *The Constant Couple*, delivered on a special end-of-the-season benefit night for Farquhar, and published as an "*Answer* to my very Good Friend, Mr. *Oldmixon;* who, having Two *PLAYS* Damn'd at the Old House, had a Mind to Curry-Favour, to have a Third Damn'd at the New." (That Oldmixon could curry favor at Lincoln's-Inn-Fields merely by denouncing Farquhar stresses the monopoly of audience attention engrossed by *The Constant Couple*.) The "Oldmixon" prologue ironically praised the playwrights for the other house: "To Starve by's *Wit*, is still the *Poet's* due; / But here are Men, whose *Wit*, is Match'd by few; / Their *Wit* both Starves Themselves, and others too" (89). Within a remarkably short time Farquhar himself was to join the great mob of playwrights living on terms of mutual aversion with the London public. But 1700 was the year of gaiety and confidence, Oldmixon's frustrations still an opportunity for laughter. Oldmixon was not amused, and twenty years after Farquhar's death was still referring to him as "modern Writer of Plays, who without Wit, Language, Learning, or Manners, wrote three or four Farces."[16]

Between 1700 and 1703, Farquhar made several forays into kinds of writing other than plays. Although he is remembered as a playwright, perhaps a fifth of his work is non-dramatic; much of that was done in these years. Nearest the stage are various prologues and epilogues which he was invited to write for other people's plays, and for which he must have been paid several pounds apiece. Most of them, like Farquhar's short verse in general, are undistinguished; the prologue to David Crauford's *Courtship A-la-mode* (1700) is interesting because it anticipates Archer's "Song of a Trifle" in *The Beaux' Stratagem* (III. iii, *154–55*):

> Custom makes Actors, Poets keep a pother,
> And Custom starves the one, and damns the other.
> Custom makes Modern Criticks snarle and bite,
> And 'tis a very Evil Custom makes 'em write.
> 'Tis Custom brings the Spark to *Sylvia*'s Lap,
> Custom undresses him, and Custom gives a Clap.

He also contributed some possibly fictitious letters and some verse to two collections, *Familiar and Courtly Letters* (1700) and *Letters of Wit, Politicks, and Morality* (1701). These experiments in non-dramatic prose and verse encouraged him to collect material for his own miscellany, *Love and Business* (1702). Here Farquhar developed his letter-writing by presenting a small epistolary novel, following a courtship from optimistic beginning to eventual bitterness and pain. These letters are written as if they had been part of a genuine correspondence, a pretense also made in *The Adventures of Covent-Garden*, or in *Love and a Bottle*, where Farquhar has the poet Lyrick say that "the Hero in Comedy is always the Poet's Character" (IV. ii, 51). To pretend to rakish experience was good business: "Mr. *Tarquahar* [*sic*] knew how necessary Lewdness was to establish his Reputation, when he expos'd *Roe-buck* in the first Play he writ for his own Character." [17] *Love and Business* also includes some letters supposed to have been written by Farquhar in Holland, one long poem ("On the Death of General Schomberg") and several shorter ones, and an extended piece of literary criticism, "A Discourse upon Comedy."

In these years, there were also three plays, all failures. *Sir Harry Wildair*, the sequel to *The Constant Couple*, was produced at Drury Lane in April, 1701. Neither the mania for *The Constant Couple* nor a superlative cast, again headed by Wilks, did this patchwork comedy much good. After some performances in April and May, it vanished from the repertory for a third of a century. *Sir Harry* was followed the next February by *The Inconstant*, a rewriting of Beaumont and Fletcher's *Wild-Goose Chase*. In this case, the fault for sparse audiences was not Farquhar's, for he improved on the original. With several good parts, including a "gay, splendid, generous, easie, fine young Gentleman" for Wilks, and a clever plot, the prospects seemed auspicious. However, the play was performed shortly before Lent, and at a time when all London was flocking to see French music and dance. Farquhar had a sixth night, but, by his own querulous statement, was left poor: "What can be a greater Compliment to our generous Nation, than to have the Lady [the French dancer Mlle. Subigny] upon her *retour* to *Paris,* boast of their splendid entertainment in *England,* of the complaisance, liberality and good nature of a People, that thronged her House so full, that she had not room to stick a Pin; and left a poor fellow that had the misfortune of being one of themselves, without one farthing, for half a years pains that he had taken for their entertainment" (221). His disappointment must have been very great. The final stroke was the death of William III, with a consequent closing of the theaters for six weeks until the coronation of Queen Anne. *The Inconstant* did not reappear in London during Farquhar's lifetime.

The third successive disaster came with *The Twin-Rivals* in December, 1702. This morality play, designed as an attack upon the vicious blindness to moral truth which many reformers thought characteristic of Restoration comedy, turned out to be not at all what the public wanted to see. They wanted to be moved or amused, not to be scraped with harsh satire. Again, Farquhar had to be content with an empty pocketbook; "*Some of the greatest Persons in* England, *both for Quality and Parts*" (287) may have praised him, but mere praise is notoriously inedible. One of those "*Persons*" probably was William Longueville, who had been a friend of Samuel Butler's, and now was Treasurer of the Inner Temple, one of the Inns of Court, which provided quarters for law students. Since the first love letter in *Love and Business* is headed from another of the Inns of Court, Gray's Inn, Farquhar may at the time have been living among law students, from whom he got the idea of writing a play with a strong legal interest. Longueville certainly gave him advice. Although the best suggestions of these friends evidently could not salvage *The Twin-Rivals,* Farquhar's new sense of the meaning and power of law was to become the mallet with which he created his two last comedies, *The Recruiting Officer* and *The Beaux' Stratagem.* But these reflections would have been cold comfort to a hungry Farquhar.

At this ebb, Farquhar blundered badly. He married. The woman, Margaret Pemell, was a widow with two children and no money of her own to maintain them. Farquhar must have known about the children, but the poverty came as a surprise. "His Wife," says his earliest biographer, "through the Reputation of a great Fortune, trick'd him into Matrimony. This was chiefly the Fault of her Love, which was so violent for him, that she resolv'd to leave nothing untry'd to gain him." [18] A poem published in 1704 supports the authenticity of this account by advising "Bid F—r (tho' bit) to his Consort be just." [19] One hopes for her husband's sake that Margaret Farquhar had qualities worth being "just" to. He is reported to have forgiven her, pleased with her mind and heart if not her fortune; he certainly did not desert her, since he was able at his death to commend to Wilks's care the two children he had by her. On the other hand, his last letter to Wilks, begging attention for his "two helpless Girls," begs nothing for and says nothing of the girls' helpless mother. I would feel hard to put to it to conceive that the Farquhars' married life was not stained by recrimination: George's freedom had been abridged, his responsibilities increased, his money depleted, his expectations of security disappointed at a time when theatrical failures had made his insecurity apparent; worse, his confidence in his own ability to handle himself about town must have been badly damaged, for in the process of congratulating himself on having captured an heiress, he found himself a dupe. A man of twenty-five or twenty-six who could put down his resentment at every sight of the older woman to whom he owed such pain would have to be overpoweringly in love or ironically objective to a degree that strains credulity.

No one is quite sure when Farquhar married; no one is quite sure when he produced his first small attempt to support his new family, in the form of a short farce, *The Stage-Coach.* An early biographer says that Farquhar had been married about a year at the time; and since there is no record of the play's having been performed before January, 1704, it would seem that the marriage must have occurred near the beginning of 1703. However, the prologue to Mrs. Pix's *Different Widows,* published in December, 1703, seems to refer to performances of *The Stage-Coach:*

> Thither [Drury Lane] in Crouds ye flock'd to see, Sir *Harry,*
> Or any Fop dress'd *All-A-Mode de Paris;*
> So 'twas but *Droll,* it never could Miscarry.
> Finding your Palates so much out of tast,
> We [Lincoln's-Inn-Fields] fairly ventur'd for a lucky Cast;
> And *Wit* being grown by Prohibition scarce,
> Regal'd you here too with an *Irish Farce.*
> 'Twas *Farce,* and therefore pleas'd You, for a while
> Our *Teague,* and *Nicodemus* made you smile.[20]

Nicodemus Somebody is the buffonish squire in *The Stage-Coach;* Teague, a generic name for Irishmen, may refer to Macahone; and the passage surely looks as though it refers to Farquhar's having deserted Drury Lane briefly to produce his farce at Lincoln's-Inn-Fields. From this evidence, I would speculate that the Farquhars were married in the spring of 1703, after the failure of *The Twin-Rivals* had made the supposed Pemell fortune especially attractive, and that *The Stage-Coach* was written during the summer of 1703 for production in the fall.

Farquhar wrote *The Stage-Coach* with the help of his friend Peter Motteux, who had written the prologues for *The Inconstant* and *The Twin-Rivals.* It was at Lincoln's-Inn-Fields that Motteux' plays were customarily produced, so that the move to the new house may mean that Motteux did most of the work of translating the French text, Jean De la Chapelle's *Les Carosses d'Orléans,* which Farquhar adapted for their play. Motteux was particularly known as a translator (of Rabelais, as well as of French and Italian plays) and had been living in France when the original De la Chapelle farce was staged in 1681. Whatever the circumstances, Lincoln's-Inn-Fields had a bargain. The claim that *The Stage-Coach* had a run of seventy nights may be true;[21] beyond question it was one of the most popular afterpieces of the time, and continued on the stage as late as 1764. Since one-act playlets could not stand alone on an evening's program, Farquhar and Motteux probably did not make a great deal of money from it. Neither thought it worth publishing with his name on the title page. Nevertheless, it was a small success, and reassuring even if Farquhar did have to undergo the humiliation of producing a play at the "New Theatre" which he had taunted since the time of *The Constant Couple.*

In the meantime, Farquhar took two steps to make money. He joined the army as a Lieutenant of Grenadiers, at a guaranteed salary of £54.15.0 a year, about twice as much as a laborer would make, about the same as a better-paid artisan like a printer.[22] He then proceeded to Ireland, where he arranged to have *The Stage-Coach* printed for the first time. Furthermore, playing on Irish chauvinism, "he proposed publishing his works by subscription; but not meeting with encouragement according to his expectations, he was advised to have a Benefit Play, and to perform a character in it; but being in the army, was obliged to obtain the leave of the Lord Lieutenant (Duke of Ormond) which was not only granted, but the Lord Lieutenant honoured the performance with his presence; the Play was the Constant Couple, in which our author attempted the character of Sir Harry Wildair, but failed greatly in his performance, however he made near 100 l. by his Benefit." For "failed greatly in his performance," another biographer becomes more personal: "he executed the Part so lamely, as an Actor, that his Friends were asham'd for him."[23] But £100, plus the receipts from the printing of *The Stage-Coach,* was a comfortable sum for Margaret Farquhar in London.

Farquhar, ready to assume his military duties, was sent in a recruiting party to the English midlands, while literary ill-wishers wrote verses like "it's nobler in red to make a Campaign/ Than to butcher an innocent Muse." He was a good campaigner in red. His colonel, Lord Orrery, testified that he "behavd himself with great Diligence and was also very Serviceable both in Raising and Recruteing ye sd. Reigmt," that "He was a Person of great Ingenuity."[24] As to the innocent Muse, Farquhar, did not lay martial hands on her until 1705, when he started work on *The Recruiting Officer.* The play was dedicated "To All Friends round The Wrekin," the steep hill outside Shrewsbury, and a number of those friends appeared in it:

Some little Turns of Humour that I met with almost within the Shade of that famous Hill, gave the rise to this Comedy; and People were apprehensive, that, by the Example of some others, I would make the Town merry at the expence of the Country Gentlemen: But they forgot that I was to write a Comedy, not a Libel; and that whilst I held to Nature, no Person of any Character in your Country could suffer by being expos'd. I have drawn the Justice and the Clown in their *Puris Naturalibus;* the one an apprehensive, sturdy, brave Blockhead; and the other a worthy, honest, generous Gentleman, hearty in his Country's Cause, and of as good an Understanding as I could give him, which I must confess is far short of his own. (*41*)

A copy of a letter from an E. Blakeway dated "Shrewsbury July 4, 1765" has been interleaved in the British Museum copy of Giles Jacob's *Poetical Register;* it quotes an old Shrewsbury lady who said she remembered Farquhar on his recruiting party, and goes on to give the "living originals" of the play: "Justice Ballance is Mr Berkley then Deputy Recorder of the Town—one of the other Justices a Mr Hill an inhabitant of Shrewsbury—Mr Worthy is Mr Owen of Rusason on the borders of Shropshire—Captn Plume is Farquhar himself—Brazen unknown.—Melinda is Miss Harnage of Belsadine near the Wrekin.—Sylvia Miss Berkley Daughter of the Recorder above mentioned.—The story I suppose the Poets invention." If these identifications are accurate, they throw one trivial but pleasing sidelight on the banter between Brazen and Balance about "laconic," which may be a teasing reminiscence of Miss Berkley's Christian name, Laconia.

The Recruiting Officer had the overwhelming success that it deserved: Farquhar enjoyed three benefit nights on the 10th, the 15th, and the 20th of April, 1706, and had previously pocketed £16.2.6 for the publishing rights. The popularity of the play made it a central attraction in the theatrical war that began in late 1706, when the finest players of Drury Lane deserted to the rival company to join the three great veterans of the Restoration: Barry, Betterton, and Bracegirdle. All the noted Farquharians were among the fugitives, except for the comedian Estcourt, who had been sensational as Kite in April. On November 30, both theaters played *The Recruiting Officer,* with Wilks, Mills, Cibber, Bullock, "Jubilee Dicky" Norris, and Mrs. Oldfield representing the transplanted production, and Drury Lane countering with "the true Sergeant Kite." Until March 8, 1707, either theater might present the play. Then, *The Beaux' Stratagem* took over at the

Queen's Theatre—the new house of the company that had been at Lincoln's-Inn-Fields—countered perhaps, as on March 17, by *The Recruiting Officer* itself. On March 27, Drury Lane chose *The Recruiting Officer* to attract the public from the Queen's Theatre's *Constant Couple;* on April 17, both theaters again played *The Recruiting Officer.* And the autumn season in 1707, opening October 11, saw the Queen's Theatre doing *The Recruiting Officer* on the 13th, *The Beaux' Stratagem* on the 14th, and *The Constant Couple* on the 20th, while Drury Lane offered *The Recruiting Officer* on the 18th. These impressive facts could no longer make a difference to Farquhar, who was dead.

At some time during the fall or winter of 1706, Farquhar may have sold his lieutenancy. While his prestige had grown, his profits from the spring had been spent. His application to Ormonde, Lord-Lieutenant of Ireland, for financial assistance or a captaincy brought no results. In the meantime, he became ill. Since he seems to have been living in London, a few blocks from what is now Trafalgar Square, he was probably thought too sick to recruit or fight. In this leisure time, he made constant use of his free admission pass to the theater; then, in late November or early December, he stopped coming. "Mr. Farquhar," Colley Cibber related, "was a constant attendant on the Theatre; but Mr. Wilkes [*sic*] having missed him there, for upwards of two months, went to the house where he lodged in York-buildings [on Villiers Street, off the Strand] to enquire for him; and was informed that he had left it, but could not learn where he lived." After some days, Farquhar wrote Wilks that he had moved to St. Martin's Lane, where Wilks found him "in a most miserable situation, lodged in a back garret, and under the greatest agitation of mind." Wilks promptly urged him to write a play. "Write, says Mr. *Farquhar,* starting from his Chair! Is it possible that a Man can write common Sense, who is heartless, and has not one Shilling in his Pocket? Come, come, *George,* replied Mr. *Wilks,* banish Melancholly; draw your *Drama,* and bring it with you to Morrow, for I expect you to dine with me." [25] With this cheerful beginning, he is said to have left Farquhar twenty guineas richer, and, one would think, much heartened.

Six weeks later, at the end of January, 1707, Farquhar received £30 for the right to publish the new play, *The Beaux' Stratagem.*

Everyone has remarked with amazement Farquhar's ability to write so bright and bubbling a play during the grey winter months in a sick bed, perceiving "the Approaches of Death, before he had finished the *second* Act."[26] But his spirits won the audiences of 1707, and have won audiences ever since. Off-duty he was facing death with the same sort of evasive bravado that had marked his college joke about Christ's walking on the waters and that had recurred in some of his prefaces and dedications: "Mr. *Wilks* told Mr. *Farquhar,* that Mrs. *Oldfield* thought he had dealt too freely with the character of Mrs. *Sullen,* in giving her to *Archer* without a proper Divorce, which was not a Security for her Honour. *To salve that,* reply'd the Author, *I'll get a real Divorce—Marry her myself, and give her my Bond she shall be a real Widow in less than a Fortnight.*"[27]

Farquhar had two benefit nights from *The Beaux' Stratagem,* and it may be that some others were arranged for him; there was one on April 29. But by then, benefits could only ease his mind about his family; he was past needing money. "I have often heard him say," one biographer tells us, "that it was more pain to him, in imagining that his family might want a needful support, than the most violent death that might be inflicted upon him." The same piety fills his death-bed letter to Wilks: "Dear Bob,/ I have not any thing to leave thee to perpetuate my Memory, but two helpless Girls; look upon them sometimes, and think of him that was to the last Moment of his Life,/ Thine,/ G. Farquhar."[28] Wilks apprenticed the girls to a mantua-maker (a rather elegant seamstress, such as Wilks's own wife had been); a benefit was arranged for the family, and a small pension paid them; Margaret Farquhar had her late husband's poem "Barcellona" to publish. Nonetheless, during the course of the eighteenth century, the family seems to have guttered out in indigence. But that is another story.

Popular legend had it that Farquhar died on the third night of *The Beaux' Stratagem,* "having broke his Heart."[29] Then, when Farquhar's burial date was published in the mid-eighteenth century as May 3, the third night story proved false, and the death was assigned to the night of his benefit, April 29. Now I fear that this touching piece of hagiography must be disclaimed. The standard modern biographies, including the *Dictionary of National Biography,* have carelessly repeated an erroneous date; in fact, the burial register of St. Martin-in-the-Fields gives the burial date as May 23, 1707, from which we can deduce that Farquhar died between May 18 and May 21. In the register, his name appears as "George Falkwere," and I am inclined to agree with the *Biographia Britannica* that this represents a phonetic spelling.[30] By eighteenth-century standards, then, the name ought to be pronounced so that the first syllable rhymes with "talk" and the second with the first syllable of "Derry." These are the facts about the man. To what extent they reveal the person behind them can only be a guess. For the rest, we may turn to the works themselves.

CHAPTER 2

The Years of Apprenticeship

I Love and a Bottle

ACCORDING to Stonehill, "*Love and a Bottle* is the most interesting play from the point of view of Farquhar's development," because it clearly demonstrates the dramatic conventions within which he worked, his "standardised sentiments," "well-worn stage tools," "stale traditions," even "plagiarisms." (xv). Whether or not one subscribes to this rather elusive reasoning, it is possible to agree that *Love and a Bottle* seems an extremely interesting play. If any evidence were needed to indicate that a very young author, schooled in a popular provincial theater, might well rely on stage conventions in trying to have a successful first play, *Love and a Bottle* would provide that evidence; I think it would also provide evidence for the deftness with which Farquhar could handle those conventions. Farquhar's work, in any genre, almost never lapses below the level of competence, and to this rule his first comedy proves no exception. Furthermore, *Love and a Bottle* expectably anticipates his later plays in structure, in dramatic techniques, and in thematic interests. It offers us at least the beginnings of a kind of dramatic grammar for reading Farquhar's comedies and tracing his development.

The first line of *Love and a Bottle,* spoken by Roebuck, the protagonist, comes from a heroic play, Dryden's *Tyrannic Love.* It maintains a tone that has already been set for the reader, if not for the audience, by Farquhar's dedication to the admiral Lord Carmarthen. The heroic tone is also implicit in Farquhar's choice of a classical epigraph, taken from a serious lament by Ovid, "Vade sed incultus, qualem decet exulis esse" ("But go uncouth, as befits an exile"). Like Ovid, Roebuck is an exile, and for that reason, if one extends the implications of the epigraph, is *incultus.* As he himself points out, his exile and penury have barred him from the heroic role that he otherwise might have played. Society, we are told, is to blame, for it will not value the bold man, as Roebuck tells the crippled soldier: "the merciful Bullet, more kind than thy ungrateful Country, has given thee a Debenter [debenture] in thy broken Leg, from which thou canst draw a more plentiful maintenance than I from all my Limbs in perfection" (I. i, 11). The "ungrateful Country" has gone so far as to disband the standing army (as it in fact had done in the late fall of 1697, about a year before this play), with the result that "the brave Officers . . . must now turn Beggars." At the beginning of the play, then, the parallel between Roebuck's poverty and that of the soldiers seems to grace him with an excuse for his actions. The favorable connotations of military bravery and liberality rest upon him, and society must be blamed for having kept his "generous Soul" too poor to give alms.

This sort of beginning leaves Farquhar really only two possibilities for development. One would be to develop the arraignment of corrupt society. He might follow Wycherley in making an embittered or cynical hero its scourge. But if one is going to damn the social order, one does not dedicate to an admiral. Furthermore, violent satire was antipathetic to Farquhar. After showing Roebuck in some agitation, "*making some turns cross the Stage in disorder*" with bloody thoughts, he brings in Lucinda and Pindress to announce that it is a "delicately fine" summer morning. Here he sets a tone that he quickly amplifies, first, by taking Roebuck out of exile through introducing a friend, Lovewell, and secondly, by suggesting that Lovewell's virtue serves him quite well in this world. From then on, *Love and a Bottle* sustains the mood of summer to the end. Farquhar has chosen the second possibility, not satire but an education toward confidence in things as they are. He has sneered at idealism, we discover, only to convince us of his own objectivity, so that we will believe his idealistic optimism. His course, then, must be to join the hero to society by the end of the play, through validating the possibility of living both decently and happily, a possibility that Roebuck at the beginning has cause to doubt.

Lovewell's appearance offers such assurances through providing live evidence of a Virtuous Young Man who is Roebuck's peer and parallel. And Lovewell's sister Leanthe, we learn, offers "a very Miracle of Beauty and Goodness," or a sensual and spiritual harmony, for the future. Mentioning her in this scene not only contradicts Roebuck's naturalistic assumption that women are virtuous only when they are too ugly to be invited to sin, but also qualifies one's impression of Lucinda, whose modesty has earlier been called into question by her banter and Pindress' comment: "your Ladyship wou'd seem to blush in the Box [at the theater], when the redness of your face proceeded from nothing but the constraint of holding your Laughter. Didn't you chide me for not putting a stronger Lace in your Stays, when you had broke one as strong as a Hempen Cord, with containing a violent Tihee at a smutty Jest in the last Play?" (I. i, 13). After the appearance of Lovewell has modified the early cynicism of the scene, Farquhar reintroduces Lucinda to speak not of bawdry but of "honourable Love."

This gradual reneging the implications of spicy or shocking scenes and attitudes typifies the whole play. To look at Farquhar's procedure in the most unflattering light, *Love and a Bottle* finds him exploiting the sexual naturalism and disillusioned wit of Restoration comedy to delight his audience during the course of the play, while he simultaneously comforts them by advising them that none of these subversive attitudes are to be taken very seriously, since everything will come out all right in the end. Along these lines, Paul E. Parnell has recently written of Colley Cibber's popular *Love's Last Shift* (1696) as a "comedy of equivocation," in which Cibber pleased aristocrats and bourgeois in his audience by pandering to the ideals of both classes. Farquhar, a hungry young man in 1698, had to please the same audience that Cibber had pleased, and he may well have borrowed from Cibber's bag of tricks.[1] The secret salacious consummation at the end of *Love and a Bottle,* all in the name of reforming the rake, certainly resembles that in *Love's Last Shift.* Whatever social conditions made Cibber prosperous also help account for Farquhar's "duplicity" in enjoying what he reprimands. If the equivocation were as pervasive in Farquhar as it is in Cibber, the integrity of his work would be severely damaged: in Cibber, the ambivalent surface tone betokens a deeper ambivalence in thematic treatment. But, as I shall point out, *Love and a Bottle* maintains thematic harmony, however scarred it is by disruptions in tone.

The thematic harmony initiates Farquhar's particular development of at least three matters, Roebuck's moral characterization, the introduction of means of judgment, and the particularization of satire. I should like to discuss each of these in order, since one leads into the next. Roebuck's moral characterization, as a man basically justifiable but *incultus,* has of course already come up, since it is the most important assumption of a plot that hangs on reforming a hero—if unjustifiable, no hero; if not *incultus,* no reform. I have already pointed out how society's failings excuse Roebuck's; Lovewell's attitudes, and even Lucinda's, tend to excuse him too in a similar way, by setting up an environment within which his actions are not unpalatably eccentric. Lucinda's gay bawdry and Lovewell's prior acquaintance with Roebuck's erstwhile mistress, Trudge, are morally more or less equivalent, given the double standard, and they provide a threshold of tolerance, so to speak, for Roebuck.

Another and subtler technique of Farquhar's is his transposition of Roebuck's sexual cynicism into the love plot between Lovewell and Lucinda. The end of the first act finds each of them reviling, not only the other, but also the sex of the other for its captiousness. "Oh Villain! Epitome of thy Sex!" cries Lucinda, while the jilted Lovewell claims that "Women are like their Maidenheads, no sooner found than lost." These echoes of Roebuck's naturalistic assumptions reverberate throughout most of the play in the lovers' unreasonable suspicions of each other. Here Farquhar shows characteristically shrewd management in doing two things at once. The audience accepts the hostility, making the climate of the play safe for Roebuck's cynical notions; but the audience also sees that the hostility arises from misunderstanding rather than from corrupt human nature, and knows that cynicism will be proved wrong. The same sort of double device also appears in the exchange of Roebuck for Lovewell during the courting of Lucinda through the middle of the play: Roebuck seems integrated with the genuine love plot, and thereby raised, while the unnecessary procedure of testing Lucinda's affections points up the folly —at Lovewell's expense—of universal cynicism. In short, through explaining and excusing Roebuck's vagaries, many of the maneuverings of the plot serve to suggest the truth of Leanthe's comment: "I may reclaim him. His follies are weakly founded, upon the Principles of Honour, where the very Foundation helps to undermine the Structure. How charming wou'd Vertue look in him, whose behaviour can add a Grace to the unseemliness of Vice!" (III. i, 39).

Leanthe's comment implies a paradox, namely, that graceful wit, even in the service of vice, displays the native good sense of the witty man, and therefore testifies to the probability of his reform whenever he sees that virtue is more sensible than vice. Here one returns by a new route to the "equivocal" drama mentioned earlier. Despite his idealism, Farquhar would as playwright lay himself open to charges of naïvete if he did not prove that he shared or responded to a "realistic" view of men and women. Moreover, the conventions of Restoration comedy, to which the audience would in large part be responsive, demanded illusionless wit based on the dominance of self-love and love of pleasure. The clear-eyed hero recognizes that men and women are "fallen," and formulates his recognition in skillful manipulation of words and actions. One of the results of the tension between opposed demands is that Roebuck must be both immersed in the affairs of the play, to be reformed, and also stand out from those affairs, as the illusionless man, to comment on them authoritatively.

Farquhar handles the situation beautifully. He satisfies the audience's taste for debunking by letting Roebuck scoff at the "whining Addresses" of conventional courtship:

> *Roeb.* An honourable Mistress! what's that?
>
> *Lov*[*ewell*]. A vertuous Lady, whom you must Love and Court; the surest method of reclaiming you.—As thus.—Those superfluous Pieces you throw away in Wine may be laid out—
>
> *Roeb.* To the Poor?
>
> *Lov.* No, no. In Sweet Powder, Cravats, Garters, Snuff-boxes, Ribbons, Coach-hire, and Chair-hire. Those idle hours which you mispend with lewd sophisticated Wenches, must be dedicated—
>
> *Roeb.* To the Church?
>
> *Lov.* No, To the innocent and charming Conversation of your vertuous Mistress; by which means, the two most exorbitant Debaucheries, Drinking and Whoring will be retrench'd.
>
> *Roeb.* A very fine Retrenchment truly! (II. i, 22)

Roebuck's words put down the artifices of love-making quite properly, just as his actions put down "courtly" jealousy, the foolish testing of Lucinda's honor. But, having ceded to Roebuck this latitude for authoritative sneers, Farquhar can make the limits of cynicism perfectly clear. He jolts Roebuck's and the public's scoffing to a stop with a confutation, as soon as virtuous love seems to be included in the category of the unnatural. The point of the play is that the favored antithesis to artificial conventions, the reality that they smother, is not sensuality but virtue. Virtue is natural.

In talking about the establishment of the natural, I have passed to my second rubric: means of judgment. Here Farquhar's dramaturgy can afford to be perfectly conventional, for Restoration comedy thrives on judgments and can be seen in large part as a complex alignment of sympathies and antipathies. Perhaps *Love and a Bottle* may nudge this alignment toward the Christian, away from the egoistic, by its constant reliance upon religious metaphor. Roebuck, at the very beginning of the play, speaks of the Devil's trying to make him turn soldier (11), jokes about the flesh and the Devil (15) and Providence (16); later there is the courtly transposition of Heaven, Hell, and charity into amorous terms (22, 23), the beaux' worship of the Devil (26), and Rigadoon's comment to Mockmode: "Oh fie, Mr. *Mockmode!* what a rustical expression that is.—Bless me!—you shou'd upon all occasions cry, Dem me. You wou'd be as nauseous to the Ladies, as one of the old Patriarks, if you us'd that obsolete expression." And Mockmode himself is compared to a heathen or Devil by Roebuck (46, 47) and by Lovewell (54). Lovewell, who has called Lucinda an angel (19)—as Roebuck has Leanthe (36)—now (56) elaborates: "I believe her Vertue so sacred that 'tis a piece of Atheism to distrust its Existence. But jealousie in Love, like the Devil in Religion, is still raising doubts which without a firm Faith in what we adore, will certainly damn us." And there are more examples. Whether these references have a primary rhetorical purpose, or whether they preserve the spoor of Farquhar the parson's son, their prominence in the diction leads the audience into a readiness for moral judgment.

Another means of stimulating judgment, perfectly usual in the "wit-comedy" of the Restoration, is the use of contrasted characters. Mockmode and Lyrick not only provide humor but also clarify one's sense of civilized and heroic behavior through their parodies of it. Mockmode is the simpler of these two, since he is merely a version of the standard Restoration fop made rawer and clumsier than usual, as suits this play. He, like Roebuck, begins as an *incultus* immigrant, but he tries to remedy his deficiencies through purely formal exercises in fencing, dancing, swearing, and so forth—borrowed, significantly, from Molière's *Bourgeois Gentilhomme*—while Roebuck has within him the true makings of a gentleman. The distinction corresponds to that between Roebuck's sturdy reliance on experience and the logical university education of Mockmode, which has taught him to "Form the Proposition by Mode and Figure." His elegance feeds only on the rinds of knowledge: he learns music by memorizing the names of the notes, as "*Alamire, Bifabemi, Cesolfa, Delasol, Ela, Effaut, Gesolrent*. I have 'em all by heart already. But I have been plaguily puzzl'd about the Etymology of these Notes; and certainly a Man cannot arrive at any perfection, unless he understands the derivation of the Terms" (II. ii, 26). It follows that their courtships of Lucinda should end in a real marriage for Roebuck (a spiritual and physical match with Leanthe) and the appearance of marriage for Mockmode (a physical mock-match with Trudge). Farquhar has made the parallelism perfectly clear throughout the play, even to the extent of having Roebuck take the name "Mockmode" for some time.

The only important originality in treatment is that Roebuck has not been made the paragon of the "mode" that Mockmode emulates. Most Restoration comic heroes were men of wit and fashion whom the fops try vainly to rival; in *Love and a Bottle,* the relationship is different, and as a result, Farquhar appears to be aspersing Mockmode's ideal as well as laughing at his awkwardness. The eventual values in the play do not glow from the marriage of an individual and a style, as they do in a comedy such as *Way of the World.* In *Love and a Bottle,* style is by-passed, and personal and social virtue justifies itself in terms of morals, not manners. Restoration fops had proved that morals and manners were, at their deepest level, inextricable; Farquhar's Mockmode begins to suggest exactly the opposite.

Lyrick has a somewhat more complex function. On one level, he serves young Farquhar as an engaging profession of modesty and objectivity— "You see, ladies and gentlemen, how well I can make fun of myself. Like you, I have no illusions." In this vein, we are offered Lyrick as the heroic poet who lives by being a prostitute (III. ii). In extending his depreciation of illusions, Farquhar implies that heroism is bombast, and studied style (40) as foolish as Mockmode's posturings and Lovewell's recipe for courtship. This is yet another side of the general attack on the artificial. On a second level, still extending what we have said, Lyrick incorporates a knowledge of artistic convention into the text of the comedy (IV. ii). "The Hero in Comedy," he tells us, "is always the Poet's Character. . . . A Compound of practical Rake, and speculative Gentleman, who always bears off the great Fortune in the Play, and Shams the Beau and 'Squire with a Whore or Chambermaid; and as the Catastrophe of all Tragedies is Death, so the end of Comedies is Marriage." Just so in *Love and a Bottle.* In part this kind of comment keeps anything from being taken too seriously; in part it whets the audience's appetite. In part, too, it is an act of candor by which Farquhar and the audience can be put on the same footing, and, having forestalled objections of conventionality, can accept the comic fable and its moral on their own grounds. One must, in a sense, discard one's objectivity once one has attained it, just as Lyrick and Roebuck, the two characters who stand out from the action and comment on it, must be drawn into it and must submit to it at the end. Lyrick's four appearances fill in, one by one, his complex function. First, there is the self-effacing lack of illusion (III. ii); then the generic consciousness (IV. ii) shading into a new idea of authorship, in which Lyrick manipulates people rather than characters; and finally, the resolution to which he must yield.

Mockmode and Lyrick, with minor characters like Bullfinch (the lecherous landlady), Rigadoon, and Pindress, serve to particularize the satire in the play. Their effect, as Farquhar foresaw, is to shift the satiric burden from society as a whole, where he tactically placed it at the beginning of the play, to their personal foibles. As I have said, the charges of social ingratitude serve largely to launch Roebuck's career with the proper tone, so that he can be shielded from censure of his anti-social gestures. But the movement of the play demands that a supposedly ungrateful and corrupt society be redeemed by the convincing loyalty and virtue of Leanthe. Farquhar cannot afford to stress social defects, therefore, and needs the minor characters to absorb the satiric energy that he has already had to build up. They divert this energy to themselves; they also limit its scope. Bullfinch, Pindress (IV. i, 48–49), and the "*Masques*" (IV. iii, 55) demonstrate the lechery of women, a constant charge of the cynical Roebuck: "This [the park] is the great Empory of Lewdness, as the Change [the Exchange] is of Knavery.— The Merchants cheat the World there, and their Wives gull them here.— I begin to think Whoring Scandalous, 'tis grown so Mechanical" (IV. iii, 55). But they also limit the lechery of women to a certain social class, as is pointed out by neighboring scenes that set the assignations with the masque and with Leanthe in opposition. Similarly, Farquhar has Lyrick take the sting out of the accusations of social ingratitude by repeating them in connection with his own mediocre work. And Mockmode validates society as the fop characteristically does, by forcing the audience to accept social standards as norms by which his obviously ridiculous behavior can be judged as such.

I have discussed the development of *Love and a Bottle* much less as a movement of plot, which seems to me secondary in this play, than as a determination and adjustment of values. Farquhar keeps the plot moving entertainingly enough, not much more but not less either, while he displays a keen sense of craftsmanship in arranging his emotional *mise en scène.* He begins, I think, with one serious miscalculation, in the character of Roebuck. The *incultus* hero is a dramatic possibility, but Farquhar takes him a bit too far. Ward speaks of Roebuck's "brutality";[2] and comments like "Heaven was pleased to lessen my affliction, by taking away the she Brat" (I. i, 16) certainly offend against what we should now consider acceptable taste. Far worse than the bruising of our modern sensibilities, which are scarcely the most significant judges of Farquhar's achievement, is the unsteadiness in the texture of the play that Roebuck's boorishness causes. The man who talks about the "she Brat" cannot be the same man who says, "Begging from a generous Soul that has not to bestow, is more tormenting than Robbery to a Miser in his abundance" (I. i, 12). I have already mentioned this wobbling of tone in connection with "comedy of equivocation." In the ending of the play, however, it becomes more than awkward; it becomes destructive. "Her superiour Vertue awes me into coldness" (V. i, 63) jars at a crucial moment against Roebuck's logic, which turns on money, blasphemy, inconstancy, and the hope of "*Rickets* and *Small-Pox,* which perhaps may carry [the squawling Children] all away" (V. i, 64). Unable to develop a character, and at this point unable to mask the lack of development, Farquhar oscillates between preserving the integrity of Roebuck and that of the play's moral.

Farquhar's resolution of his dramatic distress has points of merit, but does not even so turn out to be a very happy one. He joins sexual attractiveness and virtue in Leanthe, and uses Roebuck's marriage to her as a kind of symbolic argument for his hero's reform. Roebuck, educated through witnessing Lucinda's virtue, certainly accepts his reform through marriage, in going beyond sexual materialism:

> *Roeb.* I'm on the Rack of Pleasure, and must confess all.
> When her soft, melting, white, and yielding Waste,
> Within my pressing Arms was folded fast,
> Our lips were melted down by heat of Love,
> And lay incorporate in liquid kisses,
> Whilst in soft broken sighs, we catch'd each other's Souls.
> (V.iii, 68)

After such proofs, no wonder that he can remark, "She has convinc'd me of the bright Honour of her Sex, and I stand Champion now for the fair Female Cause" (V. iii, 70). Nonetheless, the reader cannot help feeling that Roebuck's new virtue is more glandular than spiritual. Where the benefits of virtue depend on prowess in bed, serious moral conclusions are hard come by. Farquhar ought not to be accused of equivocation in *Love and a Bottle:* however diligently he works at making an appeal as broad as Cibber's, he refuses to do so at the expense of an artistically whole play. But before he could be artistically satisfying as well, he had a considerable way to go.

II The Constant Couple

The Constant Couple shows a marked technical advance for Farquhar. He had had his fill of the rambunctious Roebuck, and looked toward a far more urbane and flexible hero, Sir Harry Wildair. Sir Harry is what the seventeenth-century French called an "honnête homme," a man who excels in a graceful and harmonious *savoir faire:* "He's a Gentleman of most happy Circumstances, born to a plentiful Estate, has had a genteel and easy Education, free from the rigidness of Teachers, and Pedantry of Schools. His florid Constitution [i.e., in the bloom of health] being never ruffled by misfortune, nor stinted in its Pleasures, has render'd him entertaining to others, and easy to himself— Turning all Passion into Gaiety of Humour, by which he chuses rather to rejoice his Friends, than be hated by any; as you shall see" (I. i, 96).[3]

In this play, too, Farquhar demonstrates an economy and speed far beyond that of *Love and a Bottle.* Angelica's virtue, Vizard's hypocrisy, and Lurewell's availability are all indicated in the first couple of minutes by Vizard and the servant; and the relationship between the Hobbesian Vizard and his unpatriotic miserly uncle Smuggler develops very rapidly thereafter. Their names, actions, and fact of kinship conspire to sketch in what they are. Then Standard's entrance picks up, in reverse order and from new points of view, the discussions of mistresses and public life that we have just heard. By the time Sir Harry comes upon the scene, Farquhar has set down a ground plan for the central concerns of the play. The method here differs sharply from that of *Love and a Bottle* in its refusal to isolate the hero and thus to force him into the sort of eccentricity that makes Roebuck so dramatically recalcitrant. Moreover, as an exile, Roebuck must accumulate his society about him as the play moves on; Sir Harry, the "honnête homme," already possesses his. As a result, minor characters can be integrated far better in *The Constant Couple* than they could be in *Love and a Bottle.* They can be tied to the action in many more ways within a full social context than within the brief train of adventures of one man. Sir Harry is the central organizing agent within that full context, more successful an ex-soldier than Standard, more cosmopolitan than the fops, more attractive a lover than his rivals, as we learn shortly after his entrance. But in each of these he is responsible to a scheme of values that he does not himself create. He is the ideal flower of a public system. His introduction makes final the social foundation of the comedy, from which the complexities can proceed.

Not only do the characters in *The Constant Couple* have a common pattern of goals, but also familial relationships in common (including courtship as at least quasi-familial) and analogous dramatic positions. The play is full of inter-connections and analogies, far more finely worked out than the simple Lovewell-Roebuck-Mockmode and Leanthe-Lucinda-Pindress groups in *Love and a Bottle.* On the very simplest level, the characters group themselves about Angelica or Lurewell, with Sir Harry and Vizard bridging the two. Except for Vizard, Angelica's would-be suitor as well as her cousin, Sir Harry is the one man who has a relationship to the Darlings that is not solely familial. The Clinchers are their cousins, and Vizard's uncle Smuggler must be at least a distant relation. Lurewell, on the other hand, has no family —we do not even learn her real name until the very end of the play, and then not very completely, unless we are to assume that her parents christened her "Lurewell Manly," a most unFarquharian combination. She lives in a world of lovers: Sir Harry, Standard, Vizard, Smuggler, and the elder Clincher.

This division of interest between two women, one young and chaste—Angelica Darling is sixteen, and unassailed because unassailable—and the other more mature and more seasoned in passion, had become conventional in Restoration tragedy, in part because of the specific talents of a pair of great actresses, Anne Bracegirdle and Elizabeth Barry. It was nowhere nearly so conventional in Restoration comedy, in which the basic unit of order tended to be the couple rather than the individual, and the basic division that of "gay" and "sober" rather than "chaste" and "passionate."[4] Farquhar's choice of an ordinarily tragic differentiation permits him to arrange his characters in terms that lend themselves to moral judgments. The simple arrangement about two women develops into a setting up of chastity/fidelity/candor against their opposites, and suggests the possibility of thematic resolution in offering the second group, represented by Lurewell, the chance of converting itself into an image of its more moral counterpart, chaste and familial. Farquhar prepares for conversion at the end of the third act (126–28), in which we see Lurewell as a kind of moral scourge, prompted by male perfidy to a surprisingly honorable revenge: "those Men, whose Pretensions I found just and honourable, I fairly dismist by letting them know my firm Resolutions never to marry. But those Villains that wou'd attempt my Honour, I've seldom fail'd to manage."

As a "person," Lurewell admits of some complexity, since she mixes the type of the vengeful woman, imported into comedy by Etherege (Loveit in *The Man of Mode*) and Congreve (Lady Touchwood in *The Double Dealer*), with enough wit to lighten the tone and enough virtue to erase all condemnation. But as an agent of rewards and punishments she is not complex. She merely remains a perfect impostor until the end of the play. In this capacity, she functions, we have seen, as a constant thematic antithesis to Angelica Darling. The opposition between the two comes up with Vizard's mentioning them at the beginning of the play ("[Lurewell's] Beauty is sufficient Cure for *Angelica's* Scorn") and provides a measure of Sir Harry's wrongheadedness in his profligacy. Despite his free and worldly ways, Sir Harry is to some extent bound to Lurewell, for whom he has gone so far as to duel in Paris, and thus thematically bound to Vizard. He accepts Vizard's implicit equation between Lurewell, seen physically, and Angelica. The equation can even be expressed through parodying Sir Harry's own description of Lurewell (I. i, 97–99). Within these carnal and materialistic terms, he imagines an Angelica who can marshal only a hypocritic virtue, who can eventually be bribed into submission.

Lurewell's thematic importance embraces other characters, too. If Vizard is one sort of extension of her duplicity, Smuggler and Clincher are clearly variants. All three are temperamentally masqueraders, suitors for her favor on the thematic level as well as personally. Their physical disguises, as Smuggler says, are symbolic: "You little Rogue, why I'm disguis'd as I am, our Sanctity is all outside, all Hypocrisy" (II. iv, 112). Lurewell then amplifies the masquerade of each in appropriate terms, Smuggler as a woman, Clincher as a porter, and Vizard as a frank villain. In so doing, she enforces upon each a delightful piece of poetic justice. Smuggler, the avaricious man, aged but lustful, puffed with his own dignity, must be sent off to Newgate on the charge of petty larceny, having been stripped of both his virility and his grave reputation. The ex-apprentice Clincher loses the clothes that are his only credentials of gentility, and must be imprisoned for having done away with his lower-class alter ego. And the juggler of masks and darkness, Vizard, finds himself trapped by both as he speaks in the dark—literally and figuratively—masked in a seducer's candor, about the high hopes that he is in fact destroying. To say that Lurewell ruins these men is to say that they symbolically ruin themselves. Their thematic analogy with her comes to its logical conclusion.

Lurewell's other suitor, Standard, represents part of her as a "person" rather than as a principle. Her seeming perfidy merely reflects his, as her eventual return to ingenuousness reflects his. And with him, as with her, the mask of perfidy has hidden genuine virtue, since only final obedience and amorous constancy have restrained Standard from marrying Miss Manly / Lurewell. This sort of parallelism, to establish certain points rather than to provide a central thematic polarity, came up in a reasonably developed form in *Love and a Bottle*. Roebuck's successive assignations with the "*Masque*" and with Leanthe/Lucinda showed Farquhar quite capable of using juxtaposition and analogy for his own ends. *The Constant Couple* employs this device for a number of purposes. One is to comment upon Sir Harry, and without really attacking him and thus staining his image, to hint that his conduct may be less than admirable.

We may look, for instance, at II. i through II. iv. Sir Harry (II. ii) offers Angelica, whom he fancies a prostitute, twenty guineas to sleep with him ("a Nest of the prettiest Goldfinches that ever chirpt in a Cage; twenty young ones, I assure you Madam"). The next scene shows Sir Harry as Lurewell's partner in duping Standard, an action that ties him to an unpleasant hypocrisy, while he professes his allegiance to superficialities: nothing, he says, could "move his Gall" but "the Resurrection of my Father to disinherit me, or an Act of Parliament against Wenching. A man of eight thousand Pound *per Annum* to be vext!" (II. iii, 108). The comment about wenching obviously continues what Angelica has just rebuked in II. ii, and that about money echoes the pretensions of the elder Clincher in II. i:

Clin. jun. I thought, Brother, you ow'd so much to the Memory of my Father, as to wear Mourning for his Death.

Clin. sen. Why so I do Fool, I wear this because I have the Estate, and you wear that, because you have not the Estate. You have cause to mourn indeed, Brother. Well Brother, I'm glad to see you, fare you well. [*Going.*

Clin. jun. Stay, stay Brother, where are you going?

Clin. sen. How natural 'tis for a Country Booby to ask impertinent Questions. Harkee Sir, is not my Father dead?

Clin. jun. Ay, ay, to my sorrow.

Clin. sen. No matter for that, he is dead, and am I not a young powder'd extravagant English Heir?

Clin. jun. Very right Sir.

Clin. sen. Why then Sir, you may be sure that I am going to the *Jubilee,* Sir.

Furthermore, Sir Harry's financial attentions to Angelica are presently taken up by Smuggler, who decides to pay Lurewell through the "*Buss and Guinea*" method (II. iv, 112).

If Sir Harry is no Clincher or Smuggler, he is no flawless rake of Restoration comedy, either. He stands liable to censure, at least implicit censure; and therefore parallel scenes serve not only, as they often do in Restoration comedy, to set off his excellencies by contrast, but also to permit his being encompassed in a moral framework. Of course, Farquhar uses parallels as foils for his hero, too. Sir Harry's swearing by Jove (e.g., II. ii, 106; II. iii, 110) makes sense in terms of power, supremacy, and manliness that are only underlined by the incongruity of having the younger Clincher mouth his overused oath, "*O Jupiter Ammon!*" The moral technique, however, seems more striking, for it indicates Farquhar's departure from the standards of Restoration wit-comedy and its admiringly displayed heroes.

Another use that Farquhar makes of parallelism illuminates a different sort of virile heroism, that of the duel. As at the beginning and end of *Love and a Bottle,* the idea of dueling is bruited inconclusively in *The Constant Couple.* Both plays bring the matter up because love and honor, in late seventeenth-century comedy as in tragedy, become paramount concerns in judging characters. The duel, as the urban version of war, offers honor its best chance of displaying itself. But the duel itself may darken the tone of comedy too much, and for Sir Harry to get involved in one might well mar his insouciance. Farquhar handles the situation by telling us about Sir Harry's bravery in a previous duel and in battle, so that his pacific calm seems good sense, not cowardice. Sir Harry is also allowed to cudgel the odious Smuggler and to throw snuff into his eyes, remarking, "How pleasant is resenting an Injury without Passion: 'Tis the Beauty of Revenge" (II. v, 116). This easy manner contrasts with Standard's in the next scene (III. i), where the cry is all for private revenge, and still further contrasts with Clincher's "design to shoot seven *Italians* a Week" in amorous quarrels: "the *Italian* grows sawcy, and I give him an *English* douse of the Face. I can Box, Sir, Box tightly, I was a Prentice, Sir,—but then, Sir, he whips out his *Stilletto,* and I whips out my *Bull-Dog*—slaps him through, trips down Stairs, turns the corner" and so on (III. i, 118). The parallel makes Standard's untoward fervor silly. If someone has missed the point here, Farquhar makes it again in IV. i where Standard's honor and Clincher's are both subdued, Standard's by reason and Clincher's by the mob (unreason). The audience is left with the impression that such pretenses to honor are "Murder and Robbery." Through Sir Harry's nonchalance, the heroic is debunked, and eventually replaced by rational virtue of a sort.

We have discussed, in terms of imposture, the thematic parallelism between Vizard's imprisonment in the closet (IV. ii) and the elder Clincher's arrest (IV. i), as well as the younger Clincher's legalism about his inheritance. Now, in the light of what has been said about the duel, we can expand this parallelism in terms of apprehending and convicting the would-be heroic. The Clinchers aspire to the heights of rakishness, Errand is a self-styled killer, and Vizard is a comic version of the Hobbesian "Statesman" common in heroic drama. "He talks as prophanely, as an Actor possess'd with a Poet," exclaims Uncle Smuggler, as Vizard spouts self-interest in high language: "Our hungry appetites, like the wild Beasts of Prey, now scour abroad, to gorge their craving Maws; the pleasure of Hypocrisie, like a chain'd Lyon, once broke loose, wildly indulges its new Freedom, ranging through all unbounded Joys" (IV. ii, 135). The exotic simile, and the pseudo-philosophical argument from "nature" implicit in the animal imagery, come directly from the grand villains of Restoration tragedy.

Yet Vizard has cast himself in the wrong play. His one chance of glory comes when the Darlings demand his blood from Sir Harry (V. i), but the gambit is declined in favor of marriage. Indeed, Sir Harry can hardly engage in the heroics that he has spent much of the scene mocking, as he accuses the Darlings of posing as characters from Nathaniel Lee's raging tragedy *The Rival Queens.* And he is in some part right in mocking their zeal—after all, has Lurewell's fall into misanthropy not been the result of taking La Calprenède's romance *Cassandra* too seriously (III. iv, 126) and thereby leaving herself exposed to disillusionment? The Darlings' proper indignation must be tempered by Sir Harry's reason, and the scene works through our pleasure at both Sir Harry's anticipated discomfiture and his present coolness before the haughty Angelica.[5] If her virtue is all the more marked by our observing the readiness with which her footmen grovel for Sir Harry's bribe, it is all the more undercut by our observing the limits of its efficacy. Romantic fancies wither in this world. Given that recognition, one realizes that the contemptuous dismissal of Vizard, who does not even get the chance of appearing at the end so that he might flounce off in style, is the only appropriate punishment for him. He must fail in making real his image of his own powers and importance on every level.

Many of the themes which have been discussed come together in the title of the play. Presumably the irony of the title was obvious to Farquhar's audience: Lurewell/Manly and Colonel Standard remain absolutely constant, like the ardent couples of *Cassandra,* but remain so through inconstancy and exploded heroisms. The curious compromise of feeling, or tempering of feeling, that results from reflection upon the title is perfectly characteristic of the kind of feeling generated by the comedy as a whole in both love plots.

The subtitle, *The Trip to the Jubilee,* caught the public fancy because it was topical and it recalled the most farcical parts of the play. However, Farquhar says in his Preface to the Reader, "*A great many quarrel at the* Trip to the Jubilee *for a* Misnomer," so that the complete relevance of that title may not have been very clear. To understand what it means, one must know that it refers to the Papal Jubilee of 1700, which was officially announced in *The London Gazette* in June, 1699, confirming rumors of its coming.[6] The London papers publicized it frequently, with "reports of the unprecedented numbers of persons who . . . travelled to Rome," so great a number that one paper claimed "that near Two

Hundred People were squeezed to Death" by the throng on opening day. The Jubilee would have been a plausible place for a would-be beau to display himself for idolators of fads and fashions.

So far it might be, as Dicky says, "the same thing with our *Lord-Mayors* Day in the City; there will be *Pageants,* and *Squibs,* and *Rary Shows,* and all that, Sir" (II. i, 105). But to Protestant England, the Papal Jubilee had other overtones. The younger Clincher is, briefly, horrified at his brother's exposing himself to the Pope, and the context in which he puts the Jubilee after he decides to go there ("I'll Court, and Swear, and Rant, and Rake, and go to the Jubilee with the best of them.") gives some sense of the English attitude toward the affair. Anti-Catholicism was compounded by the knowledge that at the Jubilee, "According to the Corrupt usage of the Church of *Rome,* are Solemn Indulgencies grated by the Pope, to all of his Communion." [7] The newspapers at the time mocked the selling of indulgences, as did songs such as this:

> Come Beaus, Virtuoso's, rich Heirs and Musicians
> Away, and in Troops to the *Jubile* jog;
> Leave Discord and Death, to the College Physicians,
> Let the Vig'rous whore on, and the impotent Flog:
> Already Rome opens her Arms to receive ye,
> And ev'ry Transgression her Lord will forgive ye.[8]

The song goes on for a half-dozen more stanzas, about the dotage on appearances, the sleaziness of relics and pardons, and the venal immorality at "old *Babylon.*"

The relation of much of this to the themes of *The Constant Couple* hardly needs belaboring. The Clinchers, Smuggler, Vizard—all might find congenial ground in a society that deifies appearances, lust, and money, and that suspends justice for the greater comfort and encouragement of the sinner. In other words, the whole play concerns trips to the Jubilee. Even Sir Harry makes his trip: his interest in Lurewell, which we must remember is made a counterpart of his interest in Angelica, has caused him to postpone "the Tour of *Italy*" specifically, and he declares that he "had rather see her *Ruell* than the Palace of *Lewis le Grand:* There's more Glory in her Smile, than in the *Jubilee at Rome;* and I would rather kiss her Hand than the *Pope's Toe*" (I. i, 97). Lurewell is an intriguing experience, to be played with, slept with, paid in gifts and flattery, and no more. Sir Harry assumes the same ends, and the same impudent impunity, with Angelica. However, all the characters find Farquhar less indulgent than Pope Innocent XII. Beginning with Standard and Lurewell, who make good their act of a dozen years before, everyone comes to the bar of accounting by the end. Here is a further ramification of the anti-romantic attitude that was discussed earlier. The romance conventions of the *rapprochement* between the separated constant couple, and even the general triumph of virtue, work as agents of realism in this new context. They are the final proof that illusions of power and freedom are likely to be found false, and that living by one's daydreams turns out to be costly.

As Sir Harry's reference to "*Lewis le Grand*" may suggest, the implications of Italian Popery are augmented by anti-French feelings. Smuggler, the religious hypocrite whose venality extends so far that gold seems part of his body (II. iv, 112), first appears in the play as an importer of contraband French wines. Later, when Sir Harry thinks Lady Darling a bawd, he naturally begins dealings with her in French (V. i, 142). This is hardly surprising since French countesses are willing to sell themselves to him at twenty-five guineas a pair "and *Je vous remercie* into the Bargain" (III. ii, 121). In short, France stands for corruption:

Viz. Why, in the City end o' th' Town we're playing the Knave to get Estates.
Stand. And in the Court end playing the Fool in spending 'em.
Wild. Just so in *Paris;* I'm glad that we're grown so modish.
Viz. We are all so reform'd, that Gallantry is taken for Vice.
Stand. And Hypocrisy for Religion.
Wild. *Alamode de Paris.* Agen. (I. i, 96)

Much of Sir Harry's foppishness and Lurewell's deceit are linked with France—Angelica is, one suspects, safely insular—while Standard's military bravery has been exercised in wars against the French. His candor and Sir Harry's frankness are expressed in downright English, as we are told, but the *double-entendres* that deceive the cudgeled Smuggler depend upon French.

I draw attention to Farquhar's use of France only in part to explicate the text, certainly not to admire any particular skill or originality in the play. There are two other reasons for mentioning it. The first is that we can learn something about Farquhar's audience: strong anti-French anti-Catholic feeling tended to be more common among the middle class than among the aristocracy that had supported the Restoration theater. The second is that Farquhar's technique of getting the audience firmly on his side through appeals to their pet prejudices, a kind of self-protection, becomes a standard part of his rhetorical arsenal. He mines opposition to the French in *Sir Harry Wildair, The Recruiting Officer,* and *The Beaux' Stratagem* as well as *The Constant Couple,* manipulating tone and satiric accusation alike through topical reference.

Because Farquhar does not have to make excuses for Sir Harry, who is less central and less unreined than Roebuck, the structure of this play differs markedly from that of *Love and a Bottle.* The problems of equivocation, of establishing means of judgment, and of attempting to supply a rudder for the tone hardly harass *The Constant Couple.* (There are slips: Sir Harry's "how wou'd that Modesty adorn Virtue, when it makes even Vice look so charming" [II. ii, 106] is painfully inept.) With a protagonist who can be criticized without being destroyed, the moral resolution works smoothly; with a much surer hand keeping the stage full and the action moving, less must be predicated on episodic injections of half-relevant but racy or silly scenes. *The Constant Couple,* in other words, builds spectacularly upon *Love and a Bottle,* scrapping some things, preserving and altering many more. It marks Farquhar's dramatic coming-of-age.

III Sir Harry Wildair

Sir Harry Wildair tried to capitalize on the popularity of *The Constant Couple.* It succeeded only in boring its audience and its readers. These two facts are intimately connected. In *Sir Harry Wildair,* Farquhar took those elements that had amused the public so long and so profitably, and expanded upon them without paying enough attention to the formal development of his play. Popular characters were doled out to a public presumably slavering for a new sight of their favorites: Standard in the first act, along with Parley and Dicky; Lurewell, heralded by chambermaids, in the second; then Sir Harry, heralded by a scattering of defeated gamblers; in the third act, Clincher. The missing characters are assiduously replaced, one by one, Vizard by the French Marquis; and the entertainment value of young Clincher and Smuggler by Beau Banter and Fireball. But young Clincher and Smuggler are also relevant to plot and theme while neither Banter nor Fireball is needed for more than local amusement, suggesting the carelessness with which *Sir Harry Wildair* is written. Even the older Clincher, now a politician, serves only a marginal purpose in the development of the play. As for the other characters, Farquhar had to try to include them although their real *raison d'être* had been lost with the skillful resolution of *The Constant Couple.* That resolution left the more peripheral Standard, Dicky, and Parley unchanged and they could pass easily into this comedy. Lurewell and Wildair, however, posed problems.

In both plays, Sir Harry follows the same pattern, from profligacy to reform. Handling him thus in the later comedy makes any sense of progress, of dialectic, almost meaningless in the earlier; yet to keep him from seeming too callous in *Sir Harry Wildair,* Farquhar had to have him indicate his tender feelings about the Angelica whose life seems to have had so little real effect upon his. The result is mildly schizophrenic. Moreover, to an audience who had seen *The Constant Couple*—and that is the very audience that Farquhar plays for—Sir Harry's manner must have become rather trite. The same problems, worsened, afflict the revived Lurewell. Comparisons between the two comedies again are invited and are damning. Lurewell's complexity, her passion of revenge with its comic and quasi-tragic potentialities, has been lost. Her climactic change is voided. She is merely a fashionable stereotyped lady; and again Farquhar is in difficulty, for the very conformity that must surround a lady of fashion denies the new Lurewell her individuality, and drives her farther from the commanding person of *The Constant Couple.*

The main thematic grouping of *Sir Harry Wildair,* France/frivolity/fashion/infidelity, comes from *The Constant Couple.* Here, like a bladder in thin air, it has swelled to fill the whole five-act comedy. Sir Harry's final comment to the Marquis sums up the matter: "Go thy ways for a true Pattern of the Vanity, Impertinence, Subtlety, and Ostentation of thy Country.— Look ye, Captain, give me thy hand; once I was a Friend to *France;* but henceforth I promise to sacrifice my Fashions, Coaches, Wigs, and Vanity, to Horses, Arms, and Equipage, and serve my King in *propria persona,* to promote a vigorous War, if there be occasion" (V. vi, 209). Infidelity ties in with this bill of complaint in any number of places, including Sir Harry's brazen comment to the Lord: "Can't we live together like good Neighbours and Christians, as they do in *France?* I lend you my Coach, I borrow yours; you Dine with me, I Sup with you; I lie with your Wife, and you lie with mine" (V. iv, 204).

Aside from its appeal to popular politics, this thematic grouping justifies itself only sporadically and spottily. Most of the time it remains too inflexible and too obvious to provide the kind of subtlety that one finds in the mingling of themes in *The Constant Couple.* On occasion, Farquhar exploits it well, as in these *double-entendres* between Parley and Standard:

> *Par.* Sir, I was running to Madamoiselle *Furbelo,* the French Milliner, for a new Burgundy for my Lady's Head.
>
> *Stand.* No, Child, you're employ'd about an old fashion'd Garniture for your Master's Head, if I mistake not your Errand.
>
> *Par.* Oh, Sir! there's the prettiest fashion lately come over! so airy, so *French,* and all that!— The Pinners are double ruffled with twelve pleats of a side, and open all from the Face; the Hair is frizl'd all up round the Head, and stands as stiff as a bodkin. Then the Favourites hang loose upon the temples, with a languishing lock in the middle. Then the Caul is extremely wide, and over all is a Cor'net rais'd very high, and all the Lappets behind. —I must fetch it presently. (I. i, 168)

The passage is not only funny, especially if Parley makes illustrative gestures as she talks, but also functional in tying French, fashions, and adultery together. Here, near the beginning of the comedy, Farquhar has subtly empowered himself to develop the formal groupings upon which the structure of the play depends. He does so disappointingly, contenting himself most of the time with direct statement, abandoning the juxtapositions and visual metaphors which had so finely guided the progress of *The Constant Couple.* The success of that play leads the reader to expectations that *Sir Harry Wildair* thwarts.

On another and far more impressive level is Farquhar's handling of a second theme that *Sir Harry Wildair* adopts, the mock-heroic. Sir Harry, after winning at cards, starts on the proper depreciatory note with a series of high-flown gallantries (II. ii, 181) which concludes "This Luck is the most Rhetorical thing in Nature." Within the context of our induced awareness of rhetoric, Standard and Fireball in the next scene, III. i, become impossible to take seriously as they plot bloody disaster to the beaux; they are also diminished by the appearance of Beau Clincher, whose unworthiness makes their furor seem inane. After these two successive scenes, III. ii poses the "florid and genteel Style" of a hundred pounds against the vapidities of unassisted language. Together Lurewell and Sir Harry mock the muse (189):

Lur. Ay, methinks I see the mournful *Melpomene* with her Handkerchief at her Eye, her Heart full of Fire, her Eyes full of Water, her Head full of Madness, and her Mouth full of Nonsense— Oh! hang it.
Wild. Ay, Madam. Then the doleful Ditties, piteous Plaints, the Daggers, the Poysons!—
Lur. Oh the Vapours!

. . . .

Wild. Oh, Madam, the most unnatural thing in the World; as fulsome as a Sack-Posset, [*Pulling her towards the Door.*] ungenteel as a Wedding-Ring, and as impudent as the naked Statue was in the Park. [*Pulls her again.*
Lur. Ay, Sir *Harry;* I hate Love that's impudent. These Poets dress it up so in their Tragedies, that no modest Woman can bear it. Your way is much the more tolerable, I must confess.
Wild. Ay, ay, Madam; I hate your rude Whining and Sighing; it puts a Lady out of countenance. [*Pulling her.*

But this last example is qualified, I think, by the audience's rejection of the lecherous tugging that Sir Harry prefers to posturing. Here Farquhar gives us not mock-heroic but overt denunciation; and while the very act of comprehending mock-heroic enforces a kind of participation in it, overt denunciation can be judged objectively. If the audience are as dubious about Sir Harry's carryings-on as has been suggested, they can move to an ambiguous position at this point, amused but unsympathetic. Wildair's unpalatable alternative helps rehabilitate the heroic, or at least the earnest. As in *Love and a Bottle,* Farquhar sharply divides moral seriousness from affectation. The audience are ready to respond as they should to Angelica's ghostly voice, which can nearly "murder my Mistress with meer Morals," as Parley says, and yet does not violate the rather precarious tone.

The tone is precarious because Farquhar has deepened it, exciting Sir Harry to real concern for Angelica's honor, even to the point of dueling the Marquis, even to the point of admitting that he is "a little out of humour" (V. v, 206). His gratuitous and bitter scoffing at the Lord's honor in V. iv has at once indicted him and indicated his own glimmering realization of his moral folly. Perhaps his fighting the Marquis, whose temperamental ally he has been, may be taken symbolically. In other words, Farquhar has readied us for conversion, both because Sir Harry may accept it and because we are beginning to find his unconverted behavior obnoxious. To a lesser extent, the same is true of Lurewell, who is understandably overcome by her husband's sudden access of dignity at the end of IV. Standard's address to Wildair, Clincher, and the Marquis also is newly grave. "Look ye, Gentlemen, I have too great a confidence in the Vertue of my Wife, to think it in the power of you, or you, Sir, to wrong my Honour: But I am bound to guard her Reputation so that no attempts be made that may provoke a Scandal; Therefore, Gentlemen, let me tell you 'tis time to desist." Sir Harry can only say, "Ay, ay; so 'tis faith" (IV. ii, 200–1).

Angelica's apparition must climax the events and clear the turbidity of tone. Both come about in part because of the context of moral gravity that Farquhar has established for her rhetoric. He has reinforced Angelica's speech, too, by establishing various empty modes of speech that contrast with the "ghost's" ominous verse: Beau Banter's Oxford and coffeehouse raillery; Clincher's vapid "news," which logically comes to rest in the drunken aphasia of "Politicks, Politicks, Brandy Politicks"; the vain screams of Lurewell as she tries to besmirch the dead Angelica to Sir Harry, which logically come to rest in the fashionable cowardice of shrieking at a mouse; and lastly the lies of that worshiper of images and seemings, the French Marquis.

Rhetorically and even psychologically, the ending of *Sir Harry Wildair* shows Farquhar working with considerable skill. As to the moral that he professes, he is nowhere nearly so successful, because of the shakiness of moral norms and moral seriousness of the characters throughout the comedy as a whole. Comparison with *The Constant Couple,* as I have said, merely makes things worse. What we have then is a patchwork play, very well done in places. Perhaps such scenes as those involving Clincher and Beau Banter succeed too well, for like the technical proficiency of Farquhar's ending, they delude one into accepting a clever surface in lieu of substance. Equally delusive are such set pieces as Fireball's "Character . . . of a fine Lady" (I. i, 165–66). In this case, Farquhar was so pleased with his cleverness that he was willing to give up nautical jargon and probability of speaker—the "character" was a sophisticated genre by 1701—as well as the uniqueness of Lurewell. Under such circumstances, even Farquhar had to fail. He may well have realized that failure later on, since he had so little confidence in *Sir Harry Wildair*'s being revived that he boldly borrowed two of its characters, improving the disguised Angelica as Silvia in *The Recruiting Officer* and the Marquis as Bellair in *The Beaux' Stratagem.*

IV *"Vivacity in the Performance": A Note*

In this examination of Farquhar's early plays we have seen him demonstrating great mastery over technique, if not quite so much over his own calculations. There remains undiscussed one area of technique that he would have considered crucial, and in which his proficiency probably was very great indeed. I am referring to the effects gained from the physical acting of the plays. All plays when read must rely on the vividness of the reader's imagination, and especially plays written for a specific company of actors.

It can be argued that an intelligent reader loses little of the more intellectual and verbal parts of a comedy, in particular if he has some knowledge about the original performance. I say this despite Farquhar's modest declaration in the preface to *The Constant Couple* that "*whenever the Stage has the misfortune to lose* [Wilks], *Sir* Harry Wildair *may go to the Jubilee,*" and Cibber's sharper observation that Wilks's brilliance was proved by "the visible Capacity which must be allow'd to an Actor, that could carry such slight Materials to such a height of Approbation: For, though the Character of *Wildair* scarce in any one Scene will stand against a just Criticism; yet in the Whole there are so many gay and false Colours of the fine Gentleman, that nothing but a vivacity in the Performance proportionably extravagant could have made them so happily glare upon a common Audience."[9] In fact, however, *The Constant Couple* did well without Wilks and *Sir Harry Wildair* did abominably with him. Furthermore, once we have his general conception of the role, which Steele recorded as "the winning Emptiness of a young Man of Good-nature and Wealth" (Spectator 370), we have learned a great deal about the bland and sprightly grace of the performance, even if its excellence cannot be recovered. Most of the subsidiary "straight" characters are equally accessible to the imagination.

However, the farther the action gets from the "straight" characters and their love plots, the less intellectual and aristocratic become its sources of humor, and the less continuous its narrative. Or to put this another way, the more foolish the characters, the more their doings seem to fit naturally into episodes—individual effects, individual stunts, individual jokes. Published texts rapidly grow insufficient to convey the comedy of these scenes, which depend heavily on grimaces and gestures, clumsiness, strutting, pratfalls, stammering, mugging, staggering, posturing, and all the other devices of physical comedy. Farquhar must have stuffed his plays with such buffoonery, for *Love and a Bottle* included the clowns Bullock, Johnson, Haynes, and Pinkethman in farcical parts; *Sir Harry Wildair* substituted Norris and Cibber for Bullock and Haynes; and *The Constant Couple* enjoyed the services of all the gentlemen mentioned above, except for Cibber.[10] How much time was taken up with farce and how many ludicrous visual effects Farquhar employed no one can say, but John Cory's comment, quoted in the last chapter, about "an Audience crowding to a JUBILEE-FARCE, and sweating to see DICKY play his Tricks," along with other similar derogations from critics, ought to warn one from underestimating the frequency of such antics.

Some of Farquhar's physical comedy, like Smuggler's cudgeling by Sir Harry Wildair, can be visualized by anyone who has seen a Punch-and-Judy show; some, like Smuggler's disguise in woman's clothing, can be visualized, but not to arouse the same joy that a stage performance might. And we can hardly reconstitute the effect of having the same "Jubilee suit," in all its extravagant splendor, worn in turn by the different-sized Pinkethman, Haynes, and Bullock; or of having the diminutive "Dicky" Norris romp alongside the towering Bullock as servant and advisor. To know that Pinkethman was short and plump helps explain the following passage from *Sir Harry Wildair:*

> [*Clincher*] And then that pretty, dear, sweet, pretty King of Sweden! What sort of Man is he, pray?
>
> *Fire.* Why, tall and slender.
>
> *Clin.* Tall and Slender! much about my pitch? heh?
>
> *Fire.* Not so gross, not altogether so low. (III. i, 186)

But even for the reader who can realize the impact the name and image of the warrior king Charles XII had made upon all Europe, the superb incongruity of Clincher's comment has only a second-hand rationalized appeal, like a joke the punch line of which needs explaining, to those whose senses cannot be immediately struck by it. And at the farthest reach from verbal expression, the farceur's tricks that made it worthwhile to cast men like Norris and Haynes in tiny parts have faded out of sight and history. Therefore, I must pass from this matter to others that offer themselves more to discourse, but I do not want to do so without at least drawing attention to that for which the silent films came two hundred years too late.

CHAPTER 3

Jeremy Collier and The Twin-Rivals

THE most important single event affecting the stage during Farquhar's lifetime was the publication in 1698 of Jeremy Collier's book *A Short View of the Immorality and Profaneness of the English Stage.* With his two-handed engine of learning and vituperation, Collier struck repeatedly at the contemporary stage, specifying and quoting from the objectionable parts of popular plays to prove that Restoration drama was immodest, profane, immoral, and disrespectful to the clergy. His authorities and references ranged in time from the earliest classical authors to men of the late seventeenth century, and in nationality over a great deal of Western Europe. On occasion, this display of learning became pedantic, but more often it enhanced the sense of torrential vigor behind his accusations.

As to Collier's prose, he shared with the men he was attacking a racy tough style, which was capable of conveying any publicly apprehensible feeling. Since he had to evoke no subtleties of reaction or tone in *A Short View,* he moved very much at his ease:

> in Tragedy (says the *Mock Astrologer* [Dryden]) *the Crimes are . . . Horrid,* so that there is a necessity for Severity and Example. And how stands the matter in *Comedy?* Quite otherwise. There the *Faults are but the sallies of Youth and the Frailties of Human Nature.* For Instance: There is nothing but a little Whoring, Pimping, Gaming, Profaness, &c. And who could be so hard hearted to give a Man any Trouble for this? Such Rigours would be strangely Inhumane! A *Poet* is a better natur'd Thing, I can assure you . . . . But to be Serious: Is Dissolution of Manners such a Peccadillo? Does a Profligate Conscience deserve nothing but Commiseration? And are People damn'd for Humane *Frailties?* I perceive the Laws of Religion and those of the *Stage* differ extreamly.[1]

In this sort of driving polemic style, unafraid of seeming coarse, undignified, insensible, or brutal, Collier prosecuted the drama of his day to great popular applause.

Attacks on the stage were nothing new in England. They had in the past almost always come from Puritans, whose dour prudishness appealed largely to other Puritans: during Cromwell's dictatorship plays were illegal. With the restoration of the monarchy, the theater had again thrived, despite broadside warnings about "Nourishing of the causes and occasions of Wantonness, as impure Lusts, Surfetting, Drunkenness, Idleness, lascivious Apparel, society with lascivious persons, leud Books, Songs, or Speeches, wanton Looks, Pictures, Stage Playes, Dancing Dalliance, &c." [2] By the time of King William's accession (1689), the Puritans' children, the new English middle class, were again moving into a position of political power. Gradually, an Anglican Church anxious to avoid a schism had softened its dogma so as to permit these old Dissenters easy entry; gradually, English cultural life grew to tolerate, to respect, to genuflect before their bourgeois taste. Men of wider respectability aided the attack upon one of the most obvious bastions of aristocratic amorality, Restoration comedy. The age was ready for Collier, and Collier, a resolute High Anglican and Tory whose hands were clean of any Puritan or middle-class taint, obliged it. His motives, politically and theologically, were pure; his denunciatory style the equal of anyone's; and his success was immense.[3]

Collier's attack threw the theaters into confusion. Replies by such playwrights as Congreve and Vanbrugh were useless, and the flurry of published argument on one side or the other—the standard bibliography of the controversy contains about sixty items[4]—merely tended to obscure the subsidiary disputants and leave Collier an unscarred victor. In the meantime, righteous citizens belonging to the Societies for the Reformation of Manners were energetically harassing the theaters and actors, trying to restrain them from alleged obscenities and profanities on stage. The theatrical companies responded with a period of experimentation, in kinds of plays and of bills, committing themselves to a commercial blindman's buff of groping for a frighteningly elusive public favor. It was at this time that Farquhar attempted to counter Collier's attack and demonstrate the moral worth potential in the theater by writing *The Twin-Rivals.* In this extraordinary comedy, he presents concretely the sort of moral fable that Collier and Collier's enemies alike claimed to favor.

No one who depended upon the drama for a livelihood could have remained cool about the controversy, and young Farquhar was no exception. He refers to it ironically in the epilogue to *Love and a Bottle* and makes the odious Smuggler "instrumental in the reformation of manners" in *The Constant Couple* (II. iii. 111; V. ii, 145). *The Adventures of Covent Garden* (1698), his little novel, finds playhouse wits agreeing "that Mr. *Collier* showed too much Malice and rancour for a Church man, and his Adversaries too little wit for the Character of Poets; that their faults transversed would show much better; Dulness being more familiar with those of Mr. *Collier's* Function, as Malice and ill nature is more adapted to the Professors of wit" (*207*). These comments are rather mild, and in fact Farquhar probably saw much justice in Collier's specific comments, although not in his zeal to uproot the stage from English life. We have already seen that Farquhar's first three plays deviated from the Restoration pattern toward a more social ethic; he felt it possible to declare in the preface to *The Constant Couple* that "*I have not displeas'd the Ladies, nor offended the Clergy; both of which are now pleas'd to say, that a Comedy may be diverting without Smut and Profaneness,*" and to repeat in the prologue, "here's no Slander,/ No Smut, no lewd-tongu'd Beau, no double Entendre."

However, Farquhar's plays would hardly have been congenial to Collier, who would have agreed with Richard Cumberland, the late eighteenth-century dramatist and critic, in shuddering at Sir Harry Wildair's "loathsome ribaldry" and "licentious manners." [5] If one reads these three early comedies while thinking of Collier's strictures against "Their [playwrights'] *Smuttiness* of *Expression;* Their *Swearing, Profainness,* and *Lewd Application* of *Scripture;* Their *Abuse* of the *Clergy;* Their *making* their *Top Characters Libertines,* and giving them *Success* in their *Debauchery,*" [6] one can see that Farquhar has incorporated most of these "Liberties" in his texts. In *Love and a Bottle,* for instance, "*Smuttiness of Expression*" flaunts itself, as where Roebuck has been told that the husband of one of the Masques is a judge:

Roeb. . . . 'Tis very hard, Madam, he shou'd not do you Justice: Has not he an Estate in Tail, Madam?

2 Mas. I seldom examine his Papers; They are a parcel of old dry shrivel'd Parchments; and this Court-hand is so devilish crabbed, I can't endure it.

Roeb. Umph!— Then I suppose, Madam, you want a young Lawyer to put your Case to. (IV.iii, 55)

The heavy sprinkling of references to God, angels, devils, etc., in that play would certainly count as "*Profainness*" with Collier; and as for mockery of the clergy, that comes up within the first fifty lines, as the crippled soldier derides clerics' keenness in knowing where charity begins and ends: "A Captain will say Dam'me, and give me Six-pence; and a Parson shall whine out God bless me, and give me not a farthing" (I. i, 11). Admittedly, all three of these offenses can be justified dramatically, and even justified morally. But Collier would counter that each of the three, however it may fit into a context, gives a kind of pleasure that violates good taste, good sense, and good moral firmness.

Insofar as Farquhar's early comedies are born from, and must cope with, the wit-comedy of the Restoration, they represent assumptions about human nature which Collier would have found deeply disturbing. The women, for instance, are directly, physcially, passionate; we have discussed the difficulties involved in Farquhar's trying to resolve *Love and a Bottle* through sexual experience. To make Roebuck's conversion credible, the language must evoke the supreme joy of sleeping with Leanthe. She is pictured in the most sensuous terms, in gasps of blank verse, as violently aroused. To Collier, such a portrayal of feminine purity would have been in execrable taste, for he found in the "naturalistic" view of women only incitements to sexual freedom. Furthermore, Farquhar seems to be accepting the notion that conversation based on sexual rapture is not only a legitimate, but the sole legitimate means of turning a rake from cynicism and vice. Otherwise, why use so precarious a resolution? Libertine roving is disavowed not because it is immoral, but because its superiority, in a libertine's terms, has been empirically disproved. And how warm and dangerous a ratification one gives to passion when one goes so far as to use its sensations as the very metaphors for moral conversion! Roebuck and Leanthe lie "incorporate in liquid kisses," "catch[ing] each other's Souls," fused physically just as they are soon to be united morally and spiritually because of the physical relationship.

The Wildair plays, which Collier might have found somewhat more palatable, nevertheless share many of the "lapses" of *Love and a Bottle.* Sir Harry can take his Angelica for a whore without making amends other than marriage, which she readily accepts, despite his earlier career. After her presumed death in *Sir Harry Wildair,* he can play a "piping hot warm Heretick" to at least six nuns in five days without much impairing his position. The men's open lust for the ladies, Lurewell and Angelica, makes it possible to read both plays like *Love and a Bottle,* as hymning the satisfaction of physical desire in marriage, the coincidence of the social with naturalistically conceived private desires. All three of the early comedies, then, present a world highly desirable to the individual male: (a) women, being chaste, can be possessed and held, but (b) this chastity does not preclude an intense and steamy physical passion; meanwhile (c) the man can possess, before the pleasures grow climactic in marriage, large numbers of sexually greedy women, including particularly the conventionally inaccessible, nuns or other men's wives. Everybody in the comedies takes this male world for granted. In fact, so much is it taken for granted that the distinction between out-and-out rakery and a virtuous passion becomes flattened. If wenching and wooing both come from the same libido, as Restoration comedy asserts and Farquhar sometimes implies, conversion is very easy and very meaningless. It involves neither sacrifice nor change of direction, and, therefore, introduction into social propriety can be quite near through a marriage and perhaps a repentence even in the most profligate moments. This statement is too extreme for Farquhar because of his veering from the Restoration pattern; but Collier would deride our making much too nice a discrimination. His moral rigor admitted of no extenuating comparisons. A counter to him had to be a sort of play different from anything Farquhar had yet written. The result was *The Twin-Rivals.*

Farquhar, constructing a prefatory apologia for his "damn'd" comedy at the end of its meager run in late December, 1702,[7] tried to explain why he had written what he did: "The Success and Countenance that Debauchery has met with in Plays, was the most Severe and Reasonable Charge against their Authors in Mr. *Collier's Short View;* and indeed this Gentleman had done the *Drama* considerable Service, had he Arraign'd the Stage only to Punish its Misdemeanours, and not to take away its Life; but there is an Advantage to be made sometimes of the Advice of an Enemy, and the only way to disappoint his Designs, is to improve upon his invective, and to make the Stage flourish by vertue of that Satyr, by which he thought to suppress it" (286). It is useless to speculate whether the praise of Collier is sincere or not. What is far more significant is that if Farquhar is to be taken literally, and I do not see why he should not be, *The Twin-Rivals* was to be written as an extension of Collier's "Satyr." Collier, arraigning the stage with great vigor and persistence, had denounced lewdness, lavished satirical invective upon the ideals behind it, and used decency (the plays of Terence, Jonson, Molière, *et al.*) only as a counterweight. Farquhar, vindicating the stage by showing its moral potentialities, wrote *The Twin-Rivals* on precisely those principles of organization, and, as I shall suggest, attacked not only "Immorality, and Profaneness" but also, by parody, the conventions of the offending immoral plays he was leaving behind.

The Twin-Rivals opens with a familar scene: "*The Curtain drawn up, discovers* Young Wou'dbe *a Dressing, and his* Valet *Buckling his Shooes.*" Scenes of the rake being dressed are among the most expressive gambits of wit-comedy: in them, the rake can preen his body and spirit before the play itself begins, so that the audience can experience his soon-to-be-employed aplomb, his carefully groomed predatory skills, his naturally artful elegance. In opening scenes like this, for instance, Dorimant (Etherege's *Man of Mode*) or Sir Humphrey Scattergood (Shadwell's *The Woman-Captain*) are given their proper places, and their preparation and anticipation are meant to be vicariously echoed by the public's. But unlike Sir Humphrey and Dorimant, Young Wou'dbe has been contrived to inspire no "identification" or sympathy. He is a hunchback. Other than that, he has the conventional equipment of the rake, the qualities which conventionally appealed for support: he is poor, sensual, and debauched; he is a clever manipulator, and, most important, a younger brother.

The younger brother is, again, a stock character in wit-comedy because he is a sympathetic underdog: if society respects priority of birth, wit-comedy erects a hierarchy of merit. Shadwell's *Squire of Alsatia,* Cibber's *Love's Last Shift,* Mrs. Pix's *The Beau Defeated,* Vanbrugh's *The Relapse* all present examples of the stereotype from the fifteen years preceding *The Twin-Rivals. The Relapse* is perhaps directly relevant. In both plays, the exploits begin after unsuccessful attempts at borrowing money, and both plays turn on an exchange of brothers; *The Relapse* was a familiar play —it had been revived at Drury Lane the month before—and it was one of those particularly attacked by Collier. The relationship is obviously tenuous, but less so than it might be if there were no hint that *The Twin-Rivals* was using the conventions of other plays to make its point. The hunchback, who was played by the actor Cibber, would have reminded everyone of one of Cibber's most famous impersonations, another hunchbacked ambitious younger brother in another Drury Lane play, Shakespeare's *Richard III.*[8] Through alluding to Shakespeare, Farquhar can add stature to Benjamin without giving him tragic dimensions within the comedy, while at the same time he slyly evokes Shakespeare's moral judgment to indict wit-comedy and its scheming underdogs.

Young Wou'dbe is a rake *manqué,* his character extruded into a hump. The actual rake in the play is the dashingly promiscuous Richmore, who has attained a certain libertine grace:

Y. W. Have you forgot, *Richmore,* how I found you one Morning, with the *Flying Post* in your hand, hunting for Physical Advertisements?

Rich. That was in the days of *Dad,* my Friend, in the days of dirty Linnen, Pit-Masks, Hedge-Taverns, and Beef-Stakes; but now I fly at nobler Game; the Ring, the Court, *Pawlet*'s and the *Park:* I despise all Women that I apprehend any danger from, less than the having my Throat cut; and shou'd scruple to Converse even with a Lady of Fortune, unless her Virtue were loud enough to give me Pride in exposing it. (I. i, 294)

The delight in exposing virtue as hypocrisy, the supposition that virtue *is* hypocrisy, marks Richmore as the Dorimant, or the Sir Harry Wildair, of *The Twin-Rivals.* All the rake's ingenuities are in his mouth:

Man[*drake*]. And will you break your Vows to *Clelia*?
Rich. Why not, when she has broke her's to me?
Man. How's that, Sir?
Rich. Why; She Swore a Hundred times never to grant me the Favour, and yet you know she broke her Word.
Man. But she lov'd Mr. *Richmore,* and that was the Reason she forgot her Oath.
Rich. And I love Mr. *Richmore,* and that is the reason I forgot mine— Why shou'd she be Angry that I follow her own Example, by doing the very same thing from the very same Motive? (I. ii, 299)

This is not only clever evasion; it also indicates Richmore's actual attitude, that love is self-interest. Clelia's love and his own are, to him, very legitimately paralleled. He and Benjamin Wou'dbe—Benjamin, the beloved youngest—differ from the virtuous characters in a way that is simpler and deeper than mere lack of scruple. Their flaw is that they accept, and act logically upon, the naturalistic view of human nature, just as the heroes of Restoration comedy do. Ten years earlier, this would have been safe enough. Now, comedy had followed pathetic tragedy in distinguishing moral from naturalistic assumptions, and in rejecting the individual self-aggrandizement that marked heroic plays and wit-comedy.

We may note that Young Wou'dbe and Richmore are Farquharian figures in a new setting. Their ideas of Love and Honour are surprisingly like Roebuck's:

Lean[*the*]. I don't believe it, Sir; you cou'd not be so hard-hearted sure: Her honourable Passion, I think, shou'd please you best.
Roeb. O Child! Boys of your age are continually reading Romances, filling your Heads with all that old bombast of Love and Honour: But when you come to my years, you'll understand better things. (III. i, 35)

They are also strikingly like Sir Harry Wildair's:

Stand[*ard*]. Sir, my Honour's concern'd.
Wild. Nay, if your Honour be concern'd with a Woman, get it out of her Hands as soon as you can. An honourable Lover is the greatest Slave in Nature; some will say, the greatest Fool. (IV. i, 129)

Both Roebuck and Sir Harry are free to beget their bastards without being forced into marriage: they are heroes; Richmore is a villain.

The differences between the earlier comedies and *The Twin-Rivals* in tone and in the view of the rake may be symbolized by two comparisons with Shakespearean passages, two naturalistic, hedonistic rationalizations for vice. The first is Sir Harry Wildair's: "but pray, Madam, be pleas'd to consider what is this same Vertue that you make such a mighty Noise about—Can your Vertue bespeak you a Front row in the Boxes? No. . . . Can your Vertue keep you a Coatch [*sic*] and Six? no, no. . . . Can your Vertue hire you a Pue in a Church? Why the very Sexton will tell you, no. Can your Vertue stake for you at Picquet? no. Then what business has a Woman with Vertue?" (V. i, 141). The original of this is obviously Falstaff's honor speech (*1 Henry IV*, V. i), and Falstaff, like Sir Harry, was conceived as waggish, droll, and salacious, although superior to a mere clown. The other speech from Farquhar is that with which Young Wou'dbe concludes Act II of *The Twin-Rivals:*

> *Y. W.* [*Solus.*] The Pride of Birth, the Heats of Appetite, and Fears of Want, are strong Temptation to Injustice— But why Injustice? —The World has broke all Civilities with me; and left me in the Eldest State of Nature, Wild, where Force, or Cunning first created Right. . . . My Brother! What is Brother? We are all so; and the first two were Enemies— He stands before me in the Road of Life to Rob me of my Pleasures— My Senses, form'd by Nature for Delight, are all alarm'd— My Sight, my Hearing, Taste, and Touch, call loudly on me for their Objects, and they shall be satisfy'd.

The reference to the "State of Nature" is probably meant to allude to Hobbes, with whom only villains (cf. Vizard) were directly associated. The speech itself, a fine speech to end an act, is rather in the manner of Edmund in *King Lear,* especially the Edmund of Nahum Tate's revised version (1681), who has become considerably more sensually motivated than was Shakespeare's, an Edmund who titles himself "a born Libertine" and who gloats, "to my hand thy [Gloster's] vast Revenues fall,/ To glut my pleasure that till now has starved." [9] The use of Edmund, especially a rakish Edmund, to give parallel tone to Young Wou'dbe is justified, for the first crime of each is to substitute a competitive and individualistic world for the proper world of social order. Such a competitive world was the assumption of wit-comedy, and its resolution "the union of public and private pride." [10] But *moral* satire cannot thrive in a competitive world: it defends not certain types of people but a certain type of social order. Its favored characters are deduced from, are exemplary of, that order; whereas those of wit-comedy must be far more independent if their eventual union with social order is to be celebrated.

If the bad characters were really to be bad, comic analogues of Richards and Edmunds, the tone of the play had to be deepened. Effective and serious satire required vices which were more than diverting follies—Farquhar remarks on this in his preface—and virtuous characters who could serve as bright contrasts. Thus this love plot had to be dignified from the usual lusty frolics. And because Restoration comedy had evolved no means for dealing with dignified virtue, techniques of representation had to be imported from tragedy. Love took on that true-hearted frenzy which was associated with tragic virtue, and frequently the characters of comedies in which such love appears refer it explicitly to contemporary tragedy.[11]

The level of generic decorum curiously changes too, and noble characters, like the Elder Wou'dbe, may at times be lent the dignity of blank verse. The wit's aphorism is replaced by its tragic counterpart, the "sentiment." Hermes, the Elder Wou'dbe, never approaches wit, even where wit was traditionally most approachable, in the making of comparisons. His resource is invective, or, euphemistically, righteous indignation: "Thou art the Worm and Maggot of the Law, bred in the bruis'd and rotten parts, and now art nourish'd on the same Corruption that produc'd thee— The *English* Law as planted first, was like the *English* Oak, shooting its spreading Arms around to shelter all that dwelt beneath its shade—but now whole Swarms of Caterpillars, like you, hang in such Clusters upon every Branch, that the once thriving Tree now sheds infectious Vermin on our Heads" (IV. i, 330).

These images are forceful, obvious, and concrete without calling attention to themselves; their impact, unlike the impact of wit, is little more than their paraphrasable content; form is no longer an important criterion. And indeed, the whole movement from the

Old Comedy to the New at the end of the seventeenth century was, like the movement from the heroic play to the pathetic tragedy twenty-five years before, an insistence on the dominance of content and a consequent rejection of the pleasing distractions of form, a shifting of interest from the way one did things to the things one did. Such a shifting of interest is plain in *The Twin-Rivals:* not only the righteousness of Hermes Wou'dbe but also the affection lavished on a faithful bourgeois, the goldsmith Fairbank, and, in a more tempered way, the faithful Irish valet Teague, gives evidence of it.

But, having testified to his hero's wholesomeness by making him a prig, Farquhar found himself in difficulties. Wit, in most of the comedies his audiences had seen, was more than a value in and of itself; it was also a badge, an indication of value, a communicative as well as a self-contained convention. Thus he was faced with the serious danger of making Richmore and Young Wou'dbe admirably witty or their moral adversaries contemptibly dull. His solution came from Steele, whose comedy *The Funeral* had, a year earlier, "founded a two-couple pattern which was followed in a whole tradition of subsequent plays." [12] Farquhar set up two complementary couples, both pairs true and sensible lovers, but one rather gayer and wittier than the other.[13] The hope is for a kind of charm by attraction. Relationships are kept uncomplicated: there are no love-chases or amatory joustings, such as Roebuck and Lovewell or Wildair and Standard engage in. They are also kept generous. Little flashes of individuality can be set off and paid for by the sweetly social.

Thus Aurelia, talking with Constance about the seduced Clelia, is permitted one sally at Clelia's expense—falling from virtue, after all, must not be encouraged:

Con. I'm glad you mention'd her [Clelia]; Don't you observe her Gayety to be much more forc'd than formerly, her Humour don't sit so easily upon her.

Aur. No, nor her Stays neither, I can assure you.

But neither must ill nature, and Aurelia cannot keep joking without a reprimand from Constance: "That's cruel, *Aurelia,* How can you make merry with her Misfortunes? I am positive she was no easy Conquest" (II. i, 303). Trueman, Aurelia's suitor, has slightly less rein: he never ventures past one flurry of stale courtly lover's wit, save when he believes (falsely, of course) that Aurelia has been unchaste. Even then his imagination suffers from a sad poverty. As a result, most of the vicarious feeling in favor of the lovers depends on convention and on their energetic opposition to Richmore and Benjamin Wou'dbe. The main action to the play is their maintaining a little quadrangle of decency which the indecent assault, and the four are less significant in themselves as lovers than as agents of moral conscience, blocking the progress of villainy. Such a pattern is, of course, completely different from anything in earlier Farquhar plays.

As a matter of fact, the love-relationships, about which the early plays crystallize, are almost superfluous for the main action here. If wit-comedy, the comedy of the individual, takes its force from the consolidation of a new society about the lovers (which is the lighter side of the general comic theme of the creation of such a new society), moral satire, the comedy of the public, takes its force from the purging of the old society by the lovers, by the agencies of social decency. *The Twin-Rivals* cannot and does not assume the "highly desirable world" of the earlier Farquhar comedies; romantic passion remains inobtrusive and love respectably Platonic; and universal naturalism or hedonism is confined to the villains' minds.

In *The Lying Lover*, produced at Drury Lane almost exactly a year after *The Twin-Rivals*, Steele tried to scout hostile laughter of the sort that satire evokes, the laughter of security, confidence, and contempt. His epilogue begins:

> OUR too advent'rous Author soar'd to Night
> Above the little Praise, Mirth to excite,
> And chose with Pity to chastise Delight.
> For Laughter's a distorted Passion, born
> Of sudden Self-Esteem, and sudden Scorn;
> Which, when 'tis o'er, the Men in Pleasure wise,
> Both him that mov'd it, and themselves despise:
> While gen'rous Pity of a painted Woe
> Makes us our selves both more approve, and know.[14]

Such a position is logically deducible from a kind of comedy dependent, in technique and ideals, upon pathetic tragedy. Yet its reasons for rejecting laughter are applicable only to wit-comedy. Moral satire frees "*Self-Esteem*" from egocentrism, frees the audience, that is, from imitating the libertine in selfish pleasure, by making the norm, the audience's point of view, external and social. One laughs as a citizen. Farquhar goes farther yet and makes one laugh as a Christian, or, at least, a theist, because he refers his norm not only to society but also, overtly, to Providence.

Without encouraging individualistic laughter, he was able to write funny parts in *The Twin-Rivals,* and did so. Johnson was assigned two roles, Balderdash and Alderman, one a hypocritically suave innkeeper who evicts the moneyless Young Wou'dbe, the other—pointedly and ingeniously given the same actor—a hypocritically suave citizen who tactfully bribes the moneyed Young Wou'dbe. Subtleman, the lawyer, played by Pinkethman, believes that the letter giveth life; here he is engaged in forging a will for Young Wou'dbe's benefit:

Y. W. Well, Mr. *Subtleman,* You are sure the Will is firm and good in Law?

Sub. I warrant you, my Lord; And for the last Words to prove it, here they are—Lookee Mr. *Clearaccount*—Yes—That is an Answer to the Question that was put to him, (you know) by those about him when he was a Dying—Yes, or no, he must have said; so we have chosen, Yes—*Yes, I have made my Will, as it may be found in the Custody of Mr.* Clearaccount *my Steward; and I desire it may stand as my Last Will and Testament*—Did you ever hear a Dying Man's Words more to the purpose? An Apoplexy! I tell you, my Lord had Intervals to the last.

Stew. Ay, But how shall these Words be prov'd?

Sub. My Lord shall speak 'um now.

Y. W. Shall he faith?

Sub. Ay, now—If the Corps ben't Bury'd—Lookee, Sir; These Words must be put into his Mouth, and drawn out again before us all; and if they won't be his last Words then;—I'll be Perjur'd.

. . . .

Y. W. But the Body is cold, and his Teeth can't be got asunder.

Sub. But what occasion has your Father for Teeth now? (II. v, 312–13)

The manipulation of this scene is quite fine, as the cynical garrulousness of forgery reveals itself first as ghoulish, and then, with its proposal to knock out the dead man's teeth, as savage. Appropriately enough, Subtleman is the bastard of a Jew, left in Lombard-street with Mrs. Mandrake to be brought up at her behest as "a good Christian." As to Mrs. Mandrake herself, played by Bullock, the transvestiary bawd did not originate in this play, but could hardly have appeared more brilliantly and mordantly elsewhere. She may be Farquhar's finest character, and again, is extremely funny in a serious Jonsonian way. Here, indeed, Farquhar is impressively like Ben Jonson, in illuminating these subsidiary villains with superbly calculated glitter: the vices satirized are cruel and cruelly treated (very markedly restraining the potential farce of the action), they are used as broad indictments (one's lawyer, one's steward, the woman who looks after one's children are venal and corrupt), and they act as "concrete universals" in their topical versions of the general sins.

A radical and original play must work to direct the feelings and attention of the audience more actively than must its conventional counterpart. Farquhar, justifying comedy through the power of his righteous intention, found that he needed a new structure. That structure was defined by the demands of the moral fable. For one thing, *The Twin-Rivals* is much tighter, much more sharply focused, more economical than anything Farquhar had written. In the early plays, subsidiary characters were primarily used to adjust the tone of the main action; here they also have that function—shyster lawyers and unctuous aldermen are stock figures—but their doings are also intimately tied to the movement of the plot. Furthermore, they carry far more vehement satire and less farce. Because the moral issues are so monochromatically clear, Farquhar could not use his old techniques of setting up meaningful parallels within the play. To some extent, his use of allusion, parallelism with matters outside the play proper, becomes a formal substitute. So does doubling of the plot. Morally, and in love, Benjamin and Richmore balance Hermes and Trueman; the family relationships of the Wou'dbes and of Richmore/Trueman play off against one another; we have the loyal servants on this side and the disloyal on that—all these help corset the play. Any shapelessness or slack that remains uncontrolled by these means, Farquhar tries to correct through highly skilled and precise pacing.

Jeremy Collier and The Twin-Rivals

The final problem for the scholar and critic is trying to suggest why *The Twin-Rivals* failed. Farquhar's own solution, that people did not want to see their darling vices reprimanded, does not hold water: prologues and epilogues, if not plays, constantly mocked and insulted the audience, and were perfectly well received. As a comedy, *The Twin-Rivals* succeeds by almost any standards, and, in comparison with other early eighteenth-century comedies, succeeds brilliantly. As a moral play, it might have pleased even a Collier, if Collier had been inclined to be pleased. Insofar as any consistent principles can be extracted from his harangues, *The Twin-Rivals* follows them. Both Collier and Farquhar believed that the function of comedy is Aesopian, and could declare that "if [the English comic authors] have left Vice unpunish'd, Vertue unrewarded, Folly unexpos'd, or Prudence unsuccessful, the Contrary of which is the *Utile* of Comedy, let them be lash'd to some purpose" (*343*). *The Twin-Rivals* sides with Collier in its inclusion of poetic justice along with ridicule: it puts vice in the pillory, and also, openly, mirrors Providence in distributing eventual rewards and punishments. Why then, since Collier was so revered, did the play fail? The answer, I think, is that Farquhar failed to understand that the public of his time was exploiting, rather than accepting, Collier's "Satyr." Collier, whatever foolishness he wrote, took a stand for moral understanding and moral dignity; the audience, which believed that it too took a stand for these things, in fact wanted only social propriety and tender feelings. In short, they wanted sentimental comedy, *comédie larmoyante,* which is moral not for the sake of God but for the sake of tears. That is not what Farquhar had provided, nor what he was inclined to provide. Unpleasant to the public and undoubtedly painful to its author, *The Twin-Rivals* died out of theatrical history. It deserved better.

CHAPTER 4

Farquhar as Imitator and Adapter

I The Adventures of Covent-Garden

FARQUHAR, if we may assume it was he, wrote *The Adventures of Covent-Garden* "In Imitation of *Scarron's* CITY ROMANCE." In fact, the *City Romance,* or *Roman Bourgeois* (1666), was attributed to Paul Scarron wrongly, by an English translator in 1671. Perhaps the error was intentional and commercial, for Scarron was well known and popular in England, while the real author, Antoine Furetière, had neither name nor following. Intentional or not, the false attribution was plausible, since Furetière, in the *Roman Bourgeois,* employed Scarron's style and structure, although he added to them, as one of his French editors remarks, "*quelque chose de plus systématique et, pour tout dire, de plus pédant.*" [1] The structure remains loose, with interpolated tales larding the novel, and with the cast of characters continually expanding and contracting as the situations change. This is very much in the picaresque fashion. So is the control exercised by the author's voice over the course of the story, just as the voices of Cervantes and Scarron, and later of Fielding, control and qualify events. For the English-speaking reader, Fielding may be the author closest in method to Furetière: both authors serve as objective, urbane, unillusioned, and unromantic historians, consciously pursing their lips at a literary tradition of romance, and parodying it.

Since Farquhar claimed to be imitating Furetière, a close look at the texture of the *Roman Bourgeois* seems necessary. Let us examine a passage from the novel, not typical in the sense that it might have been chosen at random, but representative of Furetière's mode of fiction. A girl named Lucrece has been seduced by a lord:

It cannot be said to be the fault of *Lucrece,* if the Lord kept not his word, which she had been told, was inviolable amongst persons of honour: and truely there were very many that did not blame her, because themselves had been caught in the same manner. This love lasted a while with more familiarity than formerly, and without any memorable Accident, for the Lord had no Rival to dispute against him the place he had gained, or that gave his Mistress false intelligence to his prejudice: There was neither Picture, watch, nor Bracelet of hair su[r]prised or lost, nor that passed into other hands: no absence, nor malicious report of death or inconstancy, all which are the most recurring and common Materials that build the Intrigues of Romances. Inventions that have been presented in so many formes, and so often turned and patched they can no longer be made use of.

I can, therefore, tell you no more of this Story, and though I were never so curious, all I could inform my self of would be only this, how many Turkies had been eaten at St. *Cloud,* how many dishes of strawberries and cherries in *May,* at *Vaugizard,* because the Bills of these Collations are yet to be found in the Inns where they were made, though they were sometime before discharged by the Lord, who was so good a paymaster, it derogated from his Nobility.[2]

Except perhaps at the very end of the passage, Furetière seems to be making no personal judgments. In fact he is manipulating them obliquely so as to make them appear as objective as possible. He begins with the passive voice, "it cannot be said," to imply that all society must agree, and then in the rest of the sentence supports that implication. First, the name "Lucrece" alludes surreptitiously to the chaste Roman wife who was foully raped by a prince. The connotations of the name, then, bequeath innocence and sympathy to a modern Lucrece, also the sexual victim of a treacherous Lord. Blame must be assigned to the society that has misled her: "she had been told" that lords keep promises, and has therefore fallen because of her goodness and purity, just as "very many" others have. "Inviolable," with its sexual undertones, is particularly appropriate; it intensifies the ironic ambiguity of "persons of honour," in which "honour" ought to mean something spiritual, at once the source and result of an ideal of *noblesse oblige,* though here the word merely labels the Lord's social class. (This ironic ambiguity is further developed by the use of "Nobility" in the second paragraph.) To men of real honor, there is an inviolable unity between class and conscience, word and deed, illusion and fact, ideal and reality. But Furetière's society knows only duplicity, where illusion is fatal and romance is fatal, as Lucrece and "very many" others have learned. The disillusioned make the proper moral judgments, acquitting Lucrece; and even if they acquit her to avoid having to convict themselves, they seem to form in some way the only adequate judiciary, because the only experienced one.

The reader too is expected to drop whatever illusions he has, and Furetière emphasizes this thematic point by couching it in an almost reportorial style, straightforward, unembellished, and unmetaphorical. Only "turned and patched" introduces figurative language, and that is doubly appropriate: it comes in a discussion of the devices of romance, and it is a metaphor of clothes, coverings, precisely what Furetière rejects, and we with him. The second paragraph continues the reportorial pose with its stress on fact. Turkeys and berries, St. Cloud and Vaugizard, the eventual appeal to old food bills as the only proper clue to reality for the "curious"—all are in keeping with the tough skepticism that the *Roman Bourgeois* advocates. These two paragraphs manifest that skepticism in no fewer than five ways: (1) the scorn for "the Intrigues of Romances"; (2) the exclusive use of a plain factual style; (3) the restriction to factual evidence in the narrative; (4) the quasi-legal documentation of Lucrece's innocence and society's guilt; (5) the assumption that moral illusions deceive one about social reality. Furthermore, the passage is anti-romantic in context because it deals with the middle class rather than with the traditionally royal or noble subjects of romance.

Such hard-headed rigor has led critics to compare Furetière with the nineteenth-century French realists, to call him a Balzac without vision or genius.[3] But the *Roman Bourgeois* is more complex than such critics realize. The reader, after all, knows that Furetière's carefully taken posture is artificial. If the narrator chooses the mask of objective observation at times, at other times he feels free to plunge into his characters' minds and motives: "*Lucrece* in the mean time was extreamly afflicted; she continually apprehended her misfortunes becoming publick, and perceiving there was no more hope of the Lord, resolved to take advantage of [a proposal of marriage]; and that which made her the rather give consent, was, that she had once listened to a Consultation of the same kind held at her Uncles, where the business was concluded in favour of a Maid in the like Agony." [4] Here we have Lucrece's state of mind exposed, even to the extent of rephrasing the account of a legal consultation in emotional terms ("the like Agony") that must represent Lucrece's subjective recollection rather than the objective account.

I am not suggesting that a seventeenth-century author felt the same obligation to consider single point of view that a late nineteenth-century author felt. Precisely because he did not feel that obligation, the disclaimers of omniscience in the long quotation above are significant. They assert, in this full context, the precedence of one sort of fiction, Furetière's, over another, the romance. The novel, as Furetière seems to see it, affirms certain values, such as that of viewing reality with clear eyes; these values are shared by reportage, journalism, but the novel goes beyond the report to present life more completely, as an historian would, with moral ends in view. Again, one is reminded of Fielding, whose area of omniscience, like some infinitely adjustable umbrella, sometimes shades us more, sometimes less, from a dazzling confusion. We simultaneously and paradoxically live among the characters and within the author's mind. On occasion this paradox is exploited for specific purposes. For instance, one of the characters in the *Roman Bourgeois* is named "*Philipote*, but her Romantick [name was] *Hippolita*, which is the Anagram of the other; no inconsiderbale [*sic*] good fortune for a pretended Heroine, when the Letters of her Christian Name afford a Romantick one." [5] The specific pleasure in this passage is twofold. First, one laughs at the romantic fantasy of a girl who takes an anagrammatic coincidence as in some way representing a valid connection between her everyday and would-be selves. The second, more sophisticated pleasure is in Furetière's impudence in setting up such a correspondence at all. Whereas in Philipote's experience, her christening preceded her playing "Hippolita," in the author's experience, it is the other way around. The mystic correspondence is reduced to Furetière's ingenuity, and we see fiction and illusion satirized through a more acceptable and seriously affirmed fiction. Clearly, the *Roman Bourgeois*, despite appearances, takes as its historical province not the actual but the natural, which it explores from several points of view. It is no early slice of life, but a complex presentation of empirical morality.

After so long an exposition, our discussion must land at an anticlimax, for Farquhar's "imitation" provides a much thinner and simpler texture than does the *Roman Bourgeois*. Furetière was in his forties, the friend of Boileau and Racine, and a man of the world; Farquhar, when he wrote *The Adventures of Covent-Garden*, was about twenty, still raw from a half-education in Ireland. The difference shows in the work, as Farquhar may have known when he wrote in his prefatory note: "*As for my imitating* Scarron, *I confess 'tis not* Copia vera, *as many draw their Imitations, but there is something . . . Odd in this Gentlemans Writings . . . which may puzzle an Author*" (*198*). He does manage to follow the *Roman* in at least three obvious ways: the historical style, the upper-middle-class characters, and the anti-romantic skepticism. Farquhar's epigraph, "Et quorum pars Magna fui" ("And I took a great part in these things"), indicates his claim to historical accuracy, as does a hint at the end of the prefatory note that he himself is the romantic Peregrine.[6] The claim may be true, of course, but it need not be taken literally, any more than a similar claim about his letters need be (see Chapter 5). The illusion of historicity is part of the game. In line with it, Farquhar has slightly pruned his exuberant prose. (It is still far from Furetière's austerity.) This style also suits the *haute bourgeoisie* with whom *The Adventures* deals. Generally, the diction succeeds in skirting the low, and sedulously excludes any suspicion of romantic heightening, except in moments of irony. Only when Emilia is busy ensnaring poor Peregrine, for the sake of ten guineas, do we find lushness.[7] Verse appears twice (*205, 210*), to mock romantic ecstasy and torment.

Farquhar's narrative, too, deals with swindled innocence: Peregrine, an amorous cad, dupes himself into a frustrating affair with a promiscuous coquette, Emilia, and thereby not only loses his rich mistress and his peace of mind, but is also toyed with and deceived in the most humiliating ways. But here the resemblance ends. Whereas the *Roman Bourgeois* attacks a specific habit of mind, the fabricating of illusions, *The Adventures* generalizes the morality of self-control in the conventional terms of reason versus passion. There is nothing wrong in its doing so; however, the kind of ironic effects that Furetière gets are simply not available to Farquhar with his different thematic center. Robbed of his model's greatest asset, Farquhar would have had to imitate the *Roman's* complexity by readjusting his style, reëstablishing verbal delicacies within the context of his own narrative. At the age of twenty, he could not do that successfully. It may be that he could not have done that at thirty, since mastery of the turned phrase and the precise nuance never became his forte, but then he would have offered something equally sophisticated, if different. In the *Adventures,* cruder comedy takes over. Only rarely does Farquhar achieve a complex effect, as in "his foolish wavering fancy suggested, that there cou'd be no harm in looking up to her Window, since he believ'd she stood not there; yet to what end shou'd any reasonable Man but a Glasier look at a Window, when he expected no body at it [?]" (*203*). "But a Glasier" is a nice touch, because it is so sensible and mundane as to make Peregrine's folly particularly absurd, and also because it seems to degrade Peregrine's reason below that of a tradesman. More often in *The Adventures,* vividness of language tries to take the place of wit, while verbal irony becomes hearty rather than deft.

One who is familiar with *Love and a Bottle,* which plays so pointedly with the ideas of illusion and fiction, can see what about Furetière intrigued Farquhar. But then it becomes difficult to understand why, having decided to imitate the *Roman Bourgeois,* Farquhar failed to approximate the very same teasing of illusion and fiction in the *Adventures.* The best guess might be that purely formal effects held very little interest for Farquhar. In *Love and a Bottle,* the formal development of the theme serves the moral point. In the *Roman,* the formal development, exemplifying an illusionless habit of mind, is itself the point. Nothing could have been further from the practice of a fledgling playwright in the late seventeenth century; nothing less in harmony with Farquhar's temperament, for the continuing movement in his work is toward treating form only as a kind of rhetoric, second to content. In the next section of this chapter, this demotion of form in his imitation of Beaumont and Fletcher's *Wild-Goose Chase* will be pointed out; it has already been mentioned in reference to the Elder Wou'dbe's speech. Farquhar's love letters are, I believe, the only formal exercise in his corpus, and the practice of emotionally modifying the speaking voice in letters is of course much nearer a playwright's interests than is modifying a narrative voice and point of view.

The real value of *The Adventures* lies just where one would expect, in those things that a dramatist might exploit. Some of them were exploited: Emilia became Lurewell in *The Constant Couple,* and the Captain's misadventures while dressed in porter's clothes were transferred to Beau Clincher. Farquhar might have reused, but did not, a number of morally oriented situations. For instance, Peregrine's anger over the ladies' duplicity while he himself engages in both hypocrisy (with Selinda) and philandering (with Emilia) could be dramatized effectively. So could the remarkably mordant irony by which Peregrine is persuaded to write the love letters that bring his rival, Lord C——, into Emilia's arms. Or again, one could stage the scene at the raffle, in which both Emilia and Selinda want the costly china that Peregrine has won; or the scene at the play, in which the flirtations of the one win him from the sober sense of the other, while Lord C—— hovers angrily about; or the scene with the captain at the Rose Tavern. In none of these does the effect depend on Farquhar's skillful use of language, Furetière's strong point, but rather on his ability to conceive vital dramatic situations with moral intent—Peregrine is repaid in kind for his own perfidy, the captain is no better than a porter, complete submission to amorous fortune can well be represented by a raffle.

In short, Farquhar's brief apprenticeship at the novel convinces the reader only of considerable promise as a playwright. *The Adventures* must have convinced Farquhar of the same thing. Having published a novel and produced a play at about the same time, perhaps as a probing of his talents, he abandoned fiction forever for the stage. Even in the midst of *The Adventures,* his mind seems to have turned in that direction, because he inserted the brief disquisitions on Collier and on the unities. There is some thematic point to each, it is true: the discussion of Collier shows the ill effects of passion's overcoming reason; and that of the unities, the good sense of Selinda, whom Peregrine's folly causes him to forfeit. But both discussions are drawn out further than seems necessary for the story, and both, in the light of Farquhar's future interests, strike one more as foreshadowings of the "Discourse" and *The Twin-Rivals* than as functional parts of *The Adventures.* As a very young man, Farquhar could write an amusing and lively story; as a slightly older man, he saw that amusing and lively stories would be a *cul-de-sac* for him, and wisely stopped writing them.

II The Inconstant

Beaumont and Fletcher are hardly staples of the modern repertory. Even in the university, the merits of their plays are passed over while scholars study their influence or tragicomic mode. Critics treat them as the beginning of the dramatic decline from the peaks of lofty Shakespeare and rugged Ben Jonson. Their slickness and glib simplification of ideas prompted the late R. P. Blackmur to refer to them pointedly as "the Bobbsey Twins." But the late seventeenth-century theater and critics would not have concurred. One historian, Arthur Colby Sprague, counts "thirty-nine [of their] plays . . . produced in the fifty years [from 1660 to 1710]—surely an exceptional record—and a number of these seem to have enjoyed an almost uninterrupted popularity."[8] Sprague lists some twenty adaptations and alterations of Beaumont and Fletcher written during the same period, eighteen of them actually acted. Respected critical opinion supported this popularity. Therefore, the extraordinary domination of the stage by Beaumont and Fletcher becomes of extreme importance to the understanding and criticism of the Restoration theater. In adapting them Farquhar might seem to be playing safe in two ways, by using their name and more significantly, their tried-and-true stage practice and ethos as a basis for his own work. As we shall see, this is in fact only partly so, because *The Wild-Goose Chase* was not well known and because Farquhar altered it radically.

He did not much alter the plot, at least in the first four acts. This was rich material to pirate. There was a dashing libertine's part assured for Wilks, and the low comedy of Pinkethman could be aired fully by adapting the role of the libertine's father for him. The complicated plot, with its traps and disguises and gay bawdry, must have struck Farquhar as very much the sort of thing upon which his talents could work most deftly. Nor was he competing in the popular affection with a standard repertory piece. Despite a hostile pamphleteer's remark that Farquhar had stolen from a comedy recently acted with applause, no evidence exists for any London production of *The Wild-Goose Chase* between 1668 and the late eighteenth century. Gerard Langbaine, a diligent stage historian writing in 1691, does not list it among the thirteen Beaumont and Fletcher plays that he has seen approved in the theater. John Harold Wilson calls it "a forgotten play." [9] Thus the wit and intrigue, cleverly refurbished, would seem fresh at Drury Lane. Farquhar's choice was excellent; and since his handling of it was equally so, one can forgive his asperity at having been cheated of financial success by a public *"so very fond of improving* [its] Understanding, *that the instruction of a Play does no good, when it comes in Competition with the Moral of Minuet"* (221).

The Wild-Goose Chase is based on the ideal story pattern for the vigorous male: girl meets boy, girl loses boy, girl loses boy, girl loses boy, girl gets boy. Farquhar wisely left this basic plot unaltered. The boy in Fletcher's comedy[10] is a roving libertine named Mirabel, the titular wild goose, whose eventual capture belies the implications of vain chase in the title. The girl is Oriana, who had been contracted to Mirabel before he began his travels but now finds him contracted instead to a promiscuous bachelorhood. In Act I, Mirabel returns to Paris with two companions, Pinac and Belleur; they are preceded by Oriana's brother De Gard, a sober traveler who acts as foil to their airiness. Despite De Gard's praise, it soon turns out that Mirabel has not discarded the "wild fantastic toys" or purged the "humourous fluxes" of which his father La Castre accuses him:

> . . . He was ever
> A loose and strong defier of all order,
> His Loves are wanderers, they knock at each door,
> And taste each dish, but are no residents.[11] (I. i, 319)

After Mirabel discourses appreciatively on Italian women (I. ii), La Castre enters to suggest a match between Mirabel and either Rosalura or Lilia Bianca, the two nubile daughters of his friend Natolet. Belleur and Pinac fall in love with the girls immediately, ignoring Mirabel's objections that one is too gay and the other too grave; and, beginning with II. i, the whole comedy plays off Oriana's hunt for Mirabel against the other men's hunt for the other girls. Act II gives each couple one scene to come to the fore, as Mirabel refuses Oriana, and Natolet's daughters put down their lovers, one through gaiety and the other through gravity. Act III, in one scene, is an antistrophe: the hunters devise three plots. Pinac gets a courtesan to pose as a prospective noble bride; Belleur gruffly pretends to run mad; Oriana gets De Gard to pose as a Savoy lord come to woo her. In turn, the end of III and the first two scenes of IV show the three plots thwarted on the verge of success, by the discovery of the impostures. To further the parallelism, Oriana is next given the ruse of feigning madness, but she reveals the cheat too soon for it to work. In other words, she has two schemes, one a double of Pinac's imposture, one a double of Belleur's madness, to practice on Mirabel, who has in turn been the contriver of Pinac's and Belleur's ruses. Pattern could hardly go farther without crudity.

The last act gets the goose into the pot at last, although he is preparing for flight back to Italy. Oriana poses as a wealthy Bolognese, the sister of a gentleman whose life Mirabel had saved. Now that he can look at her objectively as a stranger, Mirabel falls in love with her and proposes marriage. Oriana joyfully discovers herself and Mirabel surrenders with whimsical grace: "Well; I do take thee upon meer Compassion;/ And I do think, I shall love thee" (V. vi, 389). Like Prospero, he destroys his book —not a manual of magic but a catalogue of conquests—with the resolution. The girls give their hands to Belleur and Pinac. The play ends with everyone off to church, and with Belleur's characteristically Fletcherian *double-entendre:* "No more for *Italy;* for the *Low-Countries.*"

Fletcher does not abandon pattern in this last act. As the play begins with an arrival from Italy, the triumphant Mirabel's, so it ends with at least the pretense of such an arrival, the triumphant Oriana's. Her action in "arriving" blocks an intended departure for the same place, and restores her at the center of the play that she had begun and in the middle of which she had shared both of the ruses. Now she becomes a lodestone to compel the happy resolution of the subplots without further machinations. In less schematic terms, too, the conclusion consummates earlier events. Mirabel, home in France, has begun by praising Italian women and dispraising French: thus he is induced through the Italian disguise to join Italy and France in his choice of a wife, enjoying the union of native and foreign, of home and abroad, that he could not enjoy at the beginning. Similarly, his bravery in saving Sig. Alberto, the supposed brother of the Italian stranger, has presented him for the first time as an honorable man, and thereby anticipates an honorable conclusion. However, pattern in this last act wins out over plausibility, even plausibility in the terms of a gay comedy. Mirabel's genuine feeling for Oriana cannot be believed if he is really deceived by her Bolognese disguise; if he is not, his behavior is inexplicable. Formal appropriateness alone does not suffice to justify the denouement. This witty last act goes lame.

By "witty," I mean "ingenious," but Fletcher's plays also had a reputation for the other sort of wit, elegant and aphoristic talk. Indeed, for a playwright so highly formal to have been considered easy and natural, as Fletcher was, he would have to be able to blur form by means of dialogue, to entertain the audience distractingly moment by moment, to provide his characters with individual tunics to wear over their regimentals. Wit is the best means of individualizing elegant comic characters, for it is lighter and more flowing than obvious verse, and not degrading as idiosyncrasy would be. The girls and Mirabel are expert in the wit of similes:

> Musk-melons are the emblems of the maids;
> Now they are ripe, now cut 'em, they taste pleasantly,
> And are a dainty fruit, digested easily:
> Neglect this present time, and come to morrow,
> They are so ripe they are rotten gone, their sweetness
> Run into humour, and their taste to surfeit. (I. iii, 326)

And the texture of the dialogue is woven through with well-turned phrases.

Although his *"I took the hint from* Fletcher*'s* Wild Goose Chase" (221) is ungenerous, Farquhar's reworking of the play is at least half original with him. The general outline, of course, is the same. However, he reduces the number of characters drastically. While Mirabel and Oriana remain, Pinac entirely disappears, and the paired Lilia Bianca and Rosalura are compressed into one character, Bisarre, who shares the amorous subplot with Belleur, renamed Duretete. The two fathers, Natolet and La Castre, become one, Old Mirabel; a tutor, Lugier, vanishes; De Gard remains as Dugard. A small servant's role was enlarged for "Dicky" Norris, and Farquhar's last act required a courtesan, Lamorce—in fair trade, he gave up the courtesan who appears in one of the ruses of *The Wild-Goose Chase*. She fitted in well enough in Fletcher's moral scheme, if one can talk of such a thing, but could not be accommodated in Farquhar's.

A closer examination of *The Inconstant* will reveal the nature of Farquhar's changes. The two scenes of Act I correspond to Fletcher's, except that Farquhar introduces Old Mirabel into I. ii, to help tie the act together. Act II in turn imitates the first two scenes of Fletcher's, and picks up some material from his I. iii. Act II scene iii is cut, and Farquhar simplifies Act III to one plot instead of three. Mirabel, who has twitted his father and Bisarre, has revealed his love for Oriana by carelessly leaving "Crambo Songs, short-footed Odes, and long-legg'd Pindaricks" with "*Oriana* in every line" among his possessions. It is on this basis that Old Mirabel (not Dugard, whom Oriana is afraid to expose to Mirabel's sword) is persuaded to impersonate Oriana's noble wooer. He plays a Spanish count rather than a Savoy lord since Prince Eugen of Savoy was an English ally and Philip V a hated Bourbon. Mirabel's bravery is made clear by his choosing to quarrel with the man, unlike Fletcher's hero, who can only mutter, "This is a thundring Lord; I am glad I scap'd him," and who needs the intervention of a disaffected servant, a thin contrivance of Fletcher's, to put him out of fear.

Farquhar's fourth act has three scenes, the first two of which are not Fletcherian at all. Oriana pretends to have become a nun, and Mirabel, disguised as a friar, comes to beg "Pardon to deserve your Favour," and to plead the validity of the disavowed "Precontract"; but all is lost when Old Mirabel bursts in to denounce a trick that has made his only heir turn friar. After an interlude in IV. iii, based on Rosalura's mock penitence before Belleur (*WGC* IV. ii), Farquhar imitates Fletcher's IV. iii, the madness of Oriana. She is quite convincing, and Mirabel reacts like a member of the audience at a pathetic Restoration tragedy: "these suddain starts of undigested Words, shoot thro' my Soul with more perswasive

Force, than all the study'd Art of labour'd Eloquence" (IV. iii, 260). The cloister episode has previously led Mirabel to temporary "sanity"; he himself comments that his despair about losing Oriana has made him pious like the "*Sick Wretch*" who "*Vows all to Heaven,*" but

> *The Body is no sooner Rais'd, and Well,*
> *But the weak Soul relapses into Ill;*
> *To all its former swing of Life is led,*
> *And leaves its Vows and Promises in Bed.* (IV. ii, 257)

Farquhar's audience has twice in this act been prepared for some sort of moral realization on Mirabel's part, as Fletcher's was not. Such realizations, based on good sense as well as feeling (the motive of Fletcher's hero), urge him to denounce his earlier follies.

Although the flush of moral sense does not last long, since Oriana is again jilted, it colors Farquhar's play and differentiates it in tone and effect from Fletcher's. Farquhar intensifies this change with his rhetoric. Oriana in *The Wild-Goose Chase* has simply reacted with shame when her lover callously casts her aside upon learning that she is sane. Her counterpart launches into tragic histrionics: "tho' my former frenzy was but Counterfeit, I now shall run into a real Madness." Indeed, the whole scene has been worked in the theatrically current tragic idiom: "Speak, my charming Angel," "my Soul . . . toss'd with Storms of Passion," "Stay, my fair Innocence." All these sentences are Farquhar's Mirabel's, while Fletcher's says in the same circumstances, "What? she speaks well,/ And with another voice," "Oh fair tears, how ye take me!" and "Pray ye pardon me." The emotion may be similar, but the rhetoric is nowhere nearly so overwrought. Clearly, Farquhar has disabled himself from using Fletcher's amoral, psychologically unjustified, low-keyed fifth act. He has pointed directly to something else, and, unsurprisingly, provided it. No one could disagree with Sprague's argument that Farquhar's concluding adventure "was not quite right for *The Wild-Goose Chase,*"[12] but Farquhar did not mean it for *The Wild-Goose Chase,* not even for *The Wild-Goose Chase* with sententious insertions and sentimental fustian, for in intent and in execution, *The Inconstant* is more than that.

Farquhar's fifth act purges Fletcher's through parody. In

Fletcher, Oriana poses as a Bolognese much bedecked with jewels, whom Mirabel instantly loves. In Farquhar, Mirabel is ready to pledge himself, albeit insincerely, to a woman much bedecked with jewels who somehow reminds Duretete of a "*Curtesan*" "in *Bollognia.*" Both Mirabels postpone their travels for the jeweled woman; both are gulled by her. Surely the parallels are too striking to be ignored, although the infrequency with which *The Wild-Goose Chase* was performed would have kept them effectually concealed from the audience. They are not important in the play's rhetoric, as Farquhar's parodies in *The Twin-Rivals* or *The Beaux' Stratagem* are; however, they imply the same thing that the others do, a skepticism about the fiction being parodied and a desire to reject it for a less dubious fiction.

This private evocation of the theme of fiction/reality coincides with the central evocation of that theme in the fifth act of the play, beginning in "*the Street before the* Play-House; Mirabel *and* Duretete . . . *coming from the Play.*" Mirabel cries out in enthusiasm, "I cou'd wish that my whole Life long were the first Night of a New Play": critics have discerned the voice of Farquhar the theater buff here, but what they should have discerned is skillful preparation for the murderous "play" which is to follow. Mirabel and Lamorce have each created a different drama that represents the wishes of each. Lamorce uses illusion—her disguise—to deceive, and thus presumably to make the illusion come true by getting rich. She accepts illusion only as a total realist might. Mirabel desires no reality but that of illusion, of appearances without responsibility. Lamorce and her bravoes are projections of the characters who have lately embarrassed him, Oriana and the men assisting her. Lamorce seems to him a happy substitute. Here at last is an Oriana who can be toyed with and slept with but never married. (The real Oriana, at her low point, has been made neuter as a page.) The force of the last act comes from Mirabel's realizing the consequences of his illusory wishes, from his getting a lesson in realism; while Lamorce and the audience are given a lesson in romance through Oriana's faithfulness and derring-do. This balance between the hard-headed and the idealistic is Farquhar's theme, of course, in all three of the early plays, but he had never before contrived so complex a metaphor with which to dramatize it.

Oriana is Mirabel's true savior in every sense, as the rather heavy-handed final speech declares, since she rescues him from captivity to appearances, from death through inconstancy, as well as literally from being murdered by the bravoes. "*What liberty,*" asks Mirabel, pointing to the hapless Lamorce, "*can be so Tempting there/ As a soft, vertuous, Amorous bondage here?* [to Oriana]." Through her art of illusion, she has led him through challenges to his honor (the Spanish count), to his duty and his vows (the cloister: Mirabel himself makes the connection between the two sorts of vows), and to his reason (the fit of madness). To each illusion he has responded; from each return to reality he has backed away. Her fifth-act blending of the two has been perfectly in character. We can see from this vantage point that Farquhar has converted the tricks in *The Wild-Goose,* all of which are developments of the formal arrangement, into a series of calculated "ideological" appeals. The formal arrangement receives its neat completion in the earlier play; the moral progression receives its in the later.

Fletcher's fine choreography has been irremediably lost. Not only has the reduction of the number of couples destroyed the chance of Fletcherian parallelism, but Farquhar has also neglected almost every chance of seriously counterpointing the main plot with that involving Duretete and Bisarre. Their activities are nearly all farcical, built on the conception of Duretete as played by Bullock rather than that of Belleur as played by Lowin. Lowin, "probably . . . Burbadge's chief support" with the early seventeenth-century King's Men, was an actor of great importance as "the bluff and outspoken character, sometimes the honest friend, sometimes villain." His roles are thought to have included Shakespeare's Henry VIII and Webster's Bosola (*The Duchess of Malfi*), as well as "*Falstaffe, Morose* [in Jonson's *Epicoene*], *Vulpone,* and *Mammon* in the *Alchymist; Melancius* in the *Maid's* Tragedy." Bullock lacked the range and gravity of Lowin; he was primarily a buffoon. He had played Mockmode and the younger Clincher in Farquhar's first two comedies, while the nature of many of his other roles is clear from a mere list: Sir Tunbelly Clumsey (Vanbrugh's *Relapse*), Sir Amorous La Foole (*Epicoene*), Sir Jolly Jumble (Otway's *Soldier's Fortune*), Sir Jasper Fidget (*The Country Wife*), and even the grave-digger in *Ham-*

let. Like Lowin, he was a large portly man, but there the resemblance stopped.[13] I am not suggesting that Farquhar had to tailor Duretete for Bullock, but that his having given the part to a clown tells one a great deal about how he conceived it.

Since Duretete is a foolish man, he remains Mirabel's foil. Their relationship in the play is more or less expressed by their reactions to Bisarre. Duretete (like Mockmode) immediately becomes involved with dry pedantry: "She's mine, man; she's mine; my own Talent to a T. I'll match her in Dialecticks faith. I was seven years at the University, man; nurst up with *Barbara, Celarunt, Darii ferio, Baralipton.* Did you never know, man, that 'twas Metaphysicks made me an Ass? it was [,] faith" (II. i, 235). Mirabel's education has taught him about human nature, as shown in his answering and anticipating Bisarre by apposite passages from Virgil (III. i, 245–46). While to Duretete Bisarre remains unpredictable, the humanistic Mirabel can understand her so well as to be able to steal her individuality from her by showing her conforming to the Virgilian pattern. Through knowledge he can conquer where Duretete has been defeated: this fits with the theme of education in the play as a whole. In a simple pairing of scenes, Farquhar juxtaposes Mirabel's brave challenge to the "Spanish count" (III. ii) and Duretete's roaring at the "*two Gentlemen*" and beating them (III. iii)—honor and passion are differentiated.

The last two scenes between Duretete and Bisarre parody the main plot, although they do not comment upon it. Transvestite disguise, obedience to orders, the fight for supremacy between the man and the woman, the dangerous female bravoes of IV. iii, and the act of stripping off clothing are all related to the Mirabel-Lamorce affair. Perhaps the sexual teasing about Duretete's and Bisarre's being "examined" serves as a prologue to sexual consummation in marriage. But Farquhar rarely makes formal maneuvers for their own sake. These scenes not only heighten the events in the main plot (madness, Lamorce) by prolonging suspense, but also contrast a foolish passion with the increasing gravity of the central love. In a sense, Duretete and Bisarre siphon off the elements of the ridiculous, and make it possible for the audience to accept and respect the high rhetoric and the moral development of these last two acts.

Bisarre, unlike Lilia Bianca and Rosalura but like Duretete, serves largely as her principal's foil. In II. i, Mirabel and Oriana have a rather equal wit-combat, promising each other torments and cuckoldry; Farquhar then immediately uses Bisarre, who jeers at Duretete throughout II. ii, as a means of adjusting our response: the subplot shows us folly, shows us aberration, and we gratefully accept the more tempered world of the main plot. Bisarre is particularly necessary because Farquhar's Oriana is so bold, so much more capable of passion and charm than Fletcher's boy-actor could manage to be. Fletcher's heroine gives a simple account of her health: "You see I am not bated;/ Merry, and eat my meat" (I. i, 317). In Farquhar, there is verve in the response: "Why truly Brother I look pretty well, thank Nature and my Toylet; I have scap'd the Jaundice, Green Sickness, and the Small Pox; I eat three meals a day, am very merry when up, and sleep soundly when I'm down" (I. i, 226). By the end of the first act she has made a finer and deeper impression of her worth than can Fletcher's heroine throughout a play. Here is a creature capable of carrying off the melodrama of the last two acts. She benefits greatly from *The Inconstant's* sharp focus on a central plot and personal moral progress. Farquhar's increased reliance on individual protagonists encourages him to particularize far more than Fletcher, and he takes full advantage of the opportunity.

The difference in particularization shows up most forcibly in the creation of Old Mirabel, perhaps the finest character in the play, a foreshadowing of Justice Ballance in *The Recruiting Officer* as Oriana is of Silvia. While La Castre and Natolet of *The Wild-Goose Chase*, not regular parts of Fletcher's pattern, must be tucked into a sober middleground, Farquhar has no such compulsions. Old Mirabel provides an hilarious character study, varies the texture of the play, and gave Pinkethman a chance to show what he could do. He also has a thematic function. Just as Farquhar stresses Mirabel's personal realization of duty and honor, he stresses lineage as part of the total context of obligations within which his hero operates. Old Mirabel's constant oath, "by the Blood of the *Mirabels*"; Farquhar's alteration of Fletcher in having Mirabel arrive but not go to greet his father, an anticipatory failure of filial duty; the interruption of the cloister scene by Old Mirabel's howling for his heir; the father's willingness to pose as the Spanish count; even the boisterous reminders, both in speech and in such visual images as the giving of money, that Mirabel is his father's son—all these add to the compulsion toward marriage through emphasizing family and duty.

Young men are lusty and old men rich: therefore in a properly stable society, property and sex are inextricably linked. Old Mirabel always makes this connection, speaking from the side of money, his contribution to the running of things. His first speech sets up the guidelines: "Whilst I have Golden Pockets, then let my Hairs be Silver an they will. Adsbud, Sir, I can dance, and sing, and drink, and—no, I can't wench. But Mr. *Dugard,* no news of my Son *Bob* in all your Travels?" (I, i, 225). The unconscious association between his own impotence and his son is a lovely stroke, natural and telling, and perhaps improved by Farquhar's choice of the nickname, since it may have been (as in "dry bob") associated with the motion of coitus. Later in the play, marriage and money continue to be associated in his mind. When he chides Bob for abusing Oriana (II, i), "this tender, lovely, good-natur'd dear Rogue," the discourse proceeds to a picture, "the Effigies of the lovely *Oriana,* with ten thousand pound to her Portion—ten thousand pound, you Dog; ten thousand pound, you Rogue; how dare you refuse a Lady with ten thousand pound, you impudent Rascal." But he is no miser—quite to the contrary, he represents the sensible attitude. Farquhar's break with Restoration comedy could not be made clearer than by his elevation of the older generation from their usual position as testy dupes to the novel heights of good sense and eventual justification.

It remains to talk about the language of the play. *The Inconstant* is in prose, *The Wild-Goose Chase* in verse. Set speeches in Fletcher therefore tend toward a structure of spatial units, based on the verse line; in Farquhar, toward parallelism of syntactic structure. For instance, De Gard's and Dugard's speeches to their respective Orianas show forms governed by opposite modes of composition and thought.

> He Marry? he'll be hanged first: he knows no more
> What the conditions and the ties of Love are,
> The honest purposes and grounds of Marriage,
> Nor will know, nor be ever brought t'endeavour,
> Than I do how to build a Church; he was ever

A loose and strong defier of all order,
His loves are wanderers, they knock at each door,
And taste each dish, but are no residents. (I. i, 319)

Dug. Marriage! young *Mirabel* Marry! he'll build Churches sooner; take heed, Sister, tho your Honour stood proof to his home-bred assaults, you must keep a stricter Guard for the future; he has now got the foreign Ayre and the *Italian* Softness; his Wit's improv'd by Converse, his Behaviour finish'd by Observation, and his Assurance confirm'd by *Success.* Sister, I can assure you he has made his Conquests; and 'tis a plague upon your Sex, to be the soonest deceiv'd by those very men that you know to have been false to others. (I. i, 227)

I do not know how fruitful an observation it may be to note that the difference between Fletcher's a priori and Farquhar's a posteriori structures—content shaped by form in Fletcher's lines, vice versa in Farquhar's clauses—forms an analogue to the difference between the structures of the two plays as wholes.

Shorter sallies, where there are changes at all, are characteristically more elegant and poetic in Fletcher, brisker and racier in Farquhar. One example should suffice. When Mirabel ironically begs a servant's place with Oriana the Savoy countess, he says

But Basto, now; I know my rules and distance;
Yet, if she want an Usher; such an implement;
One that is thoroughly pac'd; a clean made Gentleman;
Can hold a hanging up; with approbation
Plant his hat formally, and wait with patience
I do beseech you, Sir. (III. i, 357)

In Farquhar, the corresponding speech goes: "I'm her Ladyship's most humble Servant; a Train and a Title, hey! room for my Lady's Coach, a front Row in the Box for her Ladyship; Lights, Lights for her Honour—now must I be a constant attender at my Lords Levee, to work my way to my Lady's Couchee—" (III. ii, 247). From its verse and elegance, *The Wild-Goose Chase* gains greatly in aural pleasure, but it lacks that comfortable jocularity through which Farquhar so easily made his characters engaging. This is one of the reasons why Fletcher's Mirabel seems so much more obnoxiously callous than Farquhar's. Admittedly, one never cares much about callousness in following the design of *The Wild-Goose Chase,* but sympathy for Mirabel and belief in his worth are essential for *The Inconstant.* Each of the plays uses language with a specific propriety that makes comparative value judgments of parts of the plays, rather than of the two total works of art, largely unprofitable.

Along with Farquhar's more spontaneous and immediate language comes a deeper and more immediate response to the characters. This is also manifested in non-verbal ways. For instance, his use of the ominous good cheer of the bravoes and the interpolated scene between Bisarre and Duretete (V. iii) increase a suspense that works to generate empathy for Mirabel, to make us feel the menace of the bravoes and to accept as relievedly as does Mirabel Oriana's victory. Since a play that moves dialectically, such as *The Inconstant,* seems more likely to use temporal devices like suspense than would a play that presents a pattern, such as *The Wild-Goose Chase,* it is unsurprising to find Farquhar drawing us in with such devices far more than does Fletcher. Similarly, Farquhar appeals to us with moment-by-moment excitement or bustle. *The Wild-Goose Chase* has only one explicit instruction for physical contact or buffoonery, Belleur's being kicked, and by its fastidiousness preserves our pleasure in its aloof contrivance. But fastidiousness never allured Farquhar. His Mirabel trips up and beats the "Spanish count," passionately seizes Oriana, and exchanges rude nose-pullings with a bravo; his Duretete beats two laughing gentlemen, minces through a scene of mock ogling, and breaks Bisarre's guinea fan, besides being "laid hold on" by her two ladies. The last act has swords and muskets. All of these are more engaging than Fletcher's dramaturgy would permit in this sort of play. One might suggest that the most important hint that Farquhar took from Fletcher was not the plot and dialogue of *The Wild-Goose Chase,* but Fletcher's practice in the art of tragicomedy.[14]

III The Stage-Coach

The last of Farquhar's borrowed work, the short farce *The Stage-Coach* (1704), does not demand much attention. Although entertaining, it is slight. One Captain Basil is waiting impatiently in the London road for accommodations into town. A wound has prevented him from riding himself to save his betrothed, Isabella, who is threatened by her uncle Micher with immediate marriage to a Lancashire booby squire. The captain is chafing at the delay, when Isabella, Micher, and the squire themselves arrive at the inn. At night, a series of contretemps in the dark offers the chance for much slapstick confusion, during which Basil and Isabella are married by a parson in the inn, and consummate their marriage with superhuman speed.

Jean De la Chapelle's comedy *Les Carosses d'Orléans* (1681) provided Farquhar and his collaborator Motteux with a model that they followed rather faithfully. Of course they naturalized the piece: Paris and Bourges became London and Lancashire, De la Chapelle's drunken Dutchman became one of Farquhar's typical Irishmen, and characters named Crispin and Bastienne became Fetch (a valet) and Dolly. There are three other sorts of changes that Farquhar made;

(1) His dialogue is crisper and more vigorous. In part this is due to the idioms of the English and French language and theater, in part to De la Chapelle's rather flat dialogue. Sometimes Farquhar expands upon the original. Cléante's "Ah Crispin la détestable voiture qu'un Carosse de Blavet" (sc. iii) appears as Basil's "What a tedious, tiresome, dull, jolting Vehicle is a Stage Coach, we that are in it are more fateagued than the beasts that Draw it" (I, *15*). At other times, he compresses the French. For example, we may take this exchange:

[*Capt.* I am thrown] into this confounded Company, a big belli'd Farmers Daughter, an Irish Wit, a canting Quaker, a City Whore, and a Country Parson.

Fet. And a disbanded Captain, Sir, for want of a stroling Lawyer, or a Nurse, and a Child to make up a clever Stage-Coach sett.

Capt. Ay, the swell'd Country Puss plagued me with her screaming and wry faces, the profound Teague with his Nonsence, the Quaker with the Spirit, the Whore with the Flesh, and the fat Parson with both. (*15, 16*)

In comparison De la Chapelle's version lacks particularization and energy. Cléante announces that he has been "persecuté par une Plaideuse qui ne parle que de ses procez; par une jeune Provinciale qui n'a jamais vû Paris, qui ne songe qu'aux ajustemens qu'elle s'y donnera, & qui avec un langage affecté vous fait cent questions impertinentes; par un Abbé qui veut faire le bel esprit, & qui ne dit que des sottises. Enfin par un Hollandois qui à peine sçait écorcher cinq ou six mots de Francois dont il vous fatigué sans cesse les oreilles: Non, quand on auroit choisi exprès des sens propres à lasser la patience d'un honneste homme, on n'eût pas fait un assemblage plus bizarre que celuy que le hazard a fait dans nostre Carosse." And to this Crispin answers with another speech about "la Provinciale's" screaming when she thinks the carriage will overturn, and the inability of the "Plaideuse" to hold her water, so that the coach must keep stopping for her "rendre des tributs à la nature." De la Chapelle belabors the joke; Farquhar makes it quick and pungent.

2) Farquhar tries far harder to characterize. De la Chapelle's foolish squire, Dodinet, enters first (sc. vii) by reacting to Angélique's little scream when she unexpectedly sees Cléante ("Qu'avez vous, Mademoiselle? est-ce que vous vous trouvez mal?"); Farquhar's Nicodemus Somebody has an analogous situation and speech ("Ha! What's the matter, my dear Wife that is to be?"), but first, the audience has been given a chance to see him laden with luggage and full of complaints: "Come, Mrs. *Isabell*, woons why don'na you come away—I've gotten your things. Bless us, what a parcel of Luggage these Women carry about them—and the poor Lover here must be subject to the Slavery of Banboxes. Why Mrs. *Isabell*—why don't you come away. I am as tired as a Scotch Pedler under his Pack" (II, *19*). And once having established his characterization. Farquhar maintains it. Dodinet's "N'est-il pas vray que j'ay fait là une belle trouvaille [?] Elle est un peu triste, mais avec le temps nous la ragaillardirons." (sc. vii) forwards the narrative, but the coarse complacent puns of Nicodemus Somebody achieve far more: "Well, how d'you like her now? hey! wo'not she make a rare Titt for *Somebody*? She's a little in the dumps at present, but we'll dump her out of that I'll warrant you" (*20*).

(3) Most significantly, Farquhar makes a better-knit play than De la Chapelle's, better-knit both in plot and in tone. In *Les Carosses d'Orléans,* the drunken Dutchman who lies in the same room as Cléante is unaware of anything that goes on; Macahone, the analogous character in *The Stage-Coach,* serves to witness the

clandestine marriage. In turn, he, who has helped save Isabella from her fortune-hunting uncle, is appropriately saved by Basil from a fortune-hunting woman posing as a rich widow. To amuse the audience in set scenes, and to confuse the action, De la Chapelle employs the Dutchman, a country girl, and a litigant. Farquhar can eliminate the latter two, and still set the tone of folly and confusion at least as effectively through making the coachman, who is a whoremonger in both versions, a swindler too (*18*), and through having us hear about the landlady's exorbitant bill. These instances of avarice, together with Micher's and the "rich widow's," help fix a context from which the lovers emerge as brightly as do Cléante and Angélique from the folly at Orléans; and the job is done with far more economy and force. Farquhar's use of the parson, merely an incidental fellow-traveler in De la Chapelle, to marry the lovers in the inn works as neatly as his use of the incidental chambermate Macahone as a witness.

In still more purely technical terms, Farquhar improves on De la Chapelle. Dolly, the chambermaid, appears at the very beginning of the play tacitly agreeing to some sort of assignation with Fetch, so that her help to the lovers is made plausible in a way that the help of her undeveloped counterpart Bastienne cannot be. While no reason is provided for the sluggishness of Le Cocher in *Les Carosses,* Farquhar's Jolt has been bribed by profiteering innkeepers along the London road to dally on the trip. The most cogent revision comes in the treatment of the lovers. Cléante and Angélique are allowed to run off together in scene xx (out of twenty-seven in all), and are not heard from again. Basil and Isabella, however, reappear in nightclothes—they have never left the inn—to provide a visual impression of their triumph, and to balance and conclude the action of which they have been the principals.

The Stage-Coach, which is the only play Farquhar published between 1702 and 1706, makes one hungry for the work he did not do. Not only is it a tidy and lively play, but it has a great deal of charm and wit. If, in the last analysis, it is a trifle, it is also perhaps a cheerful harbinger of the two great comedies that were yet to come.

CHAPTER 5

The Non-Dramatic Work

I *"General Schomberg"*

FARQUHAR'S ode *"On the Death of General* Schomberg *kill'd at the* Boyn" (279–82) begins inauspiciously, "What dismal Damp has overspread the War?" This is a dismal damp of a first line, and suggests a lack of control particularly dangerous in the Pindaric ode. Writers of couplets, sonnets, even blank verse, are at least gently supported by the set form within which they are working; but the Pindaric ode deliberately jettisoned any set form in order to free the author's, and thereby the reader's, exuberant fancy. The influential critic John Dennis wrote in 1695, for example, that "The Design of the Ode (I mean upon great occasions) is, like that of Heroic Poetry, to move the Reader, and cause in him admiration. Now by Heroic Poetry, the Readers mind is exalted gradually, with a more sedate and compos'd Majesty; but the Ode, by reason of the shortness of its compass, is oblig'd to fly into transport at first, and to make use immediately of all its fury, and its most violent efforts, or else it would want time to work its effect." A kind of poetry primarily designed to move the reader with "transport," "fury," and "violent efforts" obviously calls for a great deal of tact on the author's part if it is to avoid overdone silliness, if the recommended "warmth and vigour of fancy, the masterly figures, and the copiousness of imagination" [1] are going to be kept from galloping off without that control implicit in the very word "art." Fortunately, Farquhar mustered some of the proper tact, and "General Schomberg" becomes better as it proceeds.

The Pindaric ode was a natural choice of genre for Farquhar to make. Although ostensibly an imitation of the lofty but regular odes of Pindar (5th century B.C.), the Pindaric ode as it developed in England disregarded its classic model. It lost its formal regularity and became elastic, striking the reader with the sort of passionate lyricism that Dennis advises and abandoning the appearance of judgment so as to lift the spirit to admiration. Abraham Cowley (1618–1667), a popular and influential poet, initiated the revived form in mid-century; by 1706, Congreve could write "There is nothing more frequent among us, than a sort of Poems intituled Pindarique Odes." [2] Dryden, along with a bevy of lesser poets, tried his hand at the form—in Dryden's case, with immense success—and had left by the end of the century a fully established genre based on three principles already suggested: prosodic freedom, imaginative vigor, and control through verbal and metaphoric wit.

The subject of the poem, Friedrich Hermann duke of Schomberg, was a German soldier of fortune whose military prowess must have been astonishing. It won him a barony from Charles II, a county from the King of Portugal, a marshalcy from Louis XIV, and a stadtholderate from the Great Elector of Brandenburg. The English were so rapturous when he became a subject of William III's that they made him an earl, a marquis, and a duke all at once, presented him with £100,000, and privileged him to appear before the House of Commons. Then they sent him off to fight the Irish Jacobites.

These Jacobites had laid siege to Farquhar's Londonderry for 105 days in the early summer of 1689, during which time the city was hit by almost 600 bombs. "I believe there died 15000 men, women and children, many of which died for meat. But we had a great fever amongst us, and all the children died, almost whole families not one left alive," wrote an eyewitness. "One pound of oatmeal and one pound of tallow served a man a week; sometimes salt hides . . . I saw 2s. a quarter given for a little dog, horse blood at 4d. a pint; all the starch was eaten, the graves of tallow, horse flesh was a rarity, and still we resolved to hold out." Another eyewitness speaks of "Horse Flesh . . . Sold for 18s. a Pound, and very little of it to be got, a Quarter of a Dog, that fed upon the dead *Irish,* at 5s.6d., his Head at Half a Crown, a Cat at 4s. Rats, Mice, Tallow, Greaves, and all Noisome things that possibly could be Eaten at a Proportionable Rate." [3] It is no wonder that Schomberg, who arrived in Ireland shortly after this siege was lifted, was adored as a savior by people who had so much reason to hate the common enemy. Troops from Londonderry, Farquhar perhaps among them, rushed to join him; the clerical governor of Londonderry mustered English support for him, and fought (and died) with him in the field. When at the decisive battle of the Boyne (1690) Schomberg was killed under fire, he became an obvious subject for an elegiac ode written by the son of a Londonderry Protestant clergyman.

The poem itself begins to use the metric freedom of the Pindaric ode with some effectiveness through the first two stanzas, concentrating on the "grieving Voice" that trembles "As if afraid to tell/ How the great, Martial, Godlike *Schomberg* fell." These lagging trochees are now swept into a faster rhythm; "Godlike" is picked up as a motif along with the expectable "Martial"; and Farquhar's first image is of a Moses, an improved Moses who commands a "redder Sea" "not . . . to secure his Flight,/ But spight of Waves and Tides to meet, and fight." The antithesis in the near-pun on "flight" and "fight" is amplified in the rhyme, as a moderately complex parallelism develops, beginning with the couplet, "He, *Moses* like, with Sword, instead of Wand,/ This redder Sea of Gore could strait command." Rhythms here are well managed through the punctuation; "wand" and "command," rhyming, establish the idea of divine power which "sword" further augments; and "gore" is almost redeemed by its near-rhyme with "sword," which reinforces the Mosaic Red Sea image.

Stanza IV continues to connote divine right, now by describing the enemy arms in demonic terms. Cannon balls become monstrous progeny in hellish swaddling bands ("furious Offspring swath'd in curling Smoak,/ And wrapt in Bands of Fire") to plague the Mosaic host; they are made animate like Miltonic demons, with "sulphurous Ire," "wing'd with Death," "flies hissing." The whole sequence of images here is ingeniously introduced by a pun on "tormented" ("Throws tormented on the Shore"), which means "hurled by an engine of war" but openly refers to the pains of hell. The pun is academic, but it is a happy stroke of poetry, very much in keeping with the late metaphysical tradition in which the Cowleyan Pindaric had originally been conceived.

Having moved attention from Schomberg's leadership to the violence of the attack upon him, Farquhar uses stanza V to picture Schomberg as an aged tower (he was seventy-five in 1690) that falls to crush the enemy beneath it. This in turn reminds the poet of Samson, another great national hero, "Dragging a Train of Vengeance by each *Gyant* Arm" in stanza VI. Divine right, begun with Moses' leadership, receives its crown in Samson's suicidal triumph. The fallen temple can be seen as a ruin only "unto his Foes;/ From thence his glorious Monument arose." Yet as Schomberg was greater than Moses in action, so in martyrdom he is greater than Samson. Samson's monument *is* a ruin, seen more broadly, for it is subject to the flux of time. Time "Has eat thro' all, and even the very Ruine's gone:/ But *Schomberg's* Monument [the Boyne River] shall ne'er decay." "Monument," a hallowed word, is uniquely Schomberg's, for the river maintains its memorial identity despite all earthly mutability.

The last two stanzas complement the first two. Farquhar corrects the elegiac tone set at the beginning, demanding a suspension of "needless Grief" while "victorious Joy your Arms adorn[s]." On the hypothetical "Stygian Coast," Schomberg parades victorious before the unhappy ghosts of his military victims, paining them as he had pained their "Grosser Shapes" on earth. The poem ends with a congratulation on this state of affairs, and directions for a funeral hung with the spoils of victory, "For as he conquer'd living, so he conquering dy'd." The relationship between motion and stasis expressed in the verbs and participles here occurs in the previous line in terms of an image: "But Lawrel Weaths fix in their blooming Pride." And as one thinks back on the ode, it is clear that the paradox of the immortal monument and of Samson's simultaneous action and passion are also comparisons of the same sort. Through such unions of seeming antitheses, Farquhar not only reorders the mixture of feelings about Schomberg, but also resolves the deadly war between divinely led good and diabolic evil in stanzas III and IV. The conclusion has been well prepared for.

"General Schomberg" is at least a competent and controlled poem. It has a unity of intent that is at once functional and inobtrusive. It is literate. On the other hand, it shows no extraordinary poetic powers, and its language remains almost entirely pedestrian and conventional, too content to prime each noun with a single expected adjective: "chilling fears," "glorious Monument," "hollow Clangours," "mighty Warriour," "stately *Triumph.*" Farquhar's talents do not seem to have extended to dignified or inspired English. The words of "General Schomberg" fail to conquer with the brilliance and ease of the man they celebrate.

II *"Barcellona"*

Farquhar's last attempt at patriotic verse was a long poem in heroic couplets, "Barcellona." It probably was not begun before April, 1706, when *The Recruiting Officer* was ready for the stage; it probably was abandoned before January, 1707, when Farquhar, in despairing poverty, must have begun work on *The Beaux' Stratagem.* While that play was being finished, his poetic hero Mordaunt (the Earl of Peterborough) fell from favor. On February 22, 1707, Peterborough was officially discharged from his posts, Admiral, General, and High Commissioner in Spain; ordered on March 14 back to England, Peterborough began a leisurely five-month trip through the continent, charming courtiers and flaunting his nonchalance. This was certainly not the occasion for anyone but a polemicist to publish verse in his favor, and the Farquhars cannot have looked to "Barcellona" for much financial help. The manuscript aged in a drawer or box until 1710, when the disintegration of the Godolphin ministry made Peterborough powerful once more, and therefore eligible to be presented with his past in six cantos at a reasonable price.

Two issues of the poem came out in 1710, one "Publish'd for the Benefit of the Author's widow and Children," one with a dedication to Peterborough by Margaret Farquhar. Whether the great Earl responded is not known. He was a vain and generous man, and both those characteristics boded well. There is also a letter from Margaret to the influential politician Harley, who was interested in rehabilitating Peterborough, which refers to Margaret's "late experience of your honour's great and generous nature" and mentions ten guineas given her from the Queen "upon the presentation of my husband's poem"; this letter is undated, but may well have to do with a gift for "Barcellona." History, however, again struck down the poem. In March, 1711, Guiscard, whom canto II praises highly, stabbed Harley during an examination for treason in Whitehall. "Barcellona" was not reissued.[4]

Unfortunately, the historical allusions in the poem make it hard for a modern reader without a brief gloss. The English were anti-Bourbon, as usual, and in the early eighteenth century, being anti-

Bourbon meant fighting on several fronts. While the Duke of Marlborough and Prince Eugen of Savoy discomfited Louis XIV in the North, Peterborough was sent to put down Gallic Popery in Spain and to deprive the Bourbon Philip V of a throne for which the English preferred the Austrian Archduke Charles. On the expedition with Peterborough were Admiral Sir Cloudesley Shovell, Rear Admiral Sir John Leake, and Prince George of Hesse-Darmstadt (Commander-in-Chief to the Archduke), all of whom appear in the poem. Don Francisco Velasco, Viceroy of Catalonia, was the adversary, confident in the strength of his fort Montjuic. Velasco's complacency had plausible warrant, for Montjuic towered upward a steep eighth of a mile. Here Peterborough's reckless fancy brought forth a triumphant plan. One September night in 1705, he and his men slowly clambered till dawn up to the very outworks of Montjuic, carelessly guarded by the assured Spaniards. By day they attacked. After skirmishes and rallyings, and the death of Darmstadt, Montjuic capitulated, and Barcelona itself, deprived of its needed citadel, followed suit. Needless to say, England was ecstatic at so great and glaring a victory over the forces of Popish darkness; and in that political ecstasy, renewed by an eyewitness account, Farquhar began his second and last sustained poetical effort.

"Barcellona" begins quite well, with the description of the newly united English and Belgian forces, whose "awful Pomp" and "Capacious Transports" lack direction and leadership. Farquhar stresses the "*differing* People," the "Loud Murmurs" and "sawcy Voice,/ [that] Arraign the best of Sovereigns [Queen Anne] in her Choice." Directly above this mass are the cautious professionals, who are little better than their underlings:

> *Some* in Experience tardy Measures make,
> First, by fresh Errors, rectifie Mistake,
> Improv'd at last, they mend as they decay,
> *Their* Judgments rise, as they rise in Pay:
> By dint of lingring time slow Captains made,
> They work upon the War, as on a Trade.
>
> . . . .
>
> They spin the War in cuning dull delay,
> By Night unravel what they wove by Day,

With lingring Steps, o'er difficulties climb,
And wait Peace issuing from the Womb of Time. (*365–66*)

To this accumulated sense of diffused power, Mordaunt is suddenly opposed: here is the swift inspired amateur, skilled in the campaigns of William III and Marlborough, but directed on the battlefield as in Parliament by "the *First Light*." His force is like that of "some full Bosom'd Flood," a suitably irresistible phenomenon of nature that swells over imposed dikes—suggestive of the unnatural artifices by which Mordaunt's enemies hope to thwart him—with "Arbitrary Tyde." Farquhar then uses this image of the sea to glide gracefully into the narrative itself, beginning with the marine embarkation of Mordaunt and Shovell. The expedition, now given a leader, sails in a climate of realistic hope, proud in its power and wary of the consequences of battle. Farquhar catches the ambivalence with his wry observation that "Mothers melt in antidated Tears."

In these first three paragraphs, which may serve to illustrate the style of the poem at its best, Farquhar used prosody with professional ease to set up rhythmic patterns and to achieve special effects. Occasionally, he modifies the verse form markedly, depending on meaning. For instance, one may take these lines:

Such *Mordaunt* was, on whom this Business lay,
Mordaunt, had Fire to o'er inform his Clay,
But not superfluous;
The *Hero* glowing at his Army's Head,
The Soldiers caught the Sparkles as they fled,
Which made each Man a *Mordaunt* that he led.

Farquhar employs the triplet, as does Dryden, to add to the force of expression, here amplified by the clever contrast in the closing rhyme, in which the sparks have fled Mordaunt so that the soldiers do not. A similar use of the triplet occurs twenty-four lines later, and is relatively frequent in the poem as a whole; although the farther along one reads, the more Farquhar's haste becomes evident in casual or even clumsy triplets without specific rhetorical functions. The short line, too, appears several times in "Barcellona." Here, with a happy turn of wit, Farquhar imitates the controlled excess of Mordaunt with the overflowing (super, fluens) line, "But not superfluous." About twenty lines later we find "Gods! how he spoke," which expresses the poet's awe and fervor by the pause of three missing feet. Both of these short lines are imitative, one of the meaning and the other of the poet's state of mind, and the reader is not surprised to find long lines of a similar sort, such as "And *Marlborough's* larger Strides on *Blenheim*'s Bloody Plain." What Farquhar had done with his arbitrary form in "General Schomberg" he now does by making free with a preëstablished form in "Barcellona."

Beginning with the fourth paragraph, Farquhar spends the rest of Canto I in preparing a setting for the action. On the most obvious level, he uses the travels of the fleet to reinforce in the reader's mind the previous humiliations of the French. "Southward they steer and shun that hostile Place,/ Where *Tourville* lost his Ships and found Disgrace," he writes, referring to the battle of La Hogue, in which the French Tourville, supporting the pretensions of James II, lost sixteen battleships and the command of the sea. Next we have Peterborough's fleet sailing across Vigo Bay, where the English under Rooke and Ormond "seiz'd the Plate of *France* and *Spain*," about a million pounds of booty. And finally the canto closes with the defense of Gibraltar, not named but introduced with a calculated allusion to Hercules, "an old *Hero* of immortal Fame." Farquhar hopes to draw a parallel between Gibraltar, "a stupendious Promontory," and Montjuic. Gibraltar has been "Six Months besieg'd, six Months defended well"; Montjuic yielded to one sparkling assault. Montjuic was successfully climbed by the English; the French are shown, in a lengthy and bloody passage, hurled upon the rocks at Gibraltar after crawling up "Like Emmets, [when] in promiscuous Swarms they creep,/ Cling to the Rocks and graple with the Steep" (*370*). As he describes their frustration and fall to the bottom of the "dreadful Precipice," Farquhar again picks up "promiscuous," ironically, listing the "Promiscuous Arms, Brains, Legs, and Trunks of Men" in grim alphabetical order, since their natural order is lost. Through this imagery he amplifies the heroism required for the English to attempt Montjuic, while through the historical review he anticipates still another Bourbon defeat. Farquhar establishes English credentials in Canto I.

Canto II, a conversation between Peterborough and the French renegade Guiscard, fresh from encouraging revolt in the Cevennes, concerns itself with the moral right and moral duty of Queen Anne's England to defeat Louis' France. It also proves the dedication of Anne's general, for while "the num'rous Chiefs themselves address/ To entertainments," Peterborough listens to Guiscard's long vigorous indictment of Louis' "Strange Arbitrary Sway," of "the dark Bastile," of a land "Where *those*, that in soft Plenty liv'd before,/ Now chain'd in Couples, naked, gaul'd and sore,/ *Jerk* at each Lash, and *lug* the bended Oar" (373).

Peace in France is a state of war. Moved by the recital, Peterborough promises to provide "Relief from *Anna*'s Hand," the hand that rules him in the present struggle to restore Spanish rights. Farquhar stresses the connection between the Queen and the hero by portraying the ship, subtly, as a little England: a "*Naval Court*" "like an *Island* with the *Forrest* crown'd" (*371*). The ship's courtiers "*sooth* and *cringe* for Gain," but their captain, like their queen, occupies himself with sterner things. Farquhar's tacit comparison of Peterborough with virtuous Anne, and rejection of any comparison between Peterborough and vicious dictatorial Louis, may be designed specifically to shield his hero from the current charge of indiscretion and impulsiveness. Or it may simply be part of a patriotic panegyric style, which often runs to extremes.

Canto III pushes the formula of praise still further by repeating the structure of II, but lifting the terms to the supernatural. In the first section of the canto, Mordaunt's divinity is played upon. His prayer brings the "stiff Gales"; he is "the Godlike Man" blessed by the gods; he, the "favourite Burden" of the "*Tritons* proud"; he, a confederate with the winds. The ruler in body and spirit over both contemplation (the council) and action (the deployment of arms), Mordaunt remains "Deaf to the Calls that clamorous Nature makes," and understandably so, since as a god he controls her. As the Batteries are erected, he seems to repeat the original creative act:

> The Ships, now lighter made, amaze the Foe,
> Put on new dreadful Forms, and taller grow:
> Upward the lofty Pines are seen to shoot,
> As when they sprouted from their Mountain Root. (378)

Barcelona, which mingles "Natures Plenty" with God's spires, as Farquhar describes it at the beginning of the canto, appears like an analogue of this man, and therefore must rightfully be his.

The images of height, the supernatural, war, nature, and religion return in the second part of Canto III with the introduction of the bloody guardian sprite of France. Like some malevolent Homeric figure, he sleeps above the mountain tops, complacent at having preserved French military power during the reign of William III. (Mordaunt, of course, does not sleep, cannot be conquered even by tyrannic demons.) In practice, this demon has only the function of aggrandizing Mordaunt as the demonism of the Jacobite enemy aggrandizes General Schomberg. Since no masculine active principle could prevail over Farquhar's hero, he can do nothing except appeal to Discord. After descending to find her in her popish disguise, a trip equivalent to the traditional epic journey to the underworld, the sketchily conceived demon vanishes. Discord, who takes over and generalizes his function, is the familiar pagan goddess Ate, with her "crested Snakes" and "flaming Eyes."

Through the introduction of Discord, Farquhar unifies the two antitheses to Mordaunt that he has been developing, that is, the lack of harmony within the allied forces, which is brought up at the beginnings of each of the first three cantos, and the armed hostility of the French, of which the reader has been reminded lengthily in Cantos II and III. Now, through the supernatural "machinery," as the eighteenth century called it, the allies' pettish caution and the intrigues of the Gallic demon become the same on the level of the narrative, just as they have been thematically interchangeable throughout the earlier section of the poem. To put it another way, Canto IV, in which Mordaunt and Darmstadt are overruled by their fearful and (unwittingly) treacherous allies is the historical acting out of the antithetical structure that underlies the whole poem. And, as the poem has resolved its imagery over and over in Mordaunt's favor, so must the historical tension in the plot of Canto IV be resolved in Canto V through the historical realm of discourse or argumentation. Mordaunt and Darmstadt have speeches in V to balance those in IV; the vision of Fortune, urging him to storm Montjuic despite the council vote, balances the earlier canvassing by the disguised Discord; and even the time, one day, is exactly balanced in this pair of cantos. The poem and the reader are ready for the climactic and successful assault that takes up the last canto of the poem and reconciles the initial conflict of the poem through Mordaunt's victory and the allegorical epiphany of Peace.

"Barcellona" then is a well-planned coherent poem. But it is painfully uneven in execution. Much of it is banal or tactless. Canto VI and to a lesser degree Canto V badly need Margaret Farquhar's prefatory excuse: *"The Author's tedious Sickness whereof he dy'd, hinder'd him from making such Corrections which he design'd especially in the Two last Canto's."* Long speeches, which would require the genius of a Milton or a Dryden to come off brilliantly, make up much of the poem; and although Farquhar does rather well with them up to the council meeting in Canto IV, the crucial moments of the poem fall into dulness. In fact, after Farquhar's happy intrusion of humor in the scenes with Discord, he never hits stride again.

On the other hand, the poem is nowhere nearly so bad as others have suggested. Aside from the sheer competence of its construction, further evidence that Farquhar was a thorough professional, "Barcellona" has many verbal pleasures to offer a sensitive reader. The "old, and long, successive lineal Ly/ Which had like Gout, or such Traditions run/ I'th'Blood, from *Father* to the infected *Son*" is surely one of them; the character of Phocas is surely another:

> She *Phocas* moves with Magisterial Mien,
> All *Confidence* without, and *none* within;
> In Speech decisive, partial in his Choice,
> Of shallow Sense, and arbitrary Voice.
> Blest with these Talents, Darlings of the Crowd,
> The forked Fabrick stalk'd and talk'd aloud;
> Swell'd like a Billow, blustering wou'd he stand
> Upon his Wooden Province, there command
> *Tyrant* at Sea, and Spaniel on the Land. (387)

One may regret that Farquhar never sharpened his hand at Augustan satire. Since he did not, we are left with the embryonic "Barcellona," maimed pleasures, and wishful thinking.

III *The Love Letters*

Farquhar's biographers have insisted on taking his letters as serious evidence for his amours; but I suspect their insistence of naïvete. The one piece of proof in favor of their contention is a brother officer's confidence, reported a half century after the fact, that one of the recipients, Penelope, was the actress Mrs. Oldfield. However, if the letters are to be accepted verbatim, Penelope is no actress, since she is addressed as "your Ladyship." Furthermore, one of the letters to Penelope is substantially the same as a letter earlier published (see *224, 306*), and a clever young man would realize that reusing published letters is ineffectual, not only crass. Finally, an anonymous contemporary of Farquhar's sneers at his "insipid imaginary Love Letters."[5] Given these facts, it would be wiser to avoid miring oneself in unsubstantiable hypotheses, and to assume that the "Farquhar" or "Damon" (after Sir Harry Wildair's practice) of the letters represents a fictional *persona*.

An examination of the seventeenth-century letter writers proves Farquhar's debt to established procedures. A native tradition, swelled by imitators of the Frenchman Voiture (1598–1648), produced a remarkable number of books of letters toward the end of the century. Their subjects and techniques closely resemble Farquhar's. *A Flying Post, With a Packet of Choice new Letters and Complements* (1678), for instance, promised a "Variety of Examples of witty and delightful Letters, upon all Occasions both of Love and Business." *Love and Business* is, of course, the title of Farquhar's miscellany. And just as the letters in *A Flying Post* were exemplary, so Farquhar's try to show and to teach various kinds of proper wit. Advice about writing the letters could be found, more or less codified, in the works of important critics like John Dennis or unimportant ones like the author of *The Lover's Secretary* (1692). Readers of *The Lover's Secretary* learned that "in Amorous and Gallant Letters you must explain your self with a tender and curious air. Ingenuity must have as great a part in them as the heart, and one must endeavour in a delicate and affecting manner to perswade the Person of whom you wou'd be beloved, that you have a real passion for her . . . you must cajole her with Address, this puts her in good humour, and inspires her with esteem for him who has known so agreeably to flatter her. . . . You chuse a subject whereon you wou'd entertain the Lady you love, and hereon write to her with a lively and natural air somewhat that is agreeable and taking." [6] Farquhar's letters are tuned to just such an epistolary ideal. Since he is so firmly within the genre, it is not surprising to find him following still another convention, the claim that the letters had really been sent. Most of the books of letters make this claim even when the reader could see perfectly well, as with letters written in rustic dialects, that they had not been sent at all. Real letters carried conviction, and satisfied the public eagerness for sniffing about in the privacy of virgins, rakes, and lords. It is the same insistence on documentary truth that is a central artistic predicate of Samuel Richardson's "editions" of Clarissa's or Harriet Byron's correspondence.

The probable degree of accuracy in the letters can be suggested by looking at "*To a Lady, whom he never saw: Being a true Relation of a Saturday Night's Adventure*" (225). This is a longish narrative in which Farquhar tells of picking up two masked ladies at the theater, and spending the night with one of them in "a *very stately Apartment*." Farquhar's part remains relatively passive, while "the Lady that was most in love with me" seeks him out at the Rose Tavern and obliquely directs Farquhar's actions until they are safely in her apartment together. She is obviously a woman of quality—the maid calls her "her Ladiship"—and rich, if she lives on Golden Square, described in an early eighteenth-century survey of London as "a very handsome open Place, railed round, and gravelled within; having very good Houses, inhabited by Gentry on all Sides." (Between 1689 and 1700, the Lords Donegal, Kingston, and Walden, the Countess of Bristol, and the Duchess of Birmingham had been resident there.) [7] To this fantasy of being chased by a wealthy titled woman, Farquhar adds the titillations of her ardor. Her maid announces the readiness of the bed with a suggestive "red-hot Warming-Pan" in hand, after which it is not surprising that the lusty Farquhar, undressing as fast as he can, still finds the lady "a-bed before me." The final piquant touch is the lady's remaining mysterious despite her elaborate passion: "[I] was forc'd to depart as great a Stranger to [her face], as when I met her first; tho' I know every other part about her so well, that I shall never forget her." Farquhar ends with a strong hint that another assignation would be welcome. This letter sounds more like nocturnal fantasy than nocturnal adventure. More important, the reader's vicarious pleasure surely is meant to hang on the totally satisfying imagination of the tale, not primarily on its truth.

The letters that Farquhar had published in 1700 and 1701 present him as a rather boisterous suppliant, full of brio and gallant candor (*221–28, 263, 268–69*). We may take the first five as an example. Farquhar has arranged them to present the greatest variety of styles—for example, the first declares briskly: "'Tis hard to find any Simpathy in *Hearts*, where there's such *Contrariety* in Opinions. I shall therefore, *Madam*, henceforth square my Sentiments to yours in every thing; and if you will quarrel without a Cause, I will oblige you, and do so too." After breaking off this neat paradox in the first letter, he takes a different tone in the second, piously dated "*Sunday-morning*": "Next to my *Prayers*, I must address my *Devotions* to you; to you whom I have offended, and to whom I must offer a *penitential Sacrifice*, if an oblation of a *bleeding Heart* can make any Attonement for my *Sin*, I offer it freely." By the third he exuberantly bursts into verse, calling "Celia" his own; drunk in the fourth, he proposes to make her his own in body as in soul; the fifth finds him wildly repentant for his drunken proposal, crying out in "*Anguish* and *Despair*" and returning to verse only to "*Curse that destructive Art, that caus'd his Doom.*" One can easily see that the letters have been written as different types, to be played off one against the other without suggesting any narrative coherence. Indeed, the "playing off" acts to deny unity to this group of five, by emphasizing the peculiar merits of each letter, each display of wit or charm or frenzied love.

The only group of Farquhar's letters that tries to do more is that published the next year, 1702, in *Love and Business* (*302–25*). Here we have a real attempt at a sort of brief epistolary novel. Placed before the collection is a head letter, ostensibly written after all the others, which serves to vouch for the truth of the narrative that follows. "I have promis'd to equip a Friend with a few Letters to help out a Collection for the Press," writes Farquhar with pretended altruism, "and there are none I dare sooner expose to the World than those to you, because your Merit may warrant their Sincerity, and because your Ladyship was pleas'd to commend them." Their value as gossip and as literature is affirmed. Like Farquhar's supposed conquest in Golden Square, this lady is of the quality, so that the letters can titillate, received as they were in the course of an actual affair. If the reader remains unmoved by this appeal, he is invited to join the lady in commending their style. Exactly the same two appeals occur in the Preface to *Clarissa,* in which Richardson quotes Belford's letter of August 4: "*Much more* lively and affecting . . . must be the Style of those who write in the height of a *present* distress . . . ; *than* the dry, narrative, unanimated Style of a person relating difficulties and dangers surmounted, can be; the relater perfectly at ease; and if himself unmoved by his own Story, not likely greatly to affect the Reader." [8] The balance between the two has changed by Richardson's time, needless to say: Farquhar's style, in the Restoration fashion, can be considered apart from the sincerity of his feelings, as Richardson's cannot. While Richardson's novels overtly and proudly moralize, Farquhar converts moral terms into solely formal ones. But one can see the direct line of development.

The letters do display a moral alertness that helps unify the group. For instance, the first love letter begins with physical deshabille on "*Tuesday Morning, one Stocking on, and t'other off.*" The next letter carries forward the motif in psychological or moral terms, for Farquhar writes that the lady's "Letter has but just come to my Hands, when, like *Prince Prettyman,* I have one Boot on and t'other off." His allusion, repeating the image of the stockings, comes from Buckingham's great spoof of Restoration heroics, *The Rehearsal,* in which an inner debate about boots mocks heroes' laborious reasonings about Love and Honour. Farquhar's tone is one of good sense, Prettyman's of romantic folly, and both focus upom the central piece of information conveyed in the letter: the witty lady has made an assignation with Farquhar at Bedlam and left him to wait there "like a Fool," a lunatic victim of his passions. The physical disarray of the stockings has been moralized, though quite lightly, and one's knowledge of the moralized imagery conditions the proper response to the following letters even when their surfaces seem innocent.

The third letter, beginning "I have been a Horseback, Madam, all this morning, which has so discompos'd my Hand and Head, that I can hardly think or write Sense," patently presents an analogy to the first two. So does the delightful letter in which Head and Heart dispute. Heart calls the lower faculties, the senses (Hands, Tongue, Lips, and—ambiguously—"some other worthy Members" that "stand up for the Heart") to his support: "they laid violent Hands, (*nemine contradicente*) upon poor Head, and knock'd out his Brains. So now, Madam, behold me as perfect a Lover as any in *Christendom*, my Heart purely dictating every Word I say; the little Rebel throws it self into your Power, and if you don't support it in the Cause it has taken up for your sake, think what will be the Condition of the Headless and Heartless *Farquhar*."

In these letters Farquhar employs the Renaissance opposition between reason and passion, or Honour and Love, or Head and Heart, but employs it only as a formal element, as the point or axis around which his snowflakes crystallize. The result is that the earlier letters turn on a continuing structure of antitheses, as with the opening of the one dated "*Sunday, after Sermon*": "I came, I saw, and was conquer'd; never had Man more to say, yet can I say nothing; where others go to save their Souls, there have I lost mine" (*306*. This sentence brings together three antitheses, the first psychological in contrasting the lover and Julius Caesar, the second verbal, and the third moral. Feeling, expression, and spiritual state—these subjects develop into the central themes of the letters, occurring singly or in pairs or in triads, frequently phrased in antitheses, almost always written with the consciousness of antithesis behind each declaration. The letter preceding "*Sunday, after Sermon*" offers a "Poetical Dialogue" that balances on the images of God and Devil, freedom and slavery. Later, in a long letter, we have the debate over the pros and cons of two maxims, treated psychologically; still later, a repetition of the Bedlam/folly motif, an antithesis to spiritual health, as Farquhar compares himself to a fawning dog, or suggests his loss of reason in drunkenness, or discusses his own illness; and later yet he plays with reversing the usual connotations of rhyme and reason, and then interpolates a description of Dryden's funeral that embodies "the Sublime and Redicule mixt in a Piece." Eventually these themes find their climactic development in the loss of love, of hope, of health, and of native land in the last letters of the sequence.

One could insist that the purpose of the letters is moral, that the antithetical structure stresses the moral antitheses rather than, as I have suggested, vice versa. In this reading, the *persona* would be undercutting his own position by unwittingly using symbolic images, like bestiality or sickness, as literal aids to his corrupt argument. I would argue against such a reading on two grounds. First, the *persona* seems too aware of moral implications to be taken as naïve. Secondly, Farquhar's moralism in his other work never operates in terms of reason and passion, an individual morality that he juggled uneasily in *The Adventures of Covent-Garden,* bypassed in the early comedies, and then replaced in the middle and later plays with a different normative system. A legacy from the seventeenth century, the morality of reason and passion could in some ways be invested, Farquhar saw, but it had lost much of its old buying power. The most judicious appraisal is that Farquhar's love letters demonstrate more moral awareness than moral intention. Like much Restoration literature they employ moral formulas purely structurally. I am supported by at least one of Farquhar's contemporaries, John Oldmixon, who assumed that the letters were meant to display fine wit, not to moralize against its abuse: "What think ye," he wrote, "of our Poet's Delicacy and Wit, who in a gallant Letter to his Mistress, tells her, *He's gall'd with riding, Love is forging Darts in his Belly; he's a Dog in a Doublet,* &c. There's a deal of graver Nonsense with it, but it being mostly *blasphemy,* I dare not repeat it." [9]

These letters, like those that Farquhar had written earlier, are arranged so as to display variety in style and wit, although their order here also fits the natural progression of the narrative. As Oldmixon says, they lack delicacy, never Farquhar's forte, but they are vivid and vigorous enough to delight a modern reader. The sentences, if unfastidious, are well turned, and the sentiments convincing:

Nothing upon Earth, Madam, can Charm beyond your Wit, but your Beauty; after this not to love you, would proclaim me a Fool; and to say I did, when I thought otherwise, would pronounce me a Knave: If any Body call'd me either, I should resent it; and if you but think me either, I shall break my Heart. You have already, Madam, seen enough of me to create either a Liking or an Aversion; your Sense is above your Sex, then let your Proceeding be so likewise, and tell me plainly what I have to hope for. Were I to consult my Merit, my Humility would chide any Shadow of Hope; but after a Sight of such a Face, whose whole Composition is a smile of good Nature, why should I be so unjust as to suspect you of Cruelty: Let me either live in *London* and be happy, or retire again to my Desart to check my Vanity that drew me thence; but let me beg to receive my Sentence from your own Mouth, that I may hear you speak, and see you look at the same time, then let me be unfortunate if I can. (*306*)

In short, the letters have many of the same virtues as the plays, and those who relish the plays ought to find the letters very much to their taste.

IV *The Briscoe Letters*

Two of the letters in *Love and Business* are commendations of Holland, addressed to Farquhar's publisher Sam Briscoe, rather than to the fair Penelope. These letters claim to have been written in Holland, but the claim is doubtful, as an amateur sleuth can discover. The earlier of the two is dated "*August the 10th.* 1700. *New Stile.*, which is the equivalent of July 30 Old Style, by the Julian calendar used in England. In this letter, Farquhar writes that he boarded a ship on Wednesday, had a stormy trip on Thursday, and "On *Friday* Morning we made the Coast of *Holland.*" Since he does not say "this morning," he presumably is not writing on Friday. However, despite the rough going, it can hardly be later than Saturday morning at eleven that he claims to have disembarked at "the *Brill*" (Brielle, about twenty miles west of Rotterdam), since that town lies very near the coast, directly east of Harwich, from which Farquhar says he sailed, so that the ship would be unlikely to have made intermediate stops between the two ports. Farquhar speaks of no such intermediate stops. Yet August 10, 1700 N.S., was not a Saturday but a Tuesday. When one goes on to discover that August 10, 1700 O.S., was a Saturday, one begins to suspect that Farquhar fabricated the letter using an English calendar, and then added "*New Stile*" to the date so as to make it look genuinely foreign. The Dutch changed calendars only in 1698, so that a well-informed reader would have remembered that their dates differed from the English. Even more conclusive evidence that the letters are not genuine is supplied by

Farquhar's remarking that at Harwich he met a gentleman going as "an Express to the King, of the Duke of *Glocester*'s Death." Since this death occurred on July 30 O.S., no news of it could have been sent to King William, who was in Holland, until the very day Farquhar claims to have landed and written to Briscoe. An alternative hypothesis, that Farquhar meant to put "Old Stile" after the date of the letter, leaves one with the impossible assumption that an express messenger was sent to inform the King of a crucial matter—the Duke had been second in line for the throne of England—a week after it had happened. I think we must assume that the Briscoe letters are works of fiction.

Fictional love letters fitted into a widely established genre; fictional travel letters did not. One may suppose that Farquhar meant these to be taken as fact, and deduce that he wished to convince his readers of the truth of what he says. We are led to ask if there was any reason in 1700 or 1701 for an author to try to put forth a convincing commendation of the Dutch. The answer is yes. King William's military alliance with the Dutch had at this time come severely under fire. The English had learned to hate Holland during the commercial wars that had broken out during three successive decades before William had taken the throne, and many Englishmen now felt that their country was being duped by its Dutch king into fighting for the Dutch interest. At times, the House of Commons dragged its legislative feet when faced with bills to provision English auxiliaries for Holland.

Furthermore, there was wide resentment at the King's advancing Dutch favorites in the English court: "the admitting the Earl of *Albemarle* into the most noble Order of the Garter . . . was generally disliked . . . . many severe Reflections were then made on his Majesty, for lavishing away a Garter on his Favourite." Because of such acts of royal favoritism, Commons passed a resolution in April, 1700, after a raging debate, asking that "*no Person who was not a Native of his Dominions, except his Royal Highness Prince* George *of* Denmark [husband of the future Queen Anne], *be admitted to his Majesty's Councils in* England *or* Ireland." [10] Much public rancor came to a head in the Act of Settlement (1701), which dealt with the succession to the throne, now that the Duke of Gloucester's death had made it unlikely that a royal line could proceed from Anne. This document provided that monarchs needed parliamentary approval to leave England—a slap at William's frequent trips to Holland—and that "no person born out of the kingdoms of England, Scotland or Ireland, or the dominions thereunto belonging (although he be naturalized or made a denizen, except such as are born of English parents), shall be capable to be of the Privy Council, or a member of either House of Parliament, or to enjoy any office or place of trust either civil or military, or to have any grant of lands, tenements or hereditaments from the crown to himself or to any other or others in trust for him." [11]

In the meantime, the Tory party "studied . . . to inflame the Nation against the *Dutch*," as Bishop Burnet put it.[12] Their pamphleteers kept the Dutch people under attack as low, cunning, greedy, and conniving in trade and war. To choose one instance, John Tutchin's poem "The Foreigners" (1700) describes the Dutch as "void of Honesty and Grace,/ A Boorish, rude, and an inhumane Race." They know and worship only the coarse:

> Their hard-smoak'd Beef is their continual Meat,
> Which they with Rusk, their luscious Manna, eat;
> Such Food with their dull stomachs best agrees,
> They sing *Hosannah* to a Mare's-milk Cheese."

Taking Dryden's metaphor (in "Absalom and Achitophel") of England as Israel, Tutchin charges that the Dutch

> Exhaust our Treasure, and prolong our Wars,
> Make *Israel*'s People to themselves a prey,
> Mislead their King, and steal his Heart away:
> United Intrests thus they do divide,
> The State declines by Avarice and Pride;
> Like Beasts of Prey they ravage all the Land,
> Aquire Preferments, and usurp Command . . . .[13]

This poem of Tutchin's stimulated Defoe to write "The True Born *Englishman*" (1701), a satire on xenophobia at a time when "the Town [is] full of lampoons and invectives against Dutchmen." [14] In his defense, Defoe manages, as defenders often do, to list, perhaps even to grant, some of the attackers' arguments, such as that the Dutch are avaricious; but his main burden is that all nations, the English emphatically included, have serious faults. Farquhar's Briscoe letters, published a few months later, just after the Act of Settlement, take the opposite tack. Instead of denigrating England, they try through a pretended eyewitness account to soften public hostility to the Dutch.

From what we can guess of Farquhar's politics, his Dutch propaganda is in character. He manages to insert anti-French comments into most of his plays, including all three early ones. The Dutch favorite, the Earl of Albemarle, whose investiture with the Garter created so much English annoyance, appears as dedicatee of *Sir Harry Wildair* (Spring, 1701). Farquhar here compares William to Augustus Caesar, and the Earl to "Mecaenas, [as] *the private Councellour to those great Transactions which have made* England *so formidable to its Enemies, that* (*which I blush to own*) *it is grown jealous of its Friends*" (162). In the posthumously published "Barcellona," much praise is lavished on the Duke of Ormonde, the valiant, martial, just, graceful, loyal Duke of Ormonde, for his actions at the battle of Vigo Bay, while Admiral Sir George Rooke, who shared in the victory, receives no more than the narrative half-line, "*Rook* attacks by Sea" (*367–68*). Rooke was a High Church Tory, and therefore barred from Farquhar's Whiggish affections.[15] Even "General Schomberg," with which *Love and Business* proudly begins, must be seen in a political light, since Schomberg was a foreigner of Teutonic blood fighting bravely for England. In fact, Defoe's "True Born *Englishman*" uses him in just this guise, and may have encouraged Farquhar to set the political tone of his miscellany by beginning it as he does. The Briscoe letters come as soon after "General Schomberg" in *Love and Business* as they can without seeming blatantly political, and thus destroying their usefulness.

Once one knows how to read the letters, they pose few problems. Farquhar's usual exuberant jollity paints the Dutch as far different from the mean nigglers of Tutchin's "Foreigners." Their cleanliness glows, their skippers stand like radiant emblems of liberty and property (the Whig deities), and in short "they are gay without Levity, and fine beyond Foppery." After this general panegyric in the first letter, the second proceeds to particulars delightful to the Low Church Whig, like the substitution of social order based on trade for one based on religion: " 'Tis a pleasant thing to see Christians, Mahometans, Jews, Protestants, Papists, Armenians and Greeks, swarming together like a Hive of Bees, without one Sting of Devotion to hurt one another; they all agree about the business of this Life, because a Community in Trade is all the Interest they drive at; and they never Jostle in the Way to the Life to come, because every one takes a different Road" (289). I do not think that extensive summary or analysis of the letters is particularly important: they are carried through with Farquhar's characteristic skill in informal dialectic, as he depreciates now the English and now the French, sprinkles the account with anecdotes, impugns the reports of other travelers, all with an air of informality that masks his actual rhetorical calculations. To the middle-class readers to whom Farquhar habitually appeals, these Briscoe letters should have seemed congenial and convincing. Since by their nature they are ephemera, they can hardly have much more than an historical interest today. But their charm and their verve, and their rhetorical intelligence, make them worth a reading.

V *"Discourse upon Comedy"*

The longest and most interesting letter in *Love and Business* is the "Discourse upon Comedy." Here Farquhar makes only the most nominal pretense of corresponding with someone, perhaps following the practice of Horace in the "Art of Poetry." From the informality of the letter-writer's style, he earns the right to put forth his ideas easily and chattily. His argument itself, in tune with his spontaneous manner, derogates critics and the "rules," that is, the principles of dramatic construction received from the Greek and Roman classics. Farquhar would substitute a *consensus gentium,* the voice of the people, thus ratifying *A Trip to the Jubilee* and denigrating those stiff imitations of the ancients which cannot delight and therefore cannot teach: "To make the Moral Instructive, you must make the Story diverting; the Spleenatick Wit, the Beau Courtier, the heavy Citizen, the fine Lady, and her fine Footman, come all to be instructed, and therefore must all be diverted; and he that can do this best, and with most Applause, writes the best Comedy, let him do it by what Rules he pleases, so they be not offensive to Religion and good Manners" (338).

Farquhar's reasons for writing the "Discourse" are not absolutely clear, for despite "the strength and virulence of the constant controversy over dramatic methods," [16] no significant critic held the position that he damns. Even in France, thought of by the English as a precise and servile nation, the great Molière could write about his comedy *Les Facheux,* "It is not my intention just now to investigate if all this might be better, and if everyone who was diverted laughed according to the rules. . . . I refer the matter to the decisions of the public, and I maintain that it is as difficult to quarrel with a work that they approve as to defend one that they condemn." [17] And John Dennis, who fought for the rules full force, agreed that "regularity in a Comedy, signifies little without Diversion. The Reader himself is only judge of the last." [18] Admittedly the classics were used to chastise dramatic shapelessness, but Farquhar's nameless adversaries in the "Discourse" go much further than that. Why does he choose to attack a straw man?

There are two obvious possibilities, but the evidence is not conclusive in favor of either. The first is that he was personally irritated by the attacks against his plays, even though these attacks seem to have had no effect on his box office success. The preface to *The Constant Couple* and the prologue to *Sir Harry Wildair* give evidence that they annoyed him or at least made him feel defensive. The second is that Farquhar is continuing the satire on the university man that appears in his plays. This again is only a personal reason: the pedant and the inexperienced collegian are stock characters, part of the established store of public amusements, and therefore to attack them directly in an essay would be superfluous. A third and less obvious possibility is that the "Discourse" has oblique reference to the Collier Controversy. We know that the Controversy was something in which Farquhar was deeply interested, and it may be that he here is dealing with Collier's impeaching the artistry of Restoration drama, just as *The Twin-Rivals* deals with Collier's onslaught upon Restoration morality. Collier adduces "the Sense of Antiquity," for example, to damn Vanbrugh's failure to follow the "*Three Unities* of Time, Place, and Action"; and he frequently uses classical example to limit the scope of action and representation allowed the modern stage.[19] Furthermore, to assume that Collier is the shadow-antagonist of the "Discourse" explains Farquhar's long mockery of the purely speculative critic, since Collier, unlike Dennis, Rymer, or Oldmixon, was not himself a playwright. But again, the evidence is inconclusive.

Farquhar begins the "Discourse" with a disclaimer: he has been pressed to write although he has "no Foundation for a *Legislator*" and can offer only the "Sentiments which Hazard, not Study, brings into my Head, without any preliminary *Method* or *Cogitation*" (*326*). He has not even been able to defend his own plays. The offhand manner ingratiates him with the reader, pleading for leniency in the examination of the piece. The arguments, after all, seem casual, and ought not to be scrutinized with rigor or despised if they should happen to slip from logical to emotional appeals. In short, Farquhar is following the technique of *exordium* suggested by Quintilian: "the authority of the speaker will be particularly great if there is no suspicion that he is acting from spite or ambition, and we will also gain some unconscious support if we present ourselves as weak, unprepared, and unequal to the cleverness of our opponents" (IV. i, 8). Furthermore, his gentlemanly geniality criticizes, implicitly, the laboriousness and bookishness of his adversaries, just as his statement about "Foundation for a *Legislator*" brings up his strongest point against them, their lack of qualifications.

Farquhar goes on to say that Poetry's greatest handicap is her ingenuous openness—significantly, one might note, like his own: "Naked she came into the World, and 'tis to be fear'd, like its Professors, will go naked out." While "most of our other Arts and Sciences bear an awful Distance in their Prospect, or with a bold and glittering Varnish dazle the Eyes of the weak-sighted Vulgar," "*Poetry* alone, and chiefly the *Drama,* lies open to the Insults of all Pretenders." Her generosity, like Farquhar's, is obviously favored, and the reader can plainly see, when the matter is put forth like this, that Farquhar's tone and manner are those most congenial to her. It is he, the man of practical experience, who has shown himself judicious, he who best can speak for "that Part of the Audience, who can lay the best claim to a judicious and impartial Reflection" (*327*). Not so with the tone and manner of the scholar, whom Farquhar surreptitiously introduces in mid-paragraph, thus lessening his importance and also keeping up the pretense that the "Discourse" uses no formal argumentative structure. The scholar angrily disputes anyone's claim "to understand Poetry better than we, who have read *Homer, Virgil, Horace, Ovid,* &c. at the University," and have founded knowledge "upon the Criticisms of *Aristotle, Scaliger, Vossius,* and the like" (*328*). His anger and his rigor alike disqualify him even before Farquhar has offered arguments against him.

This section is what the classical rhetoricians call the *narratio,* or "presentation of the facts." The *narratio,* Quintilian says, must first of all be plausible, must portray events, causes, and agents naturally and believably (IV. ii, 52). The "Discourse" accordingly takes pains to show us familiar arguments and familiar distinctions. It is reasonable that there should be a diversity of opinions about poetry, and reasonable that each group makes a stock response to plays: "the Scholar calls upon us for *Decorums* and *Oeconomy;* the Courtier crys out for *Wit* and *Purity of Stile;* the Citizen for *Humour* and *Ridiculo;* . . . and the Ladies will have an Intreague" (*327*). The scholar's is no more than a stock response, both natural and undistinguished, and Farquhar's depiction of him treats him likewise as a humorous character. He has long "commiserated the Condition of the English Audience" that is forced to watch "irregular impertinence" like Vanbrugh's plays and Farquhar's, and he proceeds to produce a "regular Play" in accordance with the rules of the ancients, a play without the diversion and surprise of a double plot, without songs or dances, without varied incidents, without varied scenes. This disaster develops logically not only from the scholar's rigid arguments but also from the literary expectations aroused by Farquhar's stock pedant. Intellectual and generic patterns support one another.

As Quintilian's "credible picture of the matters at hand, that makes the audience witness the actual event" (IV. ii, 122), Farquhar's pedant is finely illustrative, plausibly suffering the curses of the players, the damning of the town, and the scorn of the booksellers. As a stock character, he reminds the reader that pedantry and the theater are old enemies. As an emblem of what not to do, he furthers the argument of the "Discourse." He also provides a paradox that will later ramify: the pedant's bored audience, Farquhar tells us, is a lewd and intriguing audience. Moral utility, which is to be a major concern in the essay, now appears for the first time, with the implicit recognition that aesthetic rigor defeats morality.

Farquhar goes on, then, to that clear, brief, full statement of his general case which Quintilian calls the *propositio* (IV. v, 26): "All the Authorities, all the Rules of Antiquity have prov'd too weak to support the Theatre, whilst others who have dispenc'd with the Criticks, and taken a Latitude in the *Œconomy* of their Plays, have been the chief Supporters of the Stage, and the Ornament of the *Drama.*" This "proposition" is double, and requires two proofs, corresponding to the classical "proof" and "refutation" (*probatio, refutatio*). Since the claims of the ancients are to be disproved, the *refutatio* comes first. The rest of the "Discourse," then, is divided in half, and proceeds to specific arguments about first the one clause, then the other, of the proposition as stated.

Aristotle, Farquhar's whipping-boy in this section of refutation, is rejected on the basis of three arguments: (a) the opinions of Aristotle's contemporaries are outmoded in law and medicine, and by analogy, Aristotle's opinions should be discarded in poetry, which changes like these professions; (b) Aristotle had no practical experience in poetry, and therefore no real knowledge of it from which to legislate about it; (c) Aristotle had a limited number of works to examine and induce rules from. Simultaneously, Farquhar uses two emotional, rather than logical, means of denigrating the Aristotelian position. First he compares the rejection of classical dogma to that of Catholic dogma: "I run as great a hazard in nibling at this *Paradox* of *Poetry,* as *Luther* did by touching *Transubstantiation,* 'tis a Mistery that the World has sweetly slept in so long, that they take it very ill to be waken'd" (*330*). And later he demotes the man Aristotle, by treating him as a self-interested and fallible man, a courtly sycophant, rather than as the marmoreal pride of antique culture. The purpose of these pieces of rhetoric is perfectly obvious, the former especially so within the context of an England both politically and ecclesiastically anti-Catholic. But they, with the three arguments listed above, have a further interest.

R. F. Jones, in defining the "stream of thought" central to seventeenth-century experimental science, isolates the sustaining principles of this stream as follows: "First was the demand for a sceptical mind, freed from all preconceptions and maintaining a critical attitude toward all ideas presented to it. Second, the need of sufficient authentic data was stressed, and observation and experimentation were insisted on as the only trustworthy means of securing these data. And third, the inductive method of reasoning was to be employed on them." [20] Farquhar's three arguments might serve as textbook exemplifications of these principles applied to the drama. Some of his subsidiary arguments, furthermore, jibe with "secondary principles" listed by Jones: opposition to the idea that nature was decaying ("the World was never more active or youthful," says Farquhar, "and true downright sense was never more Universal than at this very Day") and the principle of freedom of thought and discussion. In short, these arguments of the "Discourse" partake not only of an inner coherence but also of a specific cultural coherence, external to their form in the essay and supporting them within it. These are practical Protestant ideas, appealing to the same middle-class audience who would agree with the Protestant panegyric of "General Schomberg" and the equally Protestant propaganda of the Dutch letters also published in *Love and Business.* If that audience lacked classical learning, Farquhar did not demand it, was eager to decry it. If they had their darling tastes to defend, Farquhar found himself unabashedly one of them.

The empiricism of the "Discourse" can be shown by examining one conventional argument. Scholars have pointed out that Farquhar's "*Aristotle* was no Poet, and consequently not capable of giving Instructions in the Art of Poetry" is itself not novel. Dryden had said almost the same thing; Pope and Addison were to; and the critic Oldmixon, who disagreed, remarks: "Another remarkable Observation of Dr. *Felton*'s is, that the best *Performers are the best Judges.* He has only *Horace* against him of the Ancients, and *Dacier* of the Moderns." [21] But in fact an examination of the contexts shows that Farquhar's argumentative use of the old cliché is different. Dryden writes, in full: "poets themselves are the most proper, though I conclude not the only critics. But till some genius, as universal as Aristotle shall arise, who can penetrate into all arts and sciences, without the practice of them, I shall think it reasonable, that the judgment of an artificer in his own art should be preferable to the opinion of another man." [22]

Addison's statements of the idea, both of course later than Farquhar's (Tatler 239 and Spectator 291), reprimand ignorance in the man who "set[s] up for a Critick, without a good Insight into all the Parts of Learning." Addison specifically commends Aristotle as "the best Critick." Compared to these predecessors and contemporaries, Farquhar seems far more radically empirical. He bars all who do not write from criticizing and admits no means of learning to criticize but experience. The only measure of criticism is its accuracy in predicting the work's success in providing pleasure and utility.

Whether Farquhar himself personally subscribed to this radical empiricism we do not know. There is much evidence that he did. But given that the "Discourse" is oratory or rhetoric rather than naïve credo, his own ideas are less important than his argumentative position. He aims at a certain class of readers, a middle-class group for whom practical arguments about law, medicine, and shipbuilding would have been particularly convincing. As broad-churchmen, these readers would have laughed at Farquhar's making mock dogma of Tillotson's liberal and common-sensical sermons (*332–33*), which preached a Christianity insistent on a man's believing "nothing [besides the sacraments of baptism and communion] but what every Man's Reason either dictates to him to be necessary, or approves as highly fit and reasonable."[23] As broad-churchmen, too, they might have felt rather more sharply than the old Anglican Establishment that Collier was in large part right, and therefore have presented themselves as the most significant audience for an essay like the "Discourse," which could challenge Collier on his own grounds of morality and social usefulness.

At this point, Farquhar moves into his positive suggestions, his *probatio.* This section is heralded by a heightening of tone, audaciously achieved—perhaps with tongue in cheek—by filling the prose with the terms of Aristotelian logic: "In all Productions either Divine or Humane, the final Cause is the first Mover; because the End or Intention of any rational Action must first be consider'd, before the material or efficient Causes are put in Execution" (*335*). With a quick muddling of the meaning of "final cause," he insists on bringing us back to the origins of comedy, which he locates in Aesop's fables. At last Farquhar provides his definition of comedy, going back farther in antiquity than Aristotle to the "Philosophical *Mythology* of the Ancients" for an Aesopian dictum: comedy is a "*well-fram'd Tale handsomly told, as an agreeable Vehicle for Counsel or Reproof*" (336). "*Utile Dulci* was his Motto," says Farquhar, mixing his Aesop with his Horace, "and must be our Business."

He explains what he means at some length, wittily and even learnedly, with only this drawback, that his learning comes as direct plagiarism from Sir Roger L'Estrange's preface to his translation of Aesop (1692). Scholars have not, so far as I know, noted the thievery, but it is plain enough. L'Estrange asks "what can be said more to the Honour of this *Symbolical* Way of moralizing upon *Tales* and *Fables,* than that the Wisdom of the Antients have been still wrapt up in *Veils* and *Figures;* and their Precepts, Counsels, and salutary Monitions for the ordering of our Lives and Manners, handed down to us from all Antiquity under *Innuendo*'s and *Allusions?* For what are the *Aegyptian Hieroglyphicks,* and the whole History of the *Pagan Gods* . . . but in effect a kind of *Philosophical Mythology.*" [24] Farquhar repeats: "Here are Precepts, Admonitions, and Salutary *Innuendo*'s for the ordering of our Lives and Conversations couch'd in these *Allegories* and *Allusions.* The Wisdom of the Ancients was wrapt up in Veils and Figures; the *Aegiptian Hierogliphicks,* and the History of the Heathen Gods are nothing else" (337). Both men quote Christ's parables and Nathan's tale to David as sacred precedents for approving the Aesopian position. But plagiarism does not weaken the argument. However devious his progress, Farquhar does reach and does emphasize the fabulist view of comedy. He makes it the fulcrum of his essay.

Given that "our *Utile,* which is the End, be different from the Ancients," Farquhar goes on, "pray let our *Dulce,* which is the Means, be so too." Both are to be based empirically on the English temperament, which contains "the most unaccountable Medley of Humors among us of any People upon Earth" (337). Subject matter, mode of satire, mode of pleasing, and eventual moral must therefore be different in English comedy from those of its European congeners. Here again, as with his contention that critics must be qualified authors, Farquhar argues by developing the empirical implications of a commonly held notion. Sir William

Temple, in his essay "Of Poetry" (1692), had already remarked that English comedy provided "a greater Variety of Humour in the Picture, because there is a greater Variety in the Life. . . . [We English] have more Originals, and more that appear what they are; we have more Humour, because every Man follows his own, and takes a Pleasure, perhaps a Pride, to show it." Temple, like Farquhar, believes that the English are "unequal in our Humours, inconstant in our Passions, uncertain in our Ends, and even in our Desires." [25] But he admits this evidence only to approve the writing of humours comedies with a large varied cast of characters. There is no indication—and Temple is anything but a dogmatic critic—that the rules should be disposed of. There is no demand that the whole comic structure should be completely determined by the needs of the audience. Even the anti-Collierist argument, advanced for instance in Congreve's *Amendments of Mr. Collier's False and Imperfect Citations* (1698), that the English needed comedy to sweeten their national melancholy, merely asserts the need for theater. It does not use the facts as the "Discourse" does. In other words, through pouring old ideas into new contexts Farquhar evolves a positive program, at once novel (in method) and traditional (in aim), with the sort of empirical practicality that the new audience would find appealing.

As I have indicated, Farquhar follows the parts of the classical oration, as he had been taught to do in school, although he veils them to offer the appearance of easy negligence. The peroration is scheduled to come last, and, despite its being less clearly marked than the other parts, I think we can see its structure, beginning with the question "But are there no Rules, no Decorums to be observ'd in Comedy?" (338). This is at once a section of amplification, which Quintilian (VI. i, 52) tells us forms the greatest part of the peroration, and of Farquhar's forestalling the likely arguments of his opponents (VI. i, 20).

The first of these likely arguments is that Farquhar is recommending a state of anarchy, and this he puts down in his discussion of the shambling *The Rival Theatres,* with its Portico, Turnstile, Piaza, Spigotoso, Fossetana, Whinewell, Charmarillis, and so on. He lulls the reader by his tone of temperance: "there are Extreams in Irregularity, as dangerous to an Author, as too scrupulous a Deference to Criticism; and as I have given you an Instance of one; so I shall present you an Example of the t'other" (*339*). However he actually maintains his radical position. The gay wastrel who writes *The Rival Theatres* suffers from the same disabilities as the pedant, including that of being a stock figure of fun in stage comedies. Both are novices who scorn such accomplished work as *The Trip to the Jubilee,* both act from blindly confident vanity, and both push aside empirical reality. Like Swift's spider, they spin their plays out of their own entrails: this is obvious in the case of the wastrel, less obvious in that of the pedant until we realize that Farquhar is attacking not so much the ancients, whom he often uses and quotes from, as their dogmatic adherents. Indeed, the two types satirized here are seen as equivalents in much early eighteenth-century literature, the crowning instance being Pope's *Dunciad,* in which fop and pedant alike pay their court to Dulness. Farquhar's two bad authors devote themselves to superficialities, to the forms of comedy, without considering matters in the contexts of use and pleasure, or the real needs of real Englishmen. Their eyes turn inward, as the eyes of the vain are wont to do, and see their own desires as a universal principle.

The true universal principle is nature. Pedantic plays are unnatural; "meer Nature is offended with" the fop's slapdash construction; characters seem incoherent when one's "Knowledge of Nature" offers "no Original for such a Copy" (*340*). The peroration of the "Discourse" is unified about this norm. Having established it in his picture of the fop, the mirror image of the pedant, Farquhar darts back upon his main prey. He has made a pretense of impartiality, carrying along his attack only implicitly; now he gets back to business. The so-called unities, he points out, are only illogical and dogmatic impositions on a scheme of nature. They presume that an audience is stupidly unaware of dramatic conventions or rigidly unable to permit those conventions to be fixed by the individual play. Again, in rebutting the demand for the unities, with their tyranny of illogic, Farquhar goes back to nature, speaking of "the very Constitution of Representation" and of examining "the Nature of the thing."

In other words, through the amplification of this *peroratio,* Farquhar places within a fuller framework the empiricism upon which he has been insisting. I will discuss this fuller framework, that of natural law, more thoroughly in the chapter on *The Beaux' Stratagem.* Here it may suffice to stress three crucial components of Farquhar's argumentative principles: (1) specific form grows from function; (2) function depends upon the total context of an object—in the case of plays, upon the necessities of representation, the social use of comedy, the experience and the passions of the audience; (3) nature scrutinized by reason, reason proceeding inductively from nature, establish the proper basis for all formulations. It is from these principles that the ever-broadening empiricism of the "Discourse" springs, and in them that the essay itself must come to rest. Beginning with particular foes (like Collier) in mind, Farquhar ends by pointing to a scaffolding of ideas that was to serve him in the rest of his dramatic work. But in the "Discourse" those ideas took a peculiarly radical form, as contemporary criticisms suggest.

The "Discourse" by no means met with universal approbation. Some critics merely sneered at Farquhar's brash dismissal of the wisdom of the ancients. Others, like Farquhar's sometime friend Abel Boyer, reasoned from empirical principles to a different conclusion. In *The English Theophrastus: Or, the Manners of the Age,* Boyer discusses Farquhar under the name Curculio (or "weevil," the name of a parasite in a comedy by Plautus). Scientific hypotheses, Boyer says, must be "confirm'd by *Experience.* The same Rule holds, in some measure, in all Arts and Sciences, particularly in Dramatick Poetry. It will be a hard matter for any Man to trump up any new set of Precepts, in opposition to those of *Aristotle* and *Horace,* except by following them, he writes several approv'd Plays. The great success of the *first Part* of the *T—p* was sufficient I must confess, to justifie the Authors *Conceit;* But then the *Explosion* of the *second* ought to have cur'd him of it." Farquhar's argument that poets make the only critics is turned against him, an unsuccessful poet. Boyer goes on with other empirical arguments, pointing out that a consensus of the learned have approved the rules of Aristotle and Horace, testifying to their universality. And he ends with a typical Augustan argument, that (as Pope puts it) the rules are *"Nature Methodiz'd":* "Of all the modern Dramatick Poets the Author of the *Trip to the Jubilee* has the least Reason to turn into Ridicule *Aristotle* and *Horace,* since 'tis to their *Rules* which he has, in some measure followed, that he owed the great success of that Play. Those *Rules* are no thing but a strict imitation of Nature, which is still the same in all Ages and Nations." [26]

From the tactics of Boyer's argument one can see that Farquhar's "radical" empiricism lies not in a refusal to dogmatize, or in an insistence upon scrutiny of the facts—Boyer subscribes to both—but first in the implicit assumption that comedy should be highly particularized, and second in the procedure of reasoning from audience response. Farquhar's adoption of this radical position, as Boyer may have seen, affects his own dramatic practice only by leading him to more "natural" representations of men and manners. To the modern critic, though, the radicalism of the "Discourse" has the importance of anticipating some of the most central changes in eighteenth-century critical thought.

In the criticism of tragedy, for instance, the later seventeenth and early eighteenth centuries show an increasing emphasis on adapting tragic patterns to a specific middle-class audience and on more exact imitations of "nature." In the criticism of pastoral, liberal critics like Addison pressed for a "more accurate description of nature," "reasoning from below, from the subjective response rather than from the objective work of art or genre." [27] The supercession of the epic by the novel springs in part from the same interest in particularity and subjective response. Within these contexts, the intellectual importance of the "Discourse" is clear, despite its apparent lack of influence. The history of eighteenth-century criticism cannot be fully charted without it.

CHAPTER 6

The Recruiting Officer

WITH *The Recruiting Officer* we come to the first of the two late comedies on which Farquhar's reputation rests. The legerdemain of *The Constant Couple* and the adroit experimentalism of the middle plays, which might well fan hopes for what would come, now led to and was superseded by a new kind of comedy. Without losing the complexity and sureness that had increasingly marked his work, Farquhar left behind the harsh moral melodrama that had permeated *The Twin-Rivals* and *The Inconstant*. This is not to say that his moral interests were abandoned; they were reassessed and placed in a more comprehensive context. His powers of development and control suddenly grew, and he was enabled to write comedies among the finest and most original in English.

Since Farquhar's enlarged abilities permitted him to elaborate upon and ripen the incidents of his plot as never before, he found it relatively less important to invent striking and novel incidents. *The Recruiting Officer* in particular merely chooses a fertile situation, rich in dramatic conflict and skulduggery upon which comedy could thrive: it makes use of something perfectly familiar to Farquhar and probably to his audience, without having to contrive a set of original circumstances.

If we look at the actual recruiting act under which Farquhar himself had been working, Anno 2° and 3° Annae Reginae (March, 1703–March, 1705), we can see at hand the matrix for almost all the public military matters in the play. Cap. xix empowers three Justices of the Peace—Balance, Scale, and Scruple in the play—to "Raise and Levy such Able-bodied Men as have not any lawful Calling or Employment, or visible Means for their Maintenance, and Livelihood, to serve as Soldiers." In recompense, "the respective Officer who shall Receive such new Raised

Men, shall out of the Levy-Money pay to every Person so raised, Twenty Shillings, and to the Constable, or other Parish-Officer employed in the Raising of them, any Sum not exceeding Ten Shillings a Man." This makes explicable the constable's setting a bribe of 11s. a man in Farquhar's play: as Silvia explains, "he said that the Act allows him but ten, so the odd Shilling was clear Gains" (V. v, *105*). Volunteers were to be paid twice as much, forty shillings, so that Kite's attempt to enlist the bumpkins for only 23/6 must be regarded as governmental economy, and Plume's gift to each of two guineas—then worth a pound apiece—more strictly proper. But volunteers or press-gang, after receiving money "and Reading the said Articles of War [against mutiny and desertion], every Person so Raised, shall be deemed a Listed Soldier to all Intents and Purposes, and shall be subject to the Discipline of War, and in case of Desertion, shall be punished as a Deserter." The punishment was death. If they did not desert, they were allowed to fight for their queen and be paid a maximum of 4d. a day for "Diet and Small-Beer." *The Recruiting Officer* exploits all of this—the two parts of recruiting (getting volunteers and impressing the jobless); the legal bribes and threats; even the hardships of army life, implicit in the tricks needed to lure men otherwise faced with vagrancy or a fourteen-hour workday. Farquhar's basic plot is almost a comic documentary.

If the military affairs have been plucked from real life and then developed, Farquhar's characters come directly from contemporary fiction. They are intricate developments of well-tried prototypes. As in his earlier plays, Farquhar contrived two couples, following his practice in *The Twin-Rivals* of using one sprightly and one subdued pair. As in three of his earlier plays, he supplied a "breeches part," a role in which an actress dressed as a man. Silvia's military disguise, although new in Farquhar, might have been borrowed from any number of works: Scarron's *Comical Romance*, for instance, incorporates the story of an heiress named Sophia who disguised herself as the cavalier Don Hernando, and rose to become Viceroy of Valencia under Charles V.[1] Kite's masquerade as Copernicus the astrologer—or "Coppernose," as the Smith calls him, perhaps as Farquhar's mischievous reminiscence of Tycho Brahe's famed golden nose—has such dramatic antecedents as Foresight in Congreve's *Love for Love*, or for that matter

Face and Subtle in Jonson's *Alchemist.* Brazen, of course, can trace his family tree through a dense foliage of Restoration fops; Justice Balance, through a thinner group of crusty Restoration fathers, whose function as "blocking characters" he nominally maintains.

One of the reasons for the conventionality of the characters, besides his audience's conservatism, may be that Farquhar wrote the play rapidly. The evidence indicates that he did, whether because canvassing and cajoling for Her Majesty's Army exhausted him or because the attractions of Shrewsbury enticed away his will to write. For whatever reason, he left the play—at least the published copy—marked by carelessness. In the second act, the bumpkins change names: the first has been Costar, the second Thummas throughout the scene of their recruitment (e.g., on p. 63), but when they finally give their names to Plume at the end of the act, the first gives his as Thummas Appletree, the second his as Costar Pearmain. There is no indication in the stage directions that each indicates the other at this final moment; and to assume that Farquhar was deliberately having the men muddle their names so as to suggest their inseparability, seems like a strained reading, even in a play in which both male friendships and changes in identity recur as themes. Nor is this the only instance of Farquhar's carelessness.

Plume knows the disguised Silvia as Jack Wilfull in III. ii and IV. ii. But in the last act, he enlists her in court as Pinch, the name that she gives Justice Balance, and shows no sign of ever having seen the brisk young man that he had enlisted, with great pains, the previous day. Conversely, in the last scene of the play, Justice Balance speaks of Silvia as "Mr. *Wilfull,*" although he has only known her as Pinch. Even if one supposes that she tips Plume a wink in the courtroom scene, her father's new knowledge cannot be explained. Still a third slip comes in IV. ii. When Melinda signs her name to verify the signature given the astrologer, Lucy borrows the slip of paper "for my own Affairs," and later uses it to write Brazen her note of assignation, pretending to be her mistress. But shortly thereafter, Farquhar lets us know that Lucy, posing as Melinda, has been writing to Brazen in her own hand. Brazen then must think that Lucy's hand, "no more like *Melinda's* Character than black is to white," is Melinda's; and for Lucy to use Melinda's real writing at this point ought to alert Brazen, not fool him. In short, it seems hard not to agree that *The Recruiting Officer* "was probably hastily written and never thoroughly reviewed by the author, a man usually careful about such details." [2]

Given the casualness with which the comedy was put together, it is theoretically possible that Farquhar's use of the country, perhaps the finest stroke of inspiration in the play, may have been first prompted by an attempt to compliment the Shrewsbury folk, who had given the recruiting playwright their hospitality. Before Farquhar, provincials had almost always been treated with contempt on the Restoration stage. Congreve's Millamant, for instance, can dismiss the Shrewsbury squire Sir Willful Witwoud as a "Rustick, ruder than *Gothick*." In *The Relapse,* Vanbrugh's Sir Tunbelly Clumsey is a West-country fool whose name displays his character, just as his daughter Hoyden's displays hers. But Farquhar, masterfully, blots off the predictable contempt of the audience for the country, by bringing in the bumpkins to absorb contempt at the beginning. He thus can treat Justice Balance, who is no bumpkin, with respect. A man of the same standing and city as Sir Willful, of the same standing and familial situation as Sir Tunbelly, has been transformed into a charming and sensible gentleman, the equal of a Londoner. Justice Balance does not, of course, challenge the excellence of London, or vie with London urbanity. But the traditional bluffness and candor of the provincial melt into an engaging personality. Along with Balance, Shrewsbury itself moves out of the realm of stage caricature. All the variety and sense of real life that enhanced the traditional London scene are transferred to Shrewsbury; and Shrewsbury values become the normative values of the play. By rehabilitating the country as an analogue to, rather than as an intruder within, the world of London, Farquhar gave *The Recruiting Officer* the freshness that has captivated critics ever since. He also empowered himself to portray a wide social range of characters without at the same time having to broaden the focus of his plot.

The flower of Farquhar's Shrewsbury is Silvia. She is a kind of cross between the bumptious Hoyden Clumsey type and the gay young lady of Restoration comedy. As she says, she is "troubled with neither Spleen, Cholick, nor Vapours[;] I need no Salt for my Stomach, no Hart's-horn for my Head, nor Wash for my Complexion; I can gallop all the Morning after the Hunting Horn, and all the Evening after a Fiddle: in short, I can do every thing with my Father but drink and shoot flying; and I'm sure I can do every thing my Mother cou'd, were I put to the Tryal" (I. iii, 52).

To prepare the audience for this "natural" woman, Farquhar skillfully begins the scene with a depreciation of Melinda, who speaks first: "Welcome to Town, Cosin *Silvia* [*Salute.*] I envy'd you your Retreat in the Country; for *Shrewsbury*, methinks, and all your Heads of Shires, are the most irregular Places for living; here we have Smoak, Noise, Scandal, Affectation, and Pretension; in short, every thing to give the Spleen, and nothing to divert it." The effect here is a bit like that achieved by Swift in creating Lilliput, or by Pope in the diminished world of "The Rape of the Lock." Melinda's fashionable complaints echo fashionable complaints about London, and reinforce the treatment of Shrewsbury as analogue to London; but the self-importance of this comparison would also be ludicrous to a London audience, amusing them with Melinda's own "Affectation, and Pretension." Since the audience has been told five or ten minutes earlier that Melinda's airs result from her new riches, she seems even sillier. Within this context, the declaration of candor and good health from Silvia comes as a sympathetic corrective rather than rude excess: Silvia is accepted in the act, the necessary act, of rejecting Melinda. Silvia's values are accepted at the same time.

Thematically, Silvia binds together the two worlds of the play, Shrewsbury and the army. But before we can explore her function in this regard, we must understand the dramatic position of the army, as we have begun to understand that of Shrewsbury. *The Recruiting Officer* is a pro-war play, characterized by the same dry-eyed patriotic militarism that appears in Farquhar's other plays, and in poems like "General Schomberg" and "Barcellona." The militarism is presumed by the boast in his dedication: "The Duke of *Ormond* encourag'd the Author, and the Earl of *Orrery* approv'd the Play—My *Recruits* were *reviewed* by my *General* and my *Colonel*, and could not fail to *pass Muster*."

A minor token of it even appears, cleverly, in his epigraph, "Captique dolis, donisque coacti" ("captured by tricks and urged on by gifts"), referring to the methods of recruitment. In fact, Virgil's line (*Aen.* II, 196) is "captique dolis, lacrimisque coactis," or "captured by tricks and forced tears." The misquotation leads one to look at the epic context: Sinon, a Greek sent to deceive the Trojans into making way for the Horse, has tearfully begged for his life and promised victory for Troy if the Horse should be taken within the city walls. Looking back much later on this treachery, Aeneas remarks: "By such stratagems and Sinon's skillful perjury was the lie believed, and that nation was captured by tricks and forced tears, whom neither Diomedes nor the Larissian Achilles, neither ten years of siege nor a thousand ships, could defeat." Ingeniously, Farquhar has reversed the situation. His alert reader is referred to the foolish trust and disarmament of Troy as testimony for the necessity of English armament, and as a justification for Kite's stratagems. At the same time, the heroic comparison between beleaguered Troy and beleaguered Tummas Appletree is so grotesque as to indicate Farquhar's limited sympathy for the victims of recruitment.

Granted our historical knowledge of Farquhar's professed attitudes and his belittling the familiar distresses of recruits, we must still ask how *The Recruiting Officer* defines within itself its militaristic attitude.[3] Although Farquhar's dramatic technique forced him to be deeply aware of appraisal and judgment, he concealed neither the chicanery of recruitment nor the dangers of war. He evidently felt that he had made the army's position strong enough to withstand such realistic touches. Some of his rhetoric to this end is general. Farquhar makes his officers sprightly and clever, like Plume and Kite, or (at worst) rattle-brained, like Brazen. These men do not seem ruthless or oppressive. Furthermore, they resemble stock figures—the wit, the adroit valet, the fop—from other plays of the time, so that the audience accepts them and their tricks easily. The civilian characters within the play accept them too. However reluctant to join the army Farquhar's bumpkins are, they huzza for the Queen and declare her "greater than any King of 'em all," with a patriotic zeal that reflects upon her recruiting agents (II. iii, *60*). No one really challenges Plume's procedures; in fact, they have support from the vivacious and sensible Balance.

The rhetoric and tone of good feelings, with which *The Recruiting Officer* keeps brimming over, soften the effect of Farquhar's candor in the particular scenes of recruiting and impressment. For instance, the enlistment of Appletree and Pearmain (II. iii) is shaped like a little comedy. The two enter singing "Over the Hills and Far Away," cast themselves in fantasy as a Justice of the Peace and as the Queen, find themselves with a Carolus apiece, and then in a sudden reversal, are condemned to comic confinement: "I place you both Centinels in this place for two Hours," Kite commands them, "to watch the Motion of St. *Mary's* Clock you, and you the Motion of St. *Chad's*" (*61–62*). As they reach this nadir of mechanism and stasis through their trust in their own illusions, Plume enters as the representative of a benevolent government to right them in the name of justice and the Queen. Kite is beaten off the stage and the men properly paid, as their fantasies about being a Justice and the Queen come true, at least by proxy. As the men voluntarily enlist and go off singing "Over the Hills and Far Away" once more, the action of the first part of the scene finds itself translated into terms of free will and free movement. Perhaps the scene as a whole is ironic, for it offers the pleasures of trickery, so familiar from other comedies of the time. In another sense, however, it is not ironic. The bumpkins are happy; they have been dealt with justly; they are enlisted for country and queen. Plume has gotten what he wanted, but he has given them a version of what they had wanted too.[4]

Impressment seems crueler than trickery to a modern audience, and may have to Farquhar's also. Here, in the courtroom scene (V. v), he uses tone and rhythm to guard against misplaced pity. The scene begins and ends with encounters between Kite and the Constable, framing three cases before the court. The third is Silvia's, and as a result the audience has a focus of attention that prevents it from taking the other events of the episode very seriously: a comic tone is set in anticipation, then in actuality, by Silvia's amusing trial. Although the two cases preceding hers both involve the court's stretching the law, each is so arranged that the impediment is stated first, then ingeniously or comically dismissed. One victim cannot be legally impressed, for his wife and five children depend on him; but he is discovered to be a poacher, and then his wife disqualifies herself by declaring that "the Parish shall get nothing by sending him away, for I won't loose my Teeming Time if there be a Man left in the Parish" (*102*). The other victim cannot be legally impressed, for he has a job and a wife; but Kite wittily suggests that the man, a collier, "has no visible means of a Livelihood, for he works under-ground" (*103*). While this piece of wit holds everybody's judgment in suspense, the collier's position is completely undercut by his "wife's" admission that "We agreed that I shou'd call him Husband to avoid passing for a Whore, and that he shou'd call me Wife to shun going for a Soldier." The whoremongering rogue who shirks his duty to public and private morality alike immediately loses all sympathy. And the legality of his exemption has now been slurred over by his having felt it necessary to pretend marriage so as to dodge the draft.

Silvia, the third conscript, joins Farquhar's military myth to the traditional romance. In her father and Plume, she loves the central representatives of town and army both; and she herself, through her impersonation, can partake of both worlds. Her volunteering and impressment seem to represent her being handed over to the army by the two respective agents of civil power, the individual citizen and the state. In fact she reverses this process by drafting her father and Plume from the army to forward her romance. She is a recruiting officer in recruit's clothing: the title of the play ends up by describing her, not Plume. As things turn out, she joins the army in the one position of command that neither her Captain nor her Sergeant had thought it possible to offer as an enticement while in the midst of securing their smiths and musicians, drummers and doctors.

Thematically, her double function leads Farquhar to present Silvia hermaphroditically from the start. The girl who "can do every thing with my Father but drink and shoot flying" (I. iii, 52) "think[s] a Petticoat a mighty simple thing, and I'm heartily tir'd of my Sex," and then begins "to fancy [her] self in Breeches in good earnest" (53); her actions are "noble and generous, Manly Friendship" so that "her Sex is but a foil to her" (*51, 50*). This whole train of images points to her eventual assumption of her brother's clothes, London swagger, and sexual prowess, as well as his inheritance.

If Silvia is a sort of hermaphrodite, the army itself is sexless. (Again, I am speaking in terms of themes and images, not accusations or innuendoes.) Stonehill, in a note to III. ii, *77*, brings together a group of relevant passages, with an ominous silence about their import:

> *Sil.* What! Men kiss one another!
> *Kite.* We Officers do, 'tis our way; we live together like Man and Wife, always either kissing or fighting.

"In the same scene," says Stonehill, "Plume offers the 'recruit' as final temptation, 'You shall lie with me, you young rogue,' and kisses him. In Act IV, i, of this play, there is another such scene. [Plume seals his enlistment of Silvia with a kiss, and comments, " 'Sdeath! there's something in this Fellow that charms me."] In the final scene of Act V, Bullock offers himself to Plume in the place of his sister." Besides these instances, Brazen and Plume embrace several times, call each other "Dear," and at least once (V. iv, *99*) exchange "a Buss." But it would be silly, I think, to read this sort of thing as a continuing reference to homosexuality. Not that the Restoration stage was deeply averse to amusing an audience with sexual perversion—the subplot of *Venice Preserv'd* and the character of Coupler in *The Relapse* testify otherwise; rather that the rest of this play proves that Kite, Plume, and Brazen simply are not "sexually maladjusted," as the polite jargon of today would put it. The lying together and "bussing" of *The Recruiting Officer* are a recasting, in the idiom of the army, of the forms of civilian romance. Their function is different, because the basic social unit in the army is a platoon rather than a family, but their formal position in the military world is analogous with that of romantic gestures in the civilian world.

Once one realizes this, it becomes clear that Farquhar is furthering the analogy between military and civilian life that the dual role of Silvia suggests. War and marriage are parallel, as in Kite's comment quoted above. Earlier, Kite speaks of the "*Bed of Honour*," an analogue to, and antidote for, the marriage bed (I. i, *45–46*). "Over the Hills and Far Away" comes directly from a popular song of blighted romance, "Jockey's Lamentation": " 'Twas o'er the Hills, and far away,/ That *Jenny* stole my Heart away." [5] Plume's fathering a bastard also becomes a form of recruiting, like Kite's marriages (I. ii, *47–48*), just as Worthy's suit becomes a siege later in the same scene. Here Plume specifically makes the parallel about which I am talking:

Plume. Shake hands Brother, if you go to that—Behold me as obsequious, as thoughtful, and as constant a Coxcomb as your Worship.
Wor. For whom?
Plume. For a Regiment.

Later, Balance makes it: "For shame, Captain— You're engag'd already, wedded to the War, War is your Mistress, and it is below a Soldier to think of any other" (II. i, *55*). And in line with this, Plume can declare that though he always refuses to fight for a lady, "for a Man I'll fight Knee deep" (III. ii, *77*).

Farquhar is, on one level, making comedy out of various conventions, like the soldier's reduction of all matters into military jargon, or like the metaphor of sex as war. He is providing himself with a store of amusing *double entendres.* But on a second level, he is tightening the structure of the play, an exchange of characters between the two valid worlds presented. Both care for the stability of England, the army in its way, Justice Balance's world by its concern for law and inheritance. Socially productive sexual life jars with the army's way, but is compatible with Balance's. Therefore, Farquhar estranges sex from the army. Since the audience expects army life to be bawdy—everyone knows what scandalous things these soldiers do—Farquhar includes the Molly episode at the very beginning. But such tribute-money to the popular stereotype need not be paid, and is not, after he has made plausible the hilarious and thematically useful parodies that we have been discussing.

While Roebuck and Sir Harry Wildair must be converted to virtue by learning, Captain Plume must be reclaimed by our discovery that he really never was much of a rake at all. His women are only magnets to draw recruits, he informs us. "No, Faith, I am not that Rake that the World imagines; I have got an Air of Freedom, which People mistake for Lewdness in me, as they mistake Formality in others for Religion" (IV. i, *82*). Critics have complained that this speech is artistically crude and inconsistent, or that it marks Farquhar's selling out to the new morality and sentimentalism. Both accusations may be true—the former surely is—

but they are also superficial in their failure to understand that Plume's self-defense is thematically necessary. It is not a sudden sop to prudes, but the result of Farquhar's zeal to exculpate the army. To allow the army to corrupt, rather than merely to parody, the civil proprieties would be to undermine the strength of social order that the whole play justifies, and that makes the whole play work. If Farquhar seems to indict the army along with Plume at the beginning, in deference to the popular notion of scandal and danger, he quickly turns to a rhetoric that reverses original expectations and reclaims the honor of his army.

Silvia's dual role, we have said, suggests the analogy between military and civilian life in terms of the complex war-sex metaphor or parody. There is a second set of parallels and parodies between the army and the city, suggested by what one might call Silvia's "formal hypocrisy." By "formal" I do not mean to emphasize that her "hypocrisy" is not to be condemned, although of course it is not. I mean that in playing her dual role, she exploits social forms and social rituals such as recruitment or perhaps even wenching by participating in their letter and not their spirit. Farquhar shows us that Silvia's temperament thrives on such equivocal irony by giving her a first scene in which she subverts a quiet afternoon tea with her cousin. She is perfectly equipped to carry on her own recruiting as Plume and Kite carry on theirs, and with very much the same impish will.

In one sense, she levies a mock justice against an army that practices "hypocrisy" like hers; and in Plume's capture, Farquhar uses the standard comic plot of the cheater cheated. " 'Tis the sport," as Hamlet says, "to have the enginer/ Hoist with his own petar." The army, in recruiting, takes advantage of the analogy between the military and civil orders, subverting in one way or another a whole series of normal civilian relationships so as to transfer people from the Shrewsbury society into the regiment. The Rose episode alone exploits marriage, which Plume promises; courtship, which Rose will use to enlist her swains; the relationship between brother and sister; and the relationship between buyer and seller. In the same way, Pearmain and Appletree are marked for likely recruits by their friendship, which can be converted into the *cameraderie* typical of the military men in the play. They are eventually caught through the empty form of giving out recruiting money and Plume's rendering the forms of justice. Later in the play, Kite points out that the trades of butcher and smith can be translated into the military idiom as surgeon and gunwright, and uses the empty forms of prediction and promise to catch his men. In each case, analogies between natural civilian relationships and military ones offer victims for recruitment, who are trapped by that abuse of relationships which I have called "formal hypocrisy."

The army, by strict moral logic, should be punished in some way for these offenses against the natural order. But Farquhar and his audience approve of the army's methods; and besides, the army should not in any case be attacked. He resolves this pair of opposed claims by making Plume the happy scapegoat or surrogate for whatever moral censure the audience may care to levy against the tricks of recruiting. Silvia dupes Plume and her father, who has connived in the recruiting procedures, by turning their own methods against them. Ordinarily in comedy it is the villain who is swept away at the end by having his schemes boomerang; here Plume, and to a lesser extent Balance, "suffer" a kind of token punishment, nominally in the villain's place. As surrogate characters, standing in for the "erring" forces of government, Plume and Balance are being used by Farquhar in the same way that Pearmain and Appletree are used at the beginning of the play to absorb the audience's scorn for the provincial and thus to make possible an unprejudiced view of Shrewsbury and the Balances.

Farquhar employs other kinds of surrogacy in *The Recruiting Officer,* too. His skill with the device suggests a remarkable advance in his ability to unify his work despite the difficulties of dealing at once with three plots and a wide range of social types and situations. Silvia's disguise as Owen Balance/Jack Wilfull stands, as one might expect, as the most interesting as well as the most prominent example of surrogacy. Farquhar sets it up by including the dramatically irrelevant death of Owen. Thus robbed of a brother, she re-creates him, physically, socially, and financially. Like Viola in Shakespeare's *Twelfth Night,* she brings to life through an act of will what nature has taken away. Like Viola too, her volitive must come true.[6] Justice Balance's discovery of her hermaphroditic role, in which she is at once his hidden son and daughter, restores his daughter to him; but Balance also, in admitting Plume as Silvia's husband, restores his son and heir. Balance thus executes an act of paternal justice that stands parallel to the act of social justice executed in the courtroom scene, each one validating its own brand of recruiting.

Another surrogate relationship is that between Melinda and Silvia. This relationship depends on parallelism, but it goes beyond the simple sort of parallelism represented by, say, Plume and Worthy, in that Melinda is made to exculpate her cousin as Plume and Balance exculpate the army. I discussed above the way in which Farquhar allies the audience with Silvia at her first appearance (I. iii) by opposing her fresh candor to Melinda's pouting airs. Melinda must be made worse so that Silvia can look better. The development of the parallelism, first mentioned by Worthy (I. ii), continues to amplify this relationship: the girls are cousins, both heiresses who have been the subject of "wicked Insinuations, artful Baits, deceitful Arguments, cunning Pretences, . . . impudent Behaviour, loose Expressions, familiar Letters, [and] rude Visits," as Melinda says (V. iii, 98). But the foolish and passive cousin has first wavered at the brink of capitulation, and then, upon inheriting £20,000, grown insufferably haughty. The other cousin, who has announced to her suitor that "she wou'd have the Wedding before Consummation," has remained constant, and she gets what she wants without posturing or pain. Her service as recruit matches and mocks Melinda's service to Brazen, as her sexless night with Rose does the others' impotent flirtation. While Silvia can be the recruiting officer of the play, Melinda must eventually be recruited, as indeed, through Kite's recruiting disguise, she is. Furthermore, Melinda begins to act as she should only after being duped by the disguised Kite through her credulity about the pretended absolutism of planetary law; in the parallel situation, confronted by the actually absolute law of the state, Silvia holds to her complete supremacy and free will. Farquhar arranges each of these instances to belittle Melinda, and so to reaffirm the central position of Silvia in the play.

We may observe that in all this talk about the arrangement of affairs in *The Recruiting Officer,* nothing has been said about a process of education, such as goes on in one form or another in the early plays and *The Inconstant.* There really is no such process of education in late Farquhar. While characters may learn to mend their ways, as Melinda does or as Aimwell does in *The Beaux' Stratagem,* the plays do not turn upon individual reform. They are more interested in exhibiting an ideal system of social relationships in tune with reason and moral law. Faulty characters are not so much purged as reëstablished in proper positions. The foppish Brazen, for instance, almost suffers a marriage with the maid Lucy. In many Restoration plays, in Farquhar's *Love and a Bottle* for that matter, the sloughing of the fop in marriage to a servant or whore comes at the end of the play and is looked upon as a piece of poetic justice. *The Recruiting Officer* treats it only secondarily as poetic justice. Primarily, it is a way of pushing Brazen firmly into place. Once he accepts his proper role, he not only is entrusted with all the recruits but also is allowed for once to be perfectly accurate in spouting a genealogy, that of Balance's "Unkle that was Governour of the *Leeward* Islands" and "play'd at Billiards to a miracle" (V. vi, *109*). Such treatment is more heavily social in orientation than the usual tucking-in of loose ends with a comic resolution. Here, as we shall see in the discussion of *The Beaux' Stratagem,* Farquhar was moving toward a kind of comedy that went beyond the individual to the relational patterns of law.

CHAPTER 7

The Beaux' Stratagem

THE audacity of Farquhar's innovations in the three full-length plays preceding *The Beaux' Stratagem* was masked, in part deliberately. *The Twin-Rivals,* a brilliant if imperfect assault upon the assumptions of Restoration comedy, was supposed to be shielded by its Christian Collierist principles. This shield turned out to be flimsy, but the mishap came from miscalculation, not blind daring. In a less spectacular way, *The Inconstant* attacked the same assumptions of Restoration comedy, by sapping the ornamented parterres of Fletcher with highly individualized characters and moral seriousness. Here the deviation from Fletcher increases as the play goes on, so that Farquhar's audience was eased unwitting into the new dimension of judgment. Lastly, *The Recruiting Officer,* with its novelties of structure and technique, followed its pair of predecessors in its use of conventional plots and character types. As a practicing playwright, Farquhar must have felt himself obliged, for his own sake if not for the company's, to tone down the new and ingenious for an inertial public taste. When he began *The Beaux' Stratagem,* however, he was a dying man, and knew it. Given the state of early eighteenth-century medicine, he would have had to have been a fool not to know it, and also to know, given the state of the eighteenth-century theater, that no matter how well or how poorly his new comedy did, the want of his family could not be long assuaged. Perhaps it is this that enabled him to write so independent a play, to dress to such advantage the ideas and attitudes that had concerned him since the failure of *Sir Harry Wildair.*

When I talk about the "independence" of *The Beaux' Stratagem,* I mean that its intellectual and formal structure is openly novel. I do not mean to imply that the play spins about its own axis only, free from the constant gravitation of other plays and changing audiences. After spending years at his profession, always writing within the dramatic grammar of his time, Farquhar could not have practiced wilfulness even if he had wanted to. And there is no sign that he wanted to. On the contrary, his Aesopian theory of comedy, as he described it in the "Discourse," would have led him to conceive of comedy as a mode of rhetoric. Rhetoric has to communicate, and it can communicate only in language that people can understand, therefore a language that (in the case of plays) has been developed and refined by dramatic experiences. *The Beaux' Stratagem* has and uses a context of dramatic experiences, and, as I shall point out, a context of contemporary ideas, that provide much of the motive force behind its rhetoric.

Before discussing these contexts, however, it may be useful to discuss another kind of source, this one genetic. Shrewsbury, its setting and its people, provided the models for *The Recruiting Officer.* We know this because of Farquhar's dedication to the play, which alerts us that he has written a *roman à clef* (or *drame à clef*), and which therefore makes credible the Blakeway letter (see p. 26) that offers the key to translate art into life. Farquhar remained silent about similar sources for *The Beaux' Stratagem,* either because of his incapacitating illness or because there were none; but equivalents of the Blakeway letter have claimed that he followed an analogous procedure, and that the characters in the play are based on actual Lichfield towspeople. Some of the early biographers make unsupported claims to this effect, but the earliest piece of evidence comes from an obituary in 1759 for Thomas Bond, "servant in Sir The. Biddulph's family great part of his life." It remarks that Bond was "said to be the original from whom Mr. Farquhar took his character of Scrub in the Beaux Stra[ta]gem." A later book, Thomas Harwood's *The History and Antiquities of the Church and City of Lichfield* (1806), elaborates: "[In Bridge Street] stands the George Inn, the landlord of which, in 1707, Farquhar, in his comedy of the Beaux Stratagem, has drawn in the character of *Boniface.* . . . Lady Biddulph, who then occupied the Bishop's Palace, was supposed to have been personated in the character of *Lady Bountiful. Cherry* was the daughter of one Harrison, who kept the George." [1]

These identifications, even if they are accepted (and there is no strong reason why they should be), could add to the meaning of the play only for Lichfield antiquarians; they do not even have the same mild rhetorical significance as do those for *The Recruiting Officer,* since Farquhar did not feel that courtesy urged him to spare the feelings of innkeeper Harrison as he spares those of Justice Berkley. Nor is either Cherry or Scrub sufficiently striking a character to have gained much by having been modeled on a real person, even if the creator of Mandrake and Old Mirabel had needed that sort of artistic push. What the hypothesis of living models does indicate, whether it is true or not, is a public consciousness of Farquhar's having broken with the ideals of Restoration comedy. In Etherege and Wycherley, even in Vanbrugh and Cibber, lower-class characters exist in a conventional anonymity. Sometimes they are buffoons and sometimes ornaments of their masters' equipage, but almost never people. No one, I suspect, would accuse or credit any of those playwrights with using real men and women as Farquhar is said to have used them, as models for lower-class characters independent of their dramatic superiors and of the taint of the provinces. *The Beaux' Stratagem* follows the tack taken by *The Recruiting Officer* in lessening the social and geographical bias of Restoration comedy, and in this sense both plays look forward to Fielding rather than back to the King Charles wits.

The wits, his predecessors and contemporaries, do serve Farquhar by providing a context within which his works may be read. *The Recruiting Officer* amiably shared characters and conventions with the wits; *The Twin-Rivals* inverted and parodied their values with a vengeance. *The Beaux' Stratagem* found Farquhar going back to the method of *The Twin-Rivals,* but with more subtlety. In the earlier comedy, he had stressed a moral point through direct parodic comparison, to make clear his discontent. He now preferred to stress his aesthetic superiority to his colleagues, and thereby to win his audience to the moral position that they had found dramatically most satisfying. But so as to avoid talking in a vacuum, let me move to specific examples.

Partly because of the Collier controversy, partly because of the temper of the times that made Collier possible, the subject matter of comedy had undergone change in the decade or so before *The Beaux' Stratagem.* Playwrights dealt less and less with the dashing rakes who had enthralled the Restoration stage, and had begun to consider more specifically social matters, such as marriage. Vanbrugh's *Relapse* and *Provok'd Wife*, Cibber's *Love's Last Shift* and *Careless Husband*, Burnaby's *Reform'd Wife* and *Modish Husband*, and Steele's *Funeral* and *Tender Husband* take marital troubles as their focus, in a way that none of the comedies of Etherege or Wycherley or Congreve do.[2] Farquhar was quite in vogue. He takes advantage of this by tipping in allusions to other plays, to other men's resolutions of the problems with which he is concerned. Thereby he can implicitly call attention to the aesthetic ingenuity and moral rectitude of his own resolution, the divorce of the Sullens.

For instance, Berinthia's seduction scene with Loveless in Vanbrugh's *Relapse* probably served to prompt Mrs. Sullen's seduction scene with Archer (V. ii). The rectitude of *The Beaux' Stratagem* demands that Archer be interrupted, as Loveless and Berinthia are not; the rectitude of Mrs. Sullen demands that she refuse illicit advances, even though she has earlier told Dorinda: "Tho' to confess the Truth, I do love that Fellow;—And if I met him drest as he shou'd be, and I undrest as I shou'd be— Look'ye, Sister, I have no supernatural Gifts; I can't swear I cou'd resist the Temptation,—tho' I can safely promise to avoid it; and that's as much as the best of us can do" (IV, *170*). Now, at the height of desire and of opportunity, temptation has been unavoidable. In a similar situation, Berinthia calls out "Help, help, I'm Ravish'd, ruin'd, undone."—but she calls, as the stage direction tells us, "*Very softly.*" [3] The humor of Vanbrugh's scene comes from Berinthia's hypocrisy; but in Farquhar, where Mrs. Sullen's "Thieves, Thieves, Murder" bursts out with real conviction, the joke cannot be at her expense. Instead, Farquhar builds the scene on an incongruity that is at once funny and significant. Mrs. Sullen's cries turn out to be unexpectedly accurate, for thieves have broken into the house. The effects of the tension between Berinthia's words and motives are picked up in the tension between Mrs. Sullen's words and their undesigned meaning. By this twist, Farquhar not only keeps the joke but also unifies two plots brilliantly. Archer and the thieves are compared with each other so as to clarify Archer's moral position; but as the comparison incriminates him, his bravery simultaneously makes his crime seem milder. Farquhar's scene achieves everything its unwitting competitor could, and more. It is morally purer, and argues for its moral purity by its aesthetic superiority.

Or, to take another example of a slightly different sort from *The Relapse*, Berinthia remarks that she and her late husband lived

> Like Man and Wife, asunder;
> He lov'd the Country, I the Town.
> He Hawks and Hounds, I Coaches and Equipage.
> He Eating and Drinking, I Carding and Playing.
> He the Sound of a Horn, I the Squeak of a Fiddle.
> We were dull Company at Table, worse A-bed.
> And never agreed but once, which was about lying alone.

Farquhar picked up the speech for the countercharges of the Sullens:

> Mrs. *Sul.* In the first Place I can't drink Ale with him.
> *Sul.* Nor can I drink Tea with her.
> Mrs. *Sul.* I can't hunt with you.
> *Sul.* Nor can I dance with you.
> Mrs. *Sul.* I hate Cocking [cock-fighting] and Racing.
> *Sul.* And I abhor Ombre and Piquet [fashionable card games].
> . . . .
> Mrs. *Sul.* Is there on Earth a thing we cou'd agree in?
> *Sul.* Yes—to part. (V. iv, *189–90*)

Berinthia's pert antitheses, suggesting both her wit and her having the formulated situation well in hand, become a more emotional set of contrasts in the Sullens' exchange. The third person pronouns of the first pair of lines warm to the direct "you's" of the next and to the more vehement verbs of the pairs after that. The final solution is an aesthetic as well as an argumentative climax, made more striking by its sudden brevity. Beyond this immediate effect, Farquhar offers divorce as a natural and meaningful resolution to the discord, while Vanbrugh has mustered up nothing better than killing off Berinthia's husband before the play itself begins, and has left himself no way of resolving the marital tensions that the play itself develops. Such handling accords with Vanbrugh's declaration that the pleasure and moral of comedy "lies much more in the Characters and the Dialogue, than in the Business and the Event."[4] Farquhar, the lover of Aesop, rejected such theory, and used allusion to make the audience reject it too.

The treatment of divorce leads to consideration of an allusion that operates at the dramatic and ideological core of *The Beaux' Stratagem.* After much grave nodding in approval of his advanced discussion of ideas, scholars were confounded to learn that Farquhar had merely excerpted his thoughtful speeches about marriage from Milton's *Doctrine and Discipline of Divorce.*[5] For example, the Sullens'

> *Sull.* You're impertinent.
> Mrs. *Sull.* I was ever so, since I became one Flesh with you.
> *Sul.* One Flesh! rather two Carcasses join'd unnaturally together.
> Mrs. *Sul.* Or rather a living Soul coupled to a dead body. (III. iii, *156*)

comes from Milton's saying of a discordant couple, "instead of beeing one flesh, they will be rather two carkasses chain'd unnaturally together; or, as it may happ'n, a living soule bound to a dead corps" (II. xvi). When Mrs. Sullen complains of "the golden Links of Wedlock" and "Iron Manacles of Law," she is recalling not the proverbial "Chains of gold are stronger than chains of iron," but Milton's eloquent revision of it, "To couple hatred, therefore, though wedlock try all golden links, and borrow to her aid all the iron manacles and fetters of Law, it does but seek to twist a rope of sand" (II. xxii). Given verbal parallels as close as these—and these are not the only ones—we can safely assume that the coincidences in thought and argument between Farquhar and Milton are not fortuitous, but derivative.

Willard Connely provides one explanation fo this extensive borrowing by bringing in biographical suppositions:

> Then Farquhar got down to the question that was really on his mind: what to do with a man and wife who were mutually and hopelessly antipathetic. To all appearances, on such meagre evidence as does exist, a certain degree of antipathy had for some time been verily the position between himself and Margaret Farquhar. Writing even from his death-bed, poor Farquhar could no less write with feeling, with expostulation, if he had been bored, soured, beaten down by domestic

wrangling. But how was he to write dialogue about divorce, this quite new thing in Restoration comedy? It must sound convincing, and he had no experience of it. He had been reading both the prose and the poetry of John Milton; his head was full of him.

And so "Farquhar, in 1707, a man who if he had not already left his wife evidently wanted to, distilled [his] dialogue" from the "promulgations written in 1643, by a man whose wife had left him." [6] Connely may of course be right in supposing that Farquhar's desire for at least a vicarious divorce prompted his choice of subject. Perhaps Connely might even have been able to argue, had he chosen to, that the villain in the play has been made the husband so that Farquhar could disguise its biographical relevance, or psychologically atone for his wish to get rid of poor Margaret. Perhaps too Connely might have been able to argue that Shadwell's *Epsom Wells* (1673) ends in a separation because Mrs. Shadwell nagged Thomas, or that one of the bachelor William Burnaby's female friends was such a virago as to impel him to end his *Ladies Visiting-Day* (1701) with Sir Testy Dolt's declaration: "Well, I'll go to *Doctors Commons* [registry court] immediately, and be the first Citizen that ever had the honour of a Divorce." [7] No evidence supports any of these contentions; and, more damagingly, they not only add little to understanding the plays, but also tend to usurp the place of artistic analysis with their rather facile biographical guesses.

Farquhar's use of Milton has a purpose similar to that of his allusions to *The Relapse*. In other words, he has moral and aesthetic ends to forward, not subconscious urges to express and exorcise. Nor do I think that he is proselytizing for Milton's ideas, surely not primarily. The tone of the play is much too light to shock the audience with the miseries of enforced marriage; and, as for introducing the ideas to a wide audience, that was probably unneeded, for they were, one would suppose, familiar to the well-read citizen. Such standard works as Pierre Bayle's *Dictionary* or Baron Pufendorf's *Law of Nature and Nations*, a compendious encyclopaedia of natural law, discussed Milton's thesis. Since interest in divorce was increasing, his ideas presumably became progressively better known and, if not accepted, respectable.[8]

What Farquhar is doing is trying to justify, aided by Milton's mind and metaphors, the dubious proceedings of Mrs. Sullen and Sir Charles Freeman at the end of the play. This was in part made necessary because the eighteenth-century wife was very much her husband's subordinate:

> Women in *England,* with all their Moveable Goods so soon as they are married, are wholly *in potestate Viri,* at the Will and Disposition of the Husband.
>
> If any Goods or Chattels be given to . . . a married Woman, they all immediately become her Husband's: She can't Let, Set [deposit as security], Sell, Give away, or Alienate any thing without her Husband's Consent.
>
> Her very necessary Apparel, by the Law, is not hers in Property. If she hath any Tenure at all, . . . she holds it of, and by her Husband. . . .
>
> . . . .
>
> So the Law makes it as high a Crime, and allots the same Punishment to a Woman that shall kill her Husband, as to a Woman that shall kill her Father or Master; and that is Petit-Treason, to be burnt alive.[9]

Under these circumstances, one can see that an eighteenth-century audience might well react with hostility to Farquhar's denouement if that denouement were not prepared for. Farquhar uses Milton's ideas as his enabling clause to ratify the final action of Sir Charles and his sister.

Understanding Farquhar's use of Milton clarifies what may be yet another allusion to Vanbrugh. Stonehill tells us that "it is highly probable that the domestic infelicity between Sullen and his wife was suggested to Farquhar by Vanbrugh's *The Provok'd Wife*" (*117*). In that play, as in *The Relapse,* Vanbrugh handles the resolution of the plot carelessly. Lady Brute, the mistreated wife, acts with Constant very much as Mrs. Sullen acts with Archer, but the end of the play leaves their intrigue still uncertain, so that Sir John Brute can only remark: "after all, 'tis a Moot Point, whether I am a Cuckold or not" (V. v). Vanbrugh himself says, as Farquhar would not, "I own there is no mighty Plot in the whole matter," and leaves his play, as Farquhar would not, moral only by negative example: "the ill Consequence of [Sir John Brute's] Brutality appears in the Miscarriage of his Wife: for tho' his ill usage of her does not justify her Intrigue, her intriguing upon his ill usage, may be a Caution for some." [10] I have pointed out above how Farquhar bests Vanbrugh aesthetically, at least in terms of plausible and pleasing structure. He bests Vanbrugh morally not only by presenting morally justifiable characters, as we have seen, but also by bracing his structurally apt conclusion with Milton's argument from natural law.

Before going further, "natural law" ought to be defined. We may begin with an exposition given by John Locke, unpublished during Farquhar's life, but responsive to English thought of the time. Natural law, Locke wrote, is "a law which each can detect merely by the light planted in us by nature," that is, by reason and sense-experience. It is "the decree of the divine will . . . indicating what is and what is not in conformity with rational nature, and for this very reason commanding or prohibiting." Such a law conforms with "the natural constitution of the universe, and, particularly, with the nature of man" and therefore achieves universality "like the laws attaching to natural phenomena but unlike those of different [political] states." [11]

Of course, these laws were subject to disputation, since the "nature of man" is an ambiguous proposition to reason from. Some of the conclusions, as Pufendorf's *Elements of Jurisprudence* confesses, "can be deduced from the principles more clearly, some more obscurely, some are nearer and others further from the principles" "the truth and necessity of which results immediately from the very circumstances of human nature." [12] Nevertheless, jurists, theologians, and laymen all helped extend the province of natural law so that civil law, civil relations (buyer-seller, host-guest, etc.), and personal relations were all discussed as deductions or special cases of the universal law. *The Beaux' Stratagem* uses it to govern the latter two categories. For our purposes, we may note that natural law (a) replaces moral dogma, at least in theory, with argument based on reason and observation, (b) deals with a system of relationships instead of a code of individual behavior, (c) supplies a universal law applicable to people, or characters, of every social class or position, in a tremendous number of varied social circumstances. Farquhar accepts these tenets, and develops them theoretically and imaginatively.

The most overt statement comes from Mrs. Sullen. "Nature," she says, "is the first Lawgiver," and she proceeds to equate "Nature," (in this context) with "heaven":

> Wedlock we own ordain'd by Heaven's Decree,
> But such as Heaven ordain'd it first to be,
> Concurring Tempers in the Man and Wife
> As mutual Helps to draw the Load of Life.
> View all the Works of Providence above,
> The Stars with Harmony and Concord move;
> View all the Works of Providence below,
> The Fire, the Water, Earth, and Air, we know
> All in one Plant agree to make it grow.
> Must Man the chiefest Work of Art Divine,
> Be doom'd in endless Discord to repine?
> No, we shou'd injure Heaven by that surmise,
> Omnipotence is just, were Man but wise. (III. iii, *160*)

Like the argument of Farquhar's "Discourse," Mrs. Sullen reasons from final causes, rebelling against the marital version of the "rules," and insisting upon pragmatic definition in terms of effect upon personal lives and divine order. This insistence, shared by Milton, on the rational deduction of law from the nature of things places the discussion of divorce in *The Beaux' Stratagem* within the context of arguments from natural law. But for that context to be morally operative in the play, Farquhar must establish it. In fact, he does better. He uses its regulatory power to establish the bases of judgment in all the plots of the play, and converts the connotations of "Nature" into a central metaphor through which judgment can be embodied in aesthetically forceful terms.

All the events in the play focus on the house of Lady Bountiful. At first it is difficult to see why, for Lady Bountiful herself seems to be an extraneous character. She unravels no tanglings of the plot. She is not in general funny. The part could hardly have been inserted to please the actress who played it, Mrs. Powell, or her fans, if she had any—it is not enough of a plum for that, and not enough of a plum to be an eager exploitation of her individual talents. And Farquhar does not need Lady Bountiful's house, since the Sullens might just as well have lived together with Dorinda in their own. One can only presume that her thematic function must be of great importance. On inspection, she seems to have taken over much of the intellectual significance of Justice Balance in *The Recruiting Officer*. She is not, of course, his direct descendant, because the "problem" of *The Beaux' Stratagem* is so different from that of its predecessor. For the renewal of society that the Shrewsbury marriages portend, the justice symbolized by Balance and the army must be extended creatively and naturally through Silvia's imposture. In Lichfield, on the other hand, we begin with openhandedness and nature, and infuse it with justice. Both plays thus end by wedding justice and nature, but each play begins with a different half of the pair. Balance, who interprets nature as taking vengeance for past malfeasances (II. ii, *56*), and who judges prospective sons-in-law by worldly prudence, suggests a good but limited justice. (In his niece Melinda, this sort of near-sighted justice becomes the vindictiveness that tries to block two desired marriages.) Lady Bountiful, on the other hand, stands for a limited but benevolent nature.

Her great house, as Mrs. Sullen's complaints testify, lies in a bucolic countryside, which suits the theme of nature. Here Lady Bountiful practices the art of natural healing, unjustly scorned by her daughter-in-law as "spreading of Plaisters, brewing of Diet-drinks, and stilling Rosemary-Water" (II. i, *134*). According to the more objective Boniface, this conversion of raw nature into healing or harmonious natural artifice is highly successful:

> My Lady *Bountyful* is one of the best of Women: Her last Husband Sir *Charles Bountyful* left her worth a Thousand Pound a Year; and I believe she lays out one half on't in charitable Uses for the Good of her Neighbours; she cures Rheumatisms, Ruptures, and broken Shins in Men, Green Sickness, Obstructions, and Fits of the Mother in Women; —the Kings-Evil, Chin-Cough, and Chilblains in Children; in short, she has cured more People in and about *Litchfield* within Ten Years than the Doctors have kill'd in Twenty; and that's a bold Word. (I. i, *127*)

Her naïvete, however, which is so sparklingly plain in her treatment of the "sick" Aimwell (IV. i, *162–65*), confines her to superficial judgments of people, and deprives her of justice. It is no accident that in her house the swords of justice "won't draw" (V. iii, *182*), leaving the beaux to give the burglars their due. "Foolishly fond of her Son *Sullen*," unable therefore to be just about his faults, she must be excluded from the dialectic of the play.

Lady Bountiful is a constant cornucopia: she gives freely and unaffectedly whatever she has. The beaux, who do participate in the "dialectic," begin the play as skilled hunters (Aimwell, Archer), completely self-interested predators out to shoot and devour beauty and bounty. Their gifts are counterfeit, as Farquhar indicates by having Archer take the name "Martin," probably a reference to the expression "St. Martin's ware" ("sham finery") and an obvious undercutting of his real Christian name, Frank. We learn from their first dialogue that their allegiance is to the values of the town, where Fortune protects "*Jack Handycraft*, a handsom, well dress'd, mannerly, sharping Rogue" and leaves "poor *Jack Generous*" walking alone in "his Autumnal Perriwig, shading his melancholly Face, his Coat older than anything but its Fashion, with one Hand idle in his Pocket, and with the other picking his useless Teeth" (I. i, *128*). The beaux are keen-sighted enough to recognize the inequity, but remain totally committed to the society that promotes it: "so much Pleasure for so much Money, we have had our Penyworths, and had I Millions, I wou'd go to the same Market again. O *London, London!*" The tone is light, the gentlemen witty, the hedonism popular, so that as yet Farquhar levies no moral tax upon Aimwell and Archer. He merely sketches in their thematic opposition to Lady Bountiful, whose normative character has been the first real subject of conversation in the play.

As the play moves on, however, he so to speak squeezes them away from their self-serving hedonism through making that position morally unpleasant. To do this, Farquhar employs his technique of surrogate characters, developed to fineness in *The Recruiting Officer*. He lets the beaux' activities go on, but does not continue stressing their motives; thereby he creates a vacuum of intention into which he places surrogate characters. These surrogates, whose motives are stressed, can receive moral blame as proxies for the beaux. At the same time they induce a new moral consciousness that blocks the beaux from sinning with impunity.

Perhaps this process may begin to be seen more clearly in a specific instance of its use, the career of the innkeeper Boniface. His name is a token of his duplicity, since beside its etymology of do-good (Latin, *bonum facere*) float its English connotations of "bonny face," the handsome *appearance* of virtue.[13] Boniface seems to be the stereotyped country innkeeper, who has "liv'd in *Litchfield* Man and Boy above Eight and fifty Years," feeding "purely upon [Lichfield] Ale; I have eat my Ale, drank my Ale, and I always sleep upon Ale" (I. i, *126*). He serves sedulously and quaintly, and relays the country gossip. Without falsifying this first picture, Farquhar enriches it and qualifies it. Boniface turns out to be a highwayman, greedy and unnatural, who would "betray his Guest, and debauch his Daughter into the bargain" (I. i, *132*). He violates the natural, social, familial, and personal relationships with equanimity. His inn is appropriate for the beaux, then, for he, like them, is a hypocritical user of beauty and bounty for his own ends.

Like them, too, he is a purely sensual man. At first, Farquhar introduces Boniface's bulk merely as joke: plumpness was as funny then as it is now, and it fitted the popular idea of the lazy and untroubled country burgher. By the end of the play, however, Sir Charles Freeman can moralize the belly: "You and your Wife, Mr. Guts, may be one Flesh, because ye are nothing else—but rational Creatures have minds that must be united" (V. i, *176*). Alien to the rule of justice or nature, Boniface serves not only as a comment on the beaux but also as an antithesis to Lady Bountiful —scenically as well as thematically, because his inn is the only other setting used besides her house. Farquhar has made the polarity clear.

The principles exemplified by the inn and innkeeper must confront those exemplified by the healing manorhouse. Farquhar effects the confrontation through four variations on the theme of intrusion. Politically, the French officer Count Bellair and the chaplain "Foigard" are interlopers in Lichfield, enemies of England, abusers of hospitality, and foreign plotters against the honor of Mrs. Sullen. Archer and Aimwell, particularly Archer, are parallel to these interlopers; and Scrub's notion that the beaux are Jesuits (III. i, *144*), with the twin implication of zealous subversion and witty deceit, is at least morally just. So is Boniface's notion that the beaux, the second group of intruders, are highwaymen and therefore like his own gang, who are the third group of intruders.[14] In my discussion of Farquhar's allusions to *The Re-*

lapse, I touched upon the thematic significance of the thieves' breaking into the house "with Fire and Sword" while Archer, fired with lust and sexually armed, makes his violent attempt upon Mrs. Sullen. At this moment of juxtaposition, Scrub takes Archer, quite properly, for one of the thieves, while one of the thieves, Gibbet, unintentionally parodies Aimwell's only justification for acting as he has: "alack a day, Madam, I'm only a younger Brother, Madam; and so, Madam, if you make a Noise, I'll shoot you thro' the Head; but don't be afraid, Madam" (V. ii, *180*). Obviously, all these parallels are exculpatory as well as incriminatory: one can see that the beaux' actions differ from those of the French and the thieves, the external and internal foes of England. In other words, Farquhar's moral position uses, rather than merely expresses, its norms of nature and justice. Furthermore, the light tone prohibits us from taking the whole thing very earnestly. None the less, the parallels have moral as well as structural significance.

These three groups of interlopers are all vagrants, and in the plot oppose the fourth intruder, Mr. Sullen himself, whose beauty (Mrs. Sullen) or bounty (his strongbox) beckons them on. Sullen is not a Bountiful, as his name makes clear, but a son of Lady Bountiful's first marriage, and therefore only a half-brother to the elegant Dorinda. In a sense, then, he is a cuckoo in the Bountiful nest; thematically, he represents the selfish abuse of beauty and bounty, which excite in him only feelings of jealousy and greed. It is no wonder that he prefers Boniface's inn to the Bountiful house.

Phlegmatic melancholy makes him sullen in fact, emotionally and morally unnatural. This disease, "the spleen" or "vapours," was much fancied in the eighteenth century, as a proof of refined nervous sensibility—Cherry and Archer both unnaturally affect it (II. ii, *138;* III. iii, *153*)—but Farquhar casts these pretensions aside to treat "spleen" medically and morally as a bondage of the spirit to the body. Presumably Lady Bountiful could cure it if she were not so blind to her son's disorders, for the mental disease proceeded from a physical. One eighteenth-century physician prescribed a regimen of "*total Abstinence* from Animal Foods of all Kinds, and all Sorts of strong and fermented Liquors, keeping only to Milk, with Seeds or Grains, and the different Kinds of Vegetable Food," as well as "*Bodily Exercise* and Action . . . towards the Evening, to prepare [the patients] for their Night's quiet Rest." Sullen drinks, loafs, and stays out late: it is no wonder that his first and last lines in the play are "My Head akes consumedly." As our physician says, medical good sense can never help "*the* Voluptuous *and* Unthinking": "neither of these will ever bear or can receive any Conviction or Reasoning from such *Principles* as I lay down. But the *Laws of Nature*, and the immutable *Relations of Things*, are too stubborn to bend to such Gentlemen." [15]

These themes of disorder, or disease, infect all Sullen's actions and make them, too, unnatural. In the house of healing, he has intruded his surfeited body, his spoiled mind, and his distempered marriage. His violation of health and nature even cripples his wife, who protects her integrity by acting unnaturally herself. She intrigues with Archer and pretends to intrigue with Count Bellair; and in the bitter afterwash of her failure to make Sullen responsive, she can make "merry with the Misfortunes of other People" (IV. i, *161*). Her malicious counsel to the country woman, to cure a husband's sore leg by chopping it open, stuffing it with spices, and roasting it, plays on the supposition that husbands are beasts valuable only for the flesh. Mr. Sullen, an extension of Boniface into the Bountiful mansion, has never given his wife reason to believe otherwise.

Act IV ends with matters at their most complicated; their proper resolution seems distant and difficult, as Gibbet elevates discord into a universal principle: "it is a Maxim that Man and Wife shou'd never have it in their Power to hang one another, for if they should, the Lord have Mercy upon 'um both." Act V begins with the sudden bold arrival of Sir Charles Freeman, and the doubtful resolutions become clear. Farquhar's importing a knightly savior at the last minute does not stand as his most subtle or dexterous piece of dramatic management. The most that one can say for him is that Sir Charles functions more as a *raisonneur* and bringer of news than as an active figure. He is a narrative and thematic agent who precipitates a resolution that he has never effected. Thus he enters to enlighten Sullen about the letter and spirit of the law (V. i, *175–76*) and to suggest the final divorce. As a fleshly man, Justice of the Peace Sullen knows only the letter of the law, such as the physical act of "ly[ing] with my Wife" so as not to seem "an Atheist or a Rake"—in fact, he is a version of both, as an offender against divine and social order. By analogy, he takes metaphor (like "Sea of Truth") literally. It is no wonder that the card game he wants to play is named "All-fours." Sir Charles, not an "all fours" player, asserts spirit as well as letter. He points out that justice must proceed from nature, that is, he insists upon the procedure of natural law.

The reclamations of the last act spring from the embodiment of these newly stated principles. I have already outlined how the freeing of Mrs. Sullen depends upon natural law. Aimwell's is the next simplest and, I think, the least well conceived. The virtue of Dorinda makes him confess his artifice, and marry only when natural affection and justice are joined. In doing this, he echoes Sir Charles, whose image of proper hierarchy has compared the precedence of the mind over the body to that of the master over the servant (V. i, *176*): Aimwell tells Dorinda (V. iv, *195*) that "the Beauties of your Mind and Person have so won me from my self, that like a trusty Servant, I prefer the Interest of my Mistress to my own." The letter of love is worthless without the spirit, and therefore his pretense must be dropped. Aimwell must stop aiming and start giving, if his liberality is to make him a fit member of the Bountiful family. When he does confess, nature and justice coincide and merit is rewarded through his acceding to his viscountcy. As a minor but harmonious note we may recall that Aimwell's brother had been introduced as an undiscriminating Londoner, interested in fashion and possessions. When Aimwell confesses, the brother is dead symbolically as well as literally.

While this resolution is intellectually justifiable, Farquhar's abandoning natural probability at this point damages the less superficial logic of the play. At a moment when he is about to invoke natural law to part his mismatched couple, he asks his audience to suspend their sense of natural movement in the drama and to accept an imposed conclusion. So eager was Farquhar to make his thematic point that he mistakenly gave Aimwell the same Christian name as Sir Charles Freeman, forgetting that Archer had been calling his friend "Tom" (II, ii, *138;* III. ii, *145;* V. iv, *185*).

Archer's character admits of less reform; and even after his exploits in thief-catching, his "Adventures" are compared to those of the "House-breakers" from whom he literally, as well as morally, has received an "ugly Gash." Yet he has captured the thieves, and, even more than his besting Bellair in the competition for Mrs. Sullen, the capture certifies him as a man of merit, for he acts as an agent of order in his society. To the extent that the thieves are Archer's likenesses, he has symbolically downed and bound his own passions in them. His success, unlike Aimwell's, remains on the material level, however: he ends up with money, not a girl. On this level, Archer deals with the material world on behalf of the romantic figures. His recovery of Mrs. Sullen's fortune, for instance, depends on his ability to extend the burglary—only the stealing of the strongbox makes its proper restitution possible—but to convert its purpose to that of justice. Complacent in his new riches, he can afford to renounce Mrs. Sullen's, and to restore the honor that he would have destroyed. This action itself represents an extension and conversion of that in the boudoir scene, where Archer's burglarious lust brings Mrs. Sullen back to the honor that she might have squandered. In the same way, his unmasking of Foigard, that false protector of the faith, now is repeated and varied in his unmasking of the venal Gipsey. As with the defeat of Bellair and the testing of Mrs. Sullen, the moral order that emerged because of the Foigard episode was, as far as Archer was concerned, accidental; as with the defeat of the thieves and restoring of the fortune, the moral order that results from the Gipsey episode is intentional. Gipsey, whose name connotes the roguery that also characterizes the old Archer, gives way to Cherry, whose name suggests the fruitful nature of which the new Archer seems to be at least a fitful devotee. Even Boniface, through Archer's and Cherry's intervention, is aligned with justice, resolving the disorders of the town.

If one accepts this reading of the play, and specifically of Archer's mildly spotty reform, one can see that it is impossible for Archer to go off with Mrs. Sullen. In saying this, I must dispute the opinion of Gellert Alleman, who accepts as accurate Mrs. Oldfield's protest that Farquhar "had dealt too freely with the character of Mrs. *Sullen,* in giving her to *Archer* without a proper Divorce, which was not a Security for her Honour"; Alleman remarks that "the little anecdote is helpful because it shows the only literal interpretation of Farquhar's fifth act: the heroine goes off into justifiable adultery." [16] Given the text of the play as we now have it, however, this interpretation appears questionable. In the first place, Archer has accepted £10,000 from Aimwell, Dorinda's marriage portion, and has made the gesture of handing Mrs. Sullen's back to her: the stage picture does not encourage us to believe that they are going to live together. In the second place, the emphasis of Archer's curtain speech falls on the separation of the Sullens, not the promise of anything for the future; and even if just before this speech we have had a dance in which Archer and Mrs. Sullen are partners, the dance music, Archer's "Song of a Trifle," has made it clear how fleeting any of his affairs must be.[17] In the third place, Mrs. Sullen has been cognizant of her honor during the play, and we are not led to believe that she will change. She refers Archer to Sir Charles to "thank you for your Services, he has it in his Power" (V. iii, *184*), implying that it is not in hers. Nor does Sir Charles seem to be a man who would forward a sister's adultery. For these dramatic reasons as well as for the thematic reasons that have been discussed, "justifiable adultery" must be rejected as a sequel to the action of the play.

The Beaux' Stratagem stands as the culmination of Farquhar's brief career. I say this not only because of what Hopkins called (in a different context, of course) "the achieve of, the mastery of the thing," but also because the problems that had faced him in the earlier plays are here so beautifully developed and resolved. The adjustment of moral values could be executed on a firm and flexible basis which accommodated the wide social range within which Farquhar could most ably work. The complexities of dramatic parody, of surrogate characters, of imposture were cultivated with as much intelligence and even more daring than in *The Recruiting Officer*. And, as with *The Recruiting Officer*, the play was immensely entertaining. Farquhar's tools were in his hands, and his apprenticeship emphatically ended. Before he could use the tools or the craftsmanship, he died.

CHAPTER 8

Farquhar: The External Meaning

THE 1709 edition of Farquhar's *Works* has a laudatory frontispiece showing Ben Jonson, crowned with laurels, presenting Farquhar at the court of Apollo and the Muses. In formal arrangement, Farquhar's Irish harp balances Apollo's lyre, as his full wig does Apollo's unbound hair, and the position of his legs, Apollo's. It seems very much a confrontation between equals. Jonson holds a copy of *Bartholomew Fair,* his most vigorously and grossly realistic comedy, as is appropriate for Farquhar's own work and for the quotation from Horace's *Ars Poetica* that serves as a caption for the frame, "Tantum de medio Sumptis accedit honoris." Jonson's version of the *Ars Poetica* may provide us with a translation in context:

> I can out of knowne geare [familiar material], a fable frame,
> And so, as every man may hope the same;
> Yet he that offers at it, may sweat much,
> And toile in vaine: the excellence is such
> Of Order, and Connexion; *so much grace*
> *There comes sometimes to things of meanest place.*[1] (ll. 349–54)

That craftsmanship ("Order, and Connexion") which confers grace upon the ordinary, marks both *Bartholomew Fair* and *The Beaux' Stratagem.* The illustrator's homage to it helps clarify the motto upon Farquhar's Irish harp, "Dulce Decus," literally "sweet honor," but more specifically a reference to Horace's first Ode of Book I, where he calls his patron Maecenas his "dulce decus." Even in the presence of Apollo and Ben Jonson, his divine and artistic "patrons," Farquhar maintains his harp, his own inspiration and skill, as the agent of his sweet honor. His true patron is his genius.

If one is to take this happy compliment literally, not merely as a graphic advertising blurb, our artist is saying that Farquhar did not imitate Jonson, but achieved by his own methods what Jonson had achieved by his. This is a critical point that I should like to explore later. The artist may also be saying that we are in some way to judge Farquhar's plays as we do Jonson's; inasmuch as *Bartholomew Fair* shows Jonson's learning least of all his plays, one may suppose that the points of comparison are what the passage from the *Ars Poetica* brings up, the admirable craftsmanship of the plot, the realism of depiction and speech, and presumably the order of moral insight. Implicitly, then, if Jonson was to provide the criterion for Farquhar, one ought not to judge *The Recruiting Officer* or *The Beaux' Stratagem* by the dramatic ideals of Restoration comedy. Congreve, Wycherley, Etherege, and Vanbrugh subscribed to canons of decorum (dramatic propriety) that emphasized an ingenious variety of events rather than consistent plot, witty rather than realistic characters, and social rather than moral insight; their styles and merits differ from Jonson's or from Farquhar's, and they should not be used as yardsticks for these men.

Few critics in the eighteenth century seem to have agreed. For one thing, they accepted a hierarchy of literary kinds in which realistic comedy was ranked below "comedy of manners." Dryden, commenting on Jonson himself, says that the imitation "of folly is a lower exercise of fancy, . . . for 'tis a kind of looking downward in the poet, and representing that part of mankind which is below him." As for Jonson's language and character, "the poets of this age will be more wary than to imitate the meanness of his persons. Gentlemen will now be entertained with the follies of each other; and though they allow Cobb and Tib to speak properly, yet they are not much pleased with their tankard or with their rags. And surely their conversation can be no jest to them on the theatre, when they would avoid it in the street." [2] Pope provides the best example of this attitude in specific relation to Farquhar. Just as Congreve's excessive urbanity hinders him from depicting fools, Farquhar's excessive lowness never permits his dialogue to rise above the pert:

But in known Images of life [i.e., comedy] I guess
The labour greater, and th'Indulgence less.

Observe how seldom ev'n the best succeed:
Tell me if Congreve's Fools are Fools indeed?
What pert low Dialogue has Farqu'ar writ!
How Van[brugh] wants grace, who never wanted wit! [3]

Because he is speaking about an ideal of comedy, Pope does not discriminate between Congreve's inability to do what he tried and Farquhar's lack of desire to try something other than what he did. Intention does not matter. Although the poem grants Farquhar a rank next to Congreve among "the best," it leaves him forever doomed by his choice of style to second place. A later manifestation of this sort of criticism appears in an essay once ascribed to Goldsmith, which gave Farquhar credit for as much genius and almost as much judgment as Congreve showed, but found him far lower in "Learning" and "Versification." [4]

Other eighteenth-century critics failed to recognize a kind of dramatic skill so different from that of the Restoration playwrights. Thus a reviewer in *The Muses' Mercury* for May 1707, obviously laboring to be as generous as he could to the late Farquhar, announced that "His conduct, though not artful, was surprising; his characters, though not great, were just; his humour, though low, diverting; his dialogue, though loose and incorrect, gay and agreeable; and his wit, though not superabundant, pleasant." Another critic decided that the dialogue of *The Constant Couple* "has something too low to bear a criticism upon it, but the Gallantry, the Youth, and Gaiety of a young Man of a plentiful Fortune, is looked upon with as much Indulgence on the Stage, as in real Life, without any of those Intermixtures of Wit and Humour, which usually prepossess us in favour of such Characters in other Plays." Neither of these men can perceive Farquhar's artfulness, any more than could *The Lives of the Poets of Great Britain and Ireland* which reported that "his comedies are diverting, because his characters are natural, . . . but he has used no art in drawing them, nor does there appear any force of thinking in his performances." [5]

To insist on measuring all works by an absolute standard is a perfectly legitimate critical position; to fail to perceive artistry is a serious critical flaw. Both had the same effect in the eighteenth century, that of stifling Farquhar's serious reputation beneath a blanket of regretful disdain. Voltaire's discussion of English comedy in the *Lettres philosophiques* snubs him entirely; while Dr. Johnson's "No, Sir, I think Farquhar a man whose writings have considerable merit" very much surprised his friend Mr. Holland, who expected the usual contempt for Farquhar's works.[6] The comedies themselves were so infrequently reappraised that *A New and General Biographical Dictionary* (1798) thought itself safe in borrowing much of its commentary on Farquhar from the seventy-year-old *Works . . . To which are added some Memoirs of the Author.*

While criticism eddied thus listlessly, Farquhar's collected plays were going into more editions than those of any other playwright, comedian or tragedian, active between the Restoration and 1750. The greatest actors of the century—Garrick, Quin, Macklin, Barry, Mrs. Woffington, Mrs. Pritchard, Mrs. Clive—all appeared in his comedies. This disparity reminds one irresistibly of Farquhar's ironic commiseration with critics in his "Discourse": "What a Misfortune is it to these Gentlemen to be Natives of such an ignorant, self will'd, impertinent Island, where let a Critick and a Scholar find never so many Irregularities in a Play, yet five hundred saucy People will give him the Lie to his Face, and come to see this wicked Play Forty or Fifty times in a Year" (*341*).

The Criticks and Scholars have loosened their absolute sense of genre since the eighteenth century, and yet they have not grown much more illuminating because they have continued to neglect examining the plays closely and objectively. Some of them have replaced the generalizations of their eighteenth-century predecessors with the judicious whimsy of their own reactions: thumbs up if they prefer fresh air frolics to salons, thumbs down if not. Occasionally, biographical guesses salt their decisions: "Life was a discoloured and painful thing to him, and the only remedy was to treat it as a game . . . , a good Elizabethan romp. [He had] a fierce determination to defeat life, to rise superior to its restrictions and find an unconditioned freedom, [that] manifested itself in bursts of boisterous laughter." When the appreciative critic is intelligent, he is worth reading. But I very much doubt that one's understanding of the form and intent of a play is much enhanced by a subjective cataloguing of any reader's personal applause or dismay. The facts are not to be shied away from or warped; nor can one ignore historical context so as to try to judge seventeenth- and eighteenth-century plays by modern standards, like George Meredith's criteria for humor, or existentialist discernment.[7]

Other modern critics are at once more useful and more dangerous. These are the historical scholars, who have revived the generic criteria of the eighteenth century in the form of statements about style and development. By erecting a series of historical categories, they are able to see literary works in a sort of context, but the relative inflexibility and absolutism of the categories may distort those works made "transitional" in the system. So it has been with Farquhar, who seems to have one foot in "Restoration Comedy of Manners" and the other in "Sentimental Comedy." Scholars then have seen him shifting, sometimes clumsily and sometimes alacritously, between the two. Looked at this way, the comedies show a lack of integrity that leads one to think of their author as a man "whose temperament and environment were not much unlike those of his nineteenth-century critics, trying to write comedies like Congreve['s]." "His comedy unhappily divides itself into scenes where the Restoration attitude is for the form's sake accepted, and scenes where for the moral's sake it is condemned . . . . unconsciously torn between two irreconcilable alternatives, he finally resorts [in *The Beaux' Stratagem*], in his happiest manner, for refuge to his old device of lightly skimming the surface of his theme for fear of tumbling into a pitfall." [8]

There is keenness of insight here—admittedly transferred to imponderables about temperament from the open facts about audience demands—in recognizing Farquhar's use of tone to help him handle apparent antitheses. But that keenness is wasted and analysis frustrated when the delicacy of Farquhar's handling his own kind of play cannot be detected, cannot be conceived of, because *a priori* categories like Comedy of Manners and Sentimental Comedy admit of nothing between them. By definition, the play cannot be harmonious and thus need not be examined; by definition, the playwright must be desperate and bemused, and is worth no examination. These definitions need a rest. The whole idea of "transitional" works needs a rest, for it imposes a false measure. Any work can be considered "central," any work "transitional." Reims Cathedral can be thought of as the decadence of

Laon as well as the epitome of the "High Gothic"; Shakespeare is as much pre-Beaumont and Fletcher as they are post-Shakespearean; Johann Christian Bach offers himself as the finest example of a style, give it whatever name you will, led up to by his father's and Handel's late Baroque and followed by the clouded decadence of middle Mozart. One might call Congreve "unripe Farquhar" and discover as much disharmony of tone in him from that point of view as the *a priori* "historical" critic now finds in Farquhar, looked at as a decomposing Congreve.

However convenient the simplifications of literary history may be, and a book that has blithely talked of "Restoration Comedy" or "wit-comedy" so often is surely much obliged to them, history is in fact nominalistic. It depends on real events, real phenomena, real expressions of ideas. Its general statements should come only after the most minute and impartial inspection of particulars in context. I have tried, as much as possible, to inspect Farquhar in this way. The results, I think, have shown him a playwright of immense skill and originality. We have arrived at the point, then, at which generalizations or comparisons become salient. Perhaps it might be convenient to return to our anonymous frontispiece and its invitation to see Farquhar as a follower of Jonson's.

By now the reader ought to be convinced, if he is ever to be convinced, of Farquhar's brilliance as a manipulator of plot, so I shall not pursue that line. Farquhar's form of Jonsonian realism and moral vision, though, do need further exposition. Both realism and moral vision in Jonson depend on the theory of the humours current, at least as a part of dramatic psychology, throughout the seventeenth century. Congreve, in 1695, defined humour as "*A singular and unavoidable manner of doing, or saying any thing, Peculiar and Natural to one Man only; by which his Speech and Actions are distinguish'd from those of other men*"; but he differentiated humourous idiosyncrasy from individual affectation or habitual freakishness. Humour, unlike habit and affectation, belongs to nature and not to art, "born with us, and so of a Natural Growth, or else to be grafted into us by some accidental change in the Constitution, or revolution of the Internal Habit of Body, by which it becomes, if I may so call it, Naturaliz'd." [9] This definition coincided nicely with the one offered by Jonson in the Induction to *Every Man out of his Humour*. There the character Asper explains that within the body there is a continual flow of the four liquids "choller, melancholy, flegme, and bloud," which because of their fluid inconstancy may

> Receiue the name of Humours. Now thus farre
> It may, by *Metaphore*, apply it selfe
> Vnto the generall disposition:
> As when some one peculiar quality
> Doth so possesse a man, that it doth draw
> All his affects [feelings], his spirits, and his powers,
> In their confluctions, all to runne one way,
> This may be truly said to be a Humour.[10] (102–9)

That Jonson and Congreve start with definitions so similar serves to throw into stark relief the immense differences between them in the development of the humours. To Congreve, the humours are the finest orchard for the comic poet to pluck fruit from, since the characters subject to them can be both natural and ridiculous, in other words, plausible fools. The audience finds the characters entertaining and sympathizes with the chastening of idiosyncrasy. By this means—and I am now inducing Congreve's ideas from his practice—the witty hero can reign in a world very much like the real one. Satire serves as a means for panegyric, and vicarious superiority for the audience. For Jonson, however, the humours served a metaphysical purpose: "the man who falls into a humour becomes 'effeminate,' which is, in the traditional trope of the moral philosophers, to subvert the proper order of things by subjecting the rational soul to the appetitive soul." [11] Mind and body have their proper relationship, the violation of which is a moral fault. Here Jonson's satire focuses, on man in bondage to the arbitrary, the mechanical, the irrational.

While "in the Renaissance, 'psychology' and 'decorum' were elements of moral philosophy," [12] Farquhar's predecessors in the Restoration saw both much more narrowly as elements of technique. In their comedies, "Nature" and "natural" tended to be polarized about two related but easily differentiable meanings: (a) unaffected, gracefully achieved, as in Millamant's "Natural, easie *Suckling*" (*Way of the World* IV. iv), and (b) consonant with human needs and inclinations, as in the notion that the restraints of chastity or marriage are "unnatural." Neither meaning accounts for more than a small part of the metaphysically rich Nature presumed by Jonson as the source and reference of his comedies. Given these historical changes of thought and expression, Jonson's humour techniques for presenting a comic spectacle that would at once be natural and moral became unavailable to Farquhar, even had he wanted to make use of them. Redefinition of central terms and realignment of central interests had drained them of power.

Therefore, in the three early plays, Farquhar's insistence on treating comedy morally involved the simple imposition of moral interests upon the inherited Restoration structure. In *Love and a Bottle,* miscalculations prevented him from making the imposition graceful or convincing; in *Sir Harry Wildair,* his glibness, I think, prevented him from making it convincing. On the other hand, once one recognizes the sureness with which Farquhar undercuts Sir Harry's position in *The Constant Couple,* that play seems as successfully accomplished as its popularity might suggest. The two plays of 1702 differ markedly from the early ones. I have discussed the deliberate break of *The Twin-Rivals* from the idiom of *Love and a Bottle* and the Wildair comedies; that of *The Inconstant,* which picks up the device of fifth-act conversion, is less noticeable. But in changing Fletcher's neat amoral scheme into a fable of familial relationships and social obligations capped with a moral at the end, Farquhar has made a radical departure from Restoration practice, even from his own early practice. These comedies of 1702, especially *The Inconstant,* return to the individualism of *Love and a Bottle,* but give it a completely new twist. Both *The Inconstant* and *The Twin-Rivals* hint strongly at a return to a system of external norms. That system, which joins the moral and the natural through the idea of law, stands in back of *The Recruiting Officer* and dominates *The Beaux' Stratagem.* The fixed reference here differs from Jonson's, but like Jonson's it offers a harmony of nature and values in which dramatic representation and moral judgment may join.

Behind the technical victory of evolving a new and viable idiom for post-Restoration comedy lies a redefinition of comic form, since as we have said the elements of Jonsonian form had been drained of moral force during the seventeenth century. Farquhar makes no attempt to revive them: his excursions into the humours are quite conventional, although sometimes, as with his characterization of the melancholic Sullen, extremely successful. His originality consists in his replacing the Renaissance and Restoration emphasis on individual characters with an emphasis on relationships between characters.

The Christian concentration on the salvation of the individual soul, on man primarily responsible to his God, underlies the drama of the Renaissance, so that Elizabethan comedy and tragedy alike had dealt with the moral behavior of individuals. *Twelfth Night,* for instance, can be seen as a five act amplification of the theme of self-love as manifested in the Duke, Olivia, Malvolio, Toby, and Aguecheek. Although these characters affect one another, their comic sins are eventually referable to an absolute norm that would function just as well if they were five hermits, although if they were, their diseased passions would of course have different manifestations. The same thing is true of Shakespearean tragedy: Cleopatra, Desdemona, King Duncan are occasions for the overbearing passions of Antony and Othello and Macbeth to show themselves, and the bar before which these men are tried is that of Christian morality. The ultimate source of Shakespearean morality is what the Middle Ages called "tropological allegory," the particularization of a universal moral pattern in one man. As the seventeenth century progressed, both tragedy and comedy began to stress the censure of sin less than admiration for personal power and authority. Thus there arise the so-called heroic play in England and France, and Restoration comedy in England. Both forms turn on the assertion of personal glory, whether the hero is Dryden's Almanzor with his "I alone am King of me" or Wycherley's Horner whose pride is to be "one of the lewdest fellows" in London. While a moral nature has given way to a secularized one, in the way I have already discussed, the plays still center on the achievements of the individual. But Farquhar's do not.

In his early comedies, Farquhar tries to minimize that individualism; in his middle plays, he tries to moralize it; in his late plays, he replaces it with a drama of interrelationships. The idea of natural law, or indeed of any sort of law, supposes a system of relationships—law, as opposed to right, does not operate in isolation—and its goal is the maintenance of those relationships. Thus the punishment of individuals plays very little part in either *The Re-*

cruiting Officer or *The Beaux' Stratagem*: how easily Captain Brazen, the fop, gets off, or Lichfield's scoundrelly French! This is usually attributed to Farquhar's good humor, what one eighteenth-century critic calls his "good-natur'd Muse, not abounding over-much with Gall." Still, if one looks at the fates of Mockmode, Vizard, Smuggler, the Clinchers, and M. Marquis in the early comedies, he will see that good nature does not take one far from gall. The difference here between early and late plays is a matter of technique, not of temperament.

It might be argued, I think, that the readjustment of moral and social norms into a context of relations instead of individual absolutes was general among the Augustan writers. Maximillian Novak has recently demonstrated that Defoe, in realistic generosity to a world of fallen men, based the morality of his novels upon the principles of natural law rather than those of divine injunction.[13] In a different vein, one may examine the aphorisms of Pope's "Essay on Criticism" (1706–1711), with their insistence on judging parts only in relationship to each other, and with their own complex workings out of central terms like "wit" and "nature," in contrast to the simple series of maxims produced by such mid-seventeenth-century authors as La Rochefoucauld and Samuel Butler, or to the straightforward imitations of Horace's *Ars Poetica* written by Roscommon and Boileau.[14]

What concerns us more immediately, however, is the connection between the sort of comedy that I have been describing and the pathetic tragedy which was contemporary with it. As the heroic play died out in the 1670's, it was gradually replaced by a kind of tragedy that emphasized not the glorious deeds of the hero but his sufferings. The hero was diminished from his epic stature, and was frequently given a family and social duties. His passivity and domestication had at least two results: they were meant to make him more humanly appealing and vulnerable, but in so doing they also immersed him in a world of reciprocal actions, and raised the importance of context and surroundings in relationship to the individual. Toward the end of the seventeenth century, pathetic tragedy began to influence Restoration comedy, which had outlived its counterpart, the heroic play.

This influence also had at least two results. One was to encourage the sentimental comedy that rooted itself upon the early eighteenth-century stage, and to supply it with appropriate diction and expressive means—we have seen some of these imported into the last act of *The Inconstant* and again into Hermes Wou'dbe's blank verse in *The Twin-Rivals*. The second result was to encourage development of just such a relational comedy as we find in Farquhar's two last plays. *The Recruiting Officer* and *The Beaux' Stratagem* take over the principle of looking at the individual in context but reject the emotional goal of tears; they run, in a sense, directly parallel to the pathetic movement. In these terms, we can see that Farquhar's originality makes perfect historical sense, and can understand too that such originality might well be greeted by the London audience with so much delight. Its idiom was, in fact, their own.

Just as pathetic tragedy drifted from the florid artifices of the heroic toward an ever greater realism, Farquhar's comedies move toward a degree of natural depiction that the Restoration comedians would have shunned. There are several reasons for this. For one thing, the middle-class audience preferred characters with whom they could "identify," as modern cant puts it. Farquhar's comedies adapted their portrayal of life even more directly to bourgeois reality than Etherege's or Congreve's had to the reality of aristocrats, and pictured things as the bourgeoisie saw them rather than as the aristocrats wished they were. Not only because less artful diction suited the characters better but also because fidelity to common experience became precious to the audience, Farquhar's language loses urbanity and stylishness for an engaging spontaneity. Nature replaced artfulness, as it had done in tragedy during the last quarter of the seventeenth century. At this point, we find ourselves approaching the idea of relational drama once more. As the playwright tried more and more to imitate nature by copying it directly, relational situations tended to supplant intellectualizations and diffractions of life. Whole sets of circumstances, organized internally, replaced groupings of individual actions that referred at each point to some sort of absolute schema.

Another reason for Farquhar's realism is that the formulas of law, which suggest much about legal structure, are egalitarian: buyer and seller, murderer and victim, host and guest are all involved in relationships in which they are structurally equal, in which their individuality cannot be taken from them. "Slave" must be just as much an entity as "master." Thus the terms in which he is thinking push Farquhar to give the low characters in his comedies a kind of personal life that Restoration comedy had denied them. The servant can no longer, if he is to figure in the play, be a mere extension of his master; nor can the bumpkin exist on a different level of conception from the gentleman, a cardboard figure of clownishness grinning and scraping before a three-dimensional knight. There cannot even be the strange distinction among characters held over from romance of having a Mirabel and a Millamant in the same play with a Mincing and a Foible—the names too must be on the same level of conception. This rule of equal individuality causes the low parts of the play to be enlarged; and because of Farquhar's skill at creating widely diverse minor characters, an atmosphere of picaresque raciness blows throughout the whole comedy.[15] In such a context, the coterie appeal of verbal wit cannot thrive. All the characters must share the style of natural depiction.

Here let me pause to say that my language of cause and effect, or demand and response, represents only a way of presenting facts and my suppositions from them. Farquhar did not work his way through a play like a man in a maze, turning now toward natural law and now toward aristocratic wit to decide which lane led to the pot of gold; he certainly did not consciously evolve a network of ideas such as those that I have been trying to trace in the last few pages. Undoubtedly he worked intuitively from what interested him temperamentally and what he thought the public would like. If he was attentive to intellectual movements, and there is no sign that he was, except insofar as he had to gauge the temper of his public, most of the matters that I have been discussing would have been too blurred, too amorphous, for a man living in the early eighteenth century to come to judgments about. His choice was limited by economics and by his environment: to talk of his "ideas" in the plays is largely to construct a fiction by which to discuss the only facts we have, his actual and irrevocable achievement.

Furthermore, I cannot deny that in presenting many related reasons for a phenomenon like Farquhar's realism, I am artificially separating and schematizing the components of what was actually a single complex of ideas and emphases. It is as though one were to explain a piece of music by going through the themes, then the harmonies, then the timbres of the instruments: since language cannot deal with the simultaneity of the experience, the reader must reinterpret the formulations available to language so that he can hear the newly clarified piece of music in itself. Dealing with intellectual movements is in many ways not very different. One must begin by realizing the degree of one's crudity.

Having registered this caveat, I should like to go back to Farquhar's realism, and to turn in particular to his "pert low dialogue." Perhaps the best place to begin in dealing with the language of Restoration comedy is the brilliant analysis of Etherege's language in Dale Underwood's *Etherege and the Seventeenth-Century Comedy of Manners*. Underwood describes Etherege's language under four main rubrics:

> The language is, first of all, prevailingly "substantive" in nature. The verbs, even when they are not merely connective or "copulative," seldom carry the weight of the meaning. The weight is consistently in the nouns or in adjectives deriving from them. As a result, the language at its surface does not characteristically seem to express movement or change. The components of experience seem fixed and discrete. The sense of experience expressed by the language appears to be more a matter of "being" than "becoming." Second, it is not a sensuous language. It is only sporadically interested in projecting the immediate and concrete surfaces of experience. As a rule it deliberately abstracts that level of experience into generalized classes and categories. . . . Third, therefore, the language must be primarily concerned with establishing relationships among those [generalized classes and categories]. And [fourth] since the realities and values of the comic world are pervasively schematized, both the words and the rhetorical patterns by which their relationships are expressed also assume a schematic and oppositional character . . . the whole movement of the language becomes one of persistent parallelism or balance.[16]

Since Etherege wrote too long before Farquhar to be a fair comparison, and since Underwood's categories apply to Congreve too, we may examine comparable passages in *Way of the World* and Farquhar's plays for the purpose of illuminating "pert low dialogue" with dialogue that no one has ever thought less than exquisitely civilized.

In *The Way of the World,* I. v, Fainall and Mirabel give a "character" or set description of the eccentric knight Sir Wilfull Witwoud and his nephew:

Fain. Sir Wilfull is an odd Mixture of Bashfulness and Obstinacy. —But when he's drunk he's as loving as the Monster in the Tempest [i.e., Shakespeare's Caliban]; and much after the same manner. To give t'other his due; he has something of good Nature, and does not always want Wit.

Mira. Not always; but as often as his Memory fails him, and his common Place of Comparisons. He is a Fool with a good Memory, and some few Scraps of other Folks Wit. He is one whose Conversation can never be approv'd, yet it is now and then to be endur'd. He has indeed one good Quality, he is not Exceptious; for he so passionately affects the Reputation of understanding Raillery, that he will construe an Affront into a Jest; and call downright Rudeness and ill Language, Satire and Fire.[17]

Underwood's categories pretty clearly apply here. The verbs in Fainall's speech do very little: is, is, is, give, has, does . . . want; all the weight falls on the nouns and the two verbal adjectives, "drunk" and "loving." Mirabel's speech must be somewhat more energetic so that Congreve can build the "character" to a climax, and therefore his verbs are more striking: fails, is, is, approv'd, endur'd, has, is, affects, will construe, call. Even so, only one of the four sentences ("Conversation . . . approv'd . . . endur'd") makes its verbs do much of the work. With the possible exception of the comparison of Sir Wilfull to Caliban, the "immediate and concrete surfaces of experience" do not come into play at all, while "generalized classes and categories" hold the field. And finally, the function of the sentences in establishing relationships between the powerful nouns seems clear, as is the reflection of those relationships in the "parallelism or balance" of the sentence structure. Every sentence in both speeches manifests parallel style.

With this passage from *The Way of the World,* we may compare one from *Sir Harry Wildair,* also a "character." "Shall I tell you," says Fireball to Standard, "the Character I have heard of a fine lady?":

A fine Lady can laugh at the Death of her Husband, and cry for the loss of a Lap Dog. A fine Lady is angry without a Cause, and pleas'd without a Reason. A fine Lady has the Vapours all the Morning, and the Chollick all the Afternoon. The Pride of a fine Lady is above the merit of an understanding Head; yet her Vanity will stoop to the Adoration of a Peruke. And in fine, A fine Lady goes to Church for fashion's sake, and to the Basset-Table with Devotion; and her passion for Gaming exceeds her vanity of being thought Vertuous, or the desire of acting the contrary. (I. i, 165–66)

Perhaps this is not entirely a fair example, for the repetition of "a fine Lady" effectively removes the subject of the sentences from bearing much meaning. The temptation to use vigorous verbs thereby should increase. However, curiously enough, the only full sentence that really depends on its verbs is the first, and even there the paradox is in part carried through on the alliteration of "laugh at the Death . . . loss of a Lap Dog." "Stoop" in sentence 4 stands alone in the rest of the passage as the only hard-working verb: far stronger than its parallel in the preceding clause ("is above") and therefore weighted with contempt, "stoop" also embodies a strongly sensuous image, that of physical stooping to worship the high peruke, and leads logically into the next clause, about the lady's vanity in going to church. Otherwise, the verbs merely keep the sentences moving rhythmically and syntactically. The nouns, as in Congreve, carry the sense. Yet from this example, it surely is obvious that the "immediate and concrete surfaces of experience" are vital in Farquhar. Whereas in Congreve every common noun is abstract, Farquhar employs husbands and lapdogs, vapor, colic, perukes, and basset tables to enforce the reality of the description upon us.

Now and then, Congreve dwells on actual things. Fainall (I. v) says that "*Witwoud* grows by the Knight, like a Medlar [pear] grafted on a Crab [apple]. One will melt in your Mouth, and t'other set your Teeth on edge; one is all Pulp, and the other all Core"; to which Mirabel replies, "So one will be Rotten before he be Ripe, and the other will be Rotten without ever being Ripe at all." Or in a later scene, I. ix, Witwoud remarks that Lady Wishfort "hates *Mirabell*, worse than a Quaker hates a Parrot, or than a Fishmonger hates a hard Frost." And he is even up to talking about "the Country, where great lubberly Brothers slabber and kiss one another when they meet, like a Call of Sergeants" (II. xv). By and large, however, Congreve uses particulars for a few specific purposes: to sharpen metaphoric speech, to characterize boobies, and of course to refer to everyday objects like masks and boxes when the situation demands such references. Farquhar, in contrast, revels in his sensuous nouns; especially in the late plays, he loves speeches like Mrs. Sullen's:

He came home this Morning at his usual Hour of Four, waken'd me out of a sweet Dream of something else, by tumbling over the Tea-table, which he broke all to pieces, after his Man and he had rowl'd about the Room like sick Passengers in a Storm, he comes flounce into Bed, dead as a Salmon into a Fishmonger's Basket; his Feet cold as Ice, his Breath hot as a Furnace, and his Hands and his Face as greasy as his Flanel Night-cap.—Oh Matrimony!—He tosses up the Clothes with a barbarous swing over his Shoulders, disorders the whole Oeconomy of my Bed, leaves me half naked, and my whole Night's Comfort is the tuneable Serenade of that wakeful Nightingale, his Nose.—O the Pleasure of counting the melancholly Clock by a snoring Husband! (II.i, *135*)

"Low dialogue" in Farquhar more or less takes over the place of elegant wit. This is not to say that Farquhar could not write wittily, for he carries off the witty parts of his plays rather well, if not with the supreme polish of Wycherley or Congreve. For instance, the beaux' dialogue in Boniface's inn (I. i, *128–30*) is convincingly beau-ish. Aimwell and Archer speak with the elegant parallelism that stamps the decorum of wit:

Arch. Don't mistake me, *Aimwell,* for 'tis still my Maxim, that there is no Scandal like Rags, nor any Crime so shameful as Poverty.

Aim. The World confesses it every Day in its Practice, tho' Men won't own it for their Opinion.

They show their awareness of the town gossip in the accepted verbal fashion: "Nick Marrabone, a profess'd Pick-Pocket, and a good Bowler; but he makes a handsom Figure, and rides in his Coach, that he formerly used to ride behind." In the same vein, Jack Generous' coat is "older than any thing but its Fashion." Nearer the end of this dialogue, the beaux philosophize in the conventional verbal patterns: "Others are only Epicures in Appearances, such who shall starve their Nights to make a Figure a Days, and famish their own to feed the Eyes of others: A contrary Sort confine their Pleasures to the dark, and contract their spacious Acres to the Circuit of a Muff-string."

But Farquhar uses this excellent shuttlecocking wit only to characterize. Just as the beaux must change their opinions and interest from those which their creator so realistically provides them, so they must give up the accompanying syntax and similitudes. Their speech grows more natural and spontaneous, although never shapeless. For instance, Archer's advice to Aimwell about pressing his courtship violently (V. iii, *183*) uses balance of sentence structure only to add to the impetus of the speech; the emphasis is all on the matter, not the manner: "Press her this Minute to marry you,—now while she's hurry'd between the Palpitation of her Fear, and the Joy of her Deliverance, now while the Tide of her Spirits are at High-flood—Throw your self at her Feet; speak some *Romantick* Nonsense or other;—Address her like *Alexander* in the height of his Victory, confound her Senses, bear down her Reason, and away with her—The Priest is now in the Cellar, and dare not refuse to do the work." The staple language, so to speak, of a Farquhar comedy is this sort of sprightly and energetic, but not witty, diction.

Two reasons for Farquhar's rejecting the language of Restoration wit-comedy have already been discussed: the insistence on natural dialogue to suit natural characters, and the impulse toward establishing some sort of stylistic homogeneity in comedies filled with vital low characters. I should like to talk about two more reasons, both related to the intellectual and social functions of wit. The first of these is that Farquhar's accepting social morality made wit logically unnecessary. A witty statement, like a proverb, is a verbal indication that one knows how something else is almost sure to behave; in a witty or proverb-filled society, everyone knows how everything else is almost sure to behave. "A stitch in time saves nine" has a scientific ring to it, as a universal rule on a high level of probability and generality; so does Fainall's observation to Mirabel that "the Coldness of a losing Gamester lessens the Pleasure of the Winner" (I. i). But whereas the proverb does not insist upon actual empiricism, and can move into the realm of moral judgment or even metaphysical statement, the witty statement of the Restoration requires at least the possibility of experimental verification. Restoration wit can rarely be described as Oscar Wilde's Jack describes his in *The Importance of Being Earnest:* "It is perfectly phrased! and quite as true as any observation in civilized life should be." "Civilized life" in Restoration comedy meant truth, not the conventional tales that the great gross public was taken in by, but a truth based upon first-hand skeptical observation. The common proverb and the sententious statements of tragedy seemed empty formulas that had to be replaced, just as the conventional meanings of "honor," "virtue," "nature," and "love" had to be replaced. Wit, which was so similar in structure to the proverb, could and did supplant it artistically and intellectually.

When we come to Farquhar, especially the later Farquhar, with his use of the absolute standards of natural law, we find that he seldom has to draw upon the virtues of either proverbs or wit. He is no less empirical than the playwrights of the Restoration, but on the other hand he is sponsoring no redefinition of terms through the characters' speech. Restoration wit simply is not suitable for a play that subscribes to conventional morality. Eventually the eighteenth century developed a kind of wit that fulfilled Farquhar's empiricism and social affirmation both—this was especially true in non-dramatic works, like Pope's or Prior's—but a playwright writing when Farquhar did would have produced a very lame wit if he had tried to do the same thing. Because the audience had been well conditioned, the drama needed a cooling-off period of sorts before playwrights could introduce wit with a function radically different from that of Restoration wit.

The last reason that I shall suggest for Farquhar's abandoning Restoration wit returns to the observation that wit demonstrates intellectual control over one's environment. In Restoration comedy, where "the components of experience seem fixed and discrete," as Underwood says, the hero and the audience alike know the rules of the game. The hero then, through wit, proves his social and verbal adeptness in dealing with what he has before him. Farquhar shares with his predecessors a relatively fixed and clear area of experience, but neither the audience nor the hero knows quite how to deal with it. During the play, the audience learns rapidly; the hero takes longer, sometimes not going through a personal educative process at all. Wit is clearly impossible. Since experience in its fullest terms cannot be understood when the curtain goes up, audience and characters must be baptized again and again by reality—Farquhar's sensuous nouns do this—but cannot sustain for very long the quasi-philosophic comprehension of the world that marks the Restoration hero. Farquhar's characters rarely show much power of intellect in their formulations about the world, which is perhaps why one of the eighteenth-century critics mentioned above charges that there appears no "force of thinking in [Farquhar's] performances." Whatever force of thinking there is has been transferred from the characters' words, where it would be obvious, to the manipulation of plot, where it is far less so. The controlling intelligence behind events is always, usually only, Farquhar's.

Farquhar knows, and we know, that his characters merely illustrate a philosophical morality that they need not fully understand. The characters, however, think that they understand their world perfectly well. Therefore, their "low dialogue" is what Pope called "pert." "Pert," in the eighteenth century, had a far more pejorative sense than it does now, when people's recognition of impudence and insubordinate sauciness has been bleached by democracy. What Pope means is that Farquhar's characters speak with a kind of bright intrusiveness, that their self-assured mediocre cleverness offends the cultivated sensibility. Their lowness involves a lack of mastery which their self-confidence hides from them and leads them to betray in their language. Whether one finds the mixture of impeded competence and unimpeded blitheness offensive, as Pope presumably did, or finds it amusing, as Farquhar must have, the "pertness" is surely central to Farquhar's comic practice, and fits in perfectly well with what we have been talking about in describing its pattern.

The result of suppressing wit, of stressing low characters who might be expected to act raffishly, of thrusting the weight of empirical discovery almost entirely upon the plot, is that Farquhar wrote what we now call "situation comedy." Nothing could be more in tune with a diction depending upon things rather than ideas, or with a conception of comedy depending upon relationships rather than on individuals. Here again we may mark the way in which Farquhar altered and employed the configurations usual, if not universal, in Restoration comedy. Those plays married the wit in manipulation of events ("outwitting," as the late seventeenth century had begun to call it) with verbal wit, mastery over ideas and civilized discourse. Farquhar's demotion of verbal wit divorces these two, separating the manipulatory from the intellectual.

His heroes remain very largely in control of the immediate situations with which they find themselves faced, but they misunderstand what they ought to do: Roebuck, Sir Harry, Plume, and Aimwell have little trouble in achieving what they want to, but for each of them the love plot reveals that he can only reach knowledge by surrendering power. Roebuck and Sir Harry must give up their rakery, Plume his recruiting schemes, Aimwell his beau's stratagem. This ironic opposition between knowledge and power, so different from the Restoration pattern, shows up in the middle plays more blatantly. The last act of *The Inconstant* is a fable about this theme, and the whole structure of *The Twin-Rivals* separates those who understand from those who act. When the sense of irony is so strong as in the middle plays, "outwitting" does not bring much credit; when irony is weaker, as in the early and late plays, the hero's manipulatory skill ingratiates him with the audience despite his eventual confutation. Implicit here is an immense range of different tones which Farquhar was learning to manage, his final step in assimilating Restoration techniques to a new kind of comedy.

In this exposition of Farquhar's dramatic pattern, I have tried to reveal rather than judge. Value judgments have come up here and there as I have felt them necessary to place in perspective Farquhar's own talents and limitations, and also the potentialities and hazards of his kind of comedy. The reader ought to have a relatively clear idea of what Farquhar's genius and dramatic form could and could not do; for me to offer more would be an intrusion on that personal experience from which judgments properly emerge. Nor have I taken sides on a larger social issue, whether society lost more through the plays' refusal to pay homage to aristocratic values than it gained through their moral strength. Quite obviously, some of Farquhar's contemporaries saw these comedies as corrupters of taste; and Augustans, like any highly civilized men, recognized corruptions of taste as among the most dangerous social diseases. Whether we, from a different perspective, should view Farquhar's comedies as pernicious in broad social terms, seems to me a question of considerable importance. It is not, however, a question that this book can venture to answer.

Farquhar's antagonists probably would have found, to their dismay, that his influence grew during the course of the eighteenth century. I say "probably" because history is no more obliging than usual about offering proof of direct influence. Farquhar's moral and social ideas were quite congenial to the century, as was his pushing aside of Hobbesian cynicism for a more amiable view of human personality.[18] The great popularity of his plays, in books and on stage, must have affected other works either directly or through helping establish an atmosphere conducive to comedies like them. An examination of *The Rivals*, for instance, or *She Stoops to Conquer* will confirm that Sheridan and Goldsmith wrote on principles like Farquhar's, if not principles taken immediately from him. Connely declares that Goldsmith "turned Aimwell and Archer into Marlow and Hastings and achieved *She Stoops to Conquer*."[19] In fact resemblances go far beyond similarities of plot. Goldsmith, like Farquhar, concentrates on a scheme of natural relationships among parents, children, lovers, and travelers. Ramifications of "nature" constitute the thematic structure of the play. The city/country conflict set up at the beginning between the Hardcastles repeats that in Farquhar's two last comedies, both in statement and in resolutions. As in the Farquhar plays, the women are the chief moral educators, and as in the Farquhar plays, the brave young men must be led toward an education. Even the way the language works in Goldsmith reminds one of Farquhar. Sheridan resembles Farquhar rather less, but his plays too center upon an idea of "nature" that is handled very much as Farquhar might have, and not as any of Farquhar's predecessors might. One can say then, with full caution, that Farquhar was one of the earliest exponents of those comic ideas that inform the greatest post-Augustan comedy of the eighteenth century, and, with less caution, postulate that his personal influence was great.

If he had not died young, Farquhar would presumably have kept on writing, since he, unlike his most famous predecessors and contemporaries—Etherege, Wycherley, Congreve, Vanbrugh, Cibber—depended upon his pen for a living. How his work would have developed, what part he would have played in the literary culture of England, we cannot know. We can only wish that we and he had been given the chance to find out. "Farquhar is not a poet," wrote a Victorian lady, "and this spray from the deeps is not in him. He perceives nothing that is not." [20] We may agree; we have learned, however, not to stand quite so eagerly agape at a wash of poetic brine, but rather to reach out for enlightenment to that man who will not perceive what is not. When, like Farquhar, he will go on to perceive so much of what is, we can feel grateful.

Notes and References

1. These letters (*228–58*) were almost certainly written by one Captain Ayloffe rather than by Farquhar. See John Wilson Bowyer, *The Celebrated Mrs. Centlivre* (Durham, 1952), pp. 20–21.

2. Although I do not discuss these prologues, or the other minor poems, in this book, it seemed to me that the texts ought to be made available. In each case, I have used the first edition of the play before which the prologue appeared.

Prologue to David Crauford's *Courtship-A-la-mode* (1700):

The bus'ness of a Prologue, who can say?
I think it has no bus'ness in a Play:
For if the Play be good it need not crave it;
If bad, no Prologue on the Earth can save it.
But you plead Custom for this needless Evil,
Custom! Why ay, this Custom is the Devil.
For Custom chiefly all our ills insures;
'Tis Custom makes Men Knaves, and Women ——s.
You know the Rhime, if not, let each Man ask
His pretty little Neighbour in a Mask.
Custom makes Actors, Poets keep a pother,
And Custom starves the one, and damns the other.
Custom makes Modern Criticks snarle and bite,
And 'tis a very evil Custom makes 'em write.
'Tis Custom brings the Spark to *Sylvia's* Lap,
Custom undresses him, and Custom gives a Clap.
Why Poets write ill Plays, why Maids miscarry,
Ask why *Beaux* paint, they'll say' tis Customary.
Custom makes modern Wives break Marriage Vows,
And Custom damns most Plays at t'other House.
'Tis Custom makes our Infant Author fear,
And we plead Custom for your Kindness here.

Prologue to Francis Manning's *All for the Better: Or, the Infallible Cure* (1703):

Rejoyce the Stage—All Rural Sports are fled,
Fields cast their Green, and Trees their Beauty shed.
Nature is chill'd abroad with Winter's Rage,
And now looks only pleasing on the Stage.
Rejoyce ye *Beaux*, for now the Season comes
To hush *Bellona*, and to Silence Drums,
The Troops for Winter-quarters now come in,
And now your brisk Campaigns at home begin.
See there a Prospect of fair Wealthy Towns, [*To the Boxes.*
Stor'd with strong Magazines of Look[s] and Frowns.
Of forreign Dangers let those talk who please,
We *Beaux* will swear no Town beyond the Seas
Has kill'd us half the Men, as one of These.
But, Ladies, have a care, your time will come,
The Conquering *Venlo*[o]-Sparks are coming home.
If on the jaws of Death at honour's Call
They bravely rush'd—No pillage, but a Wall:
How would they Storm such Fortresses as those,
Whence so much sweet and wealthy Plunder flows?
Trust me, ye Fair, no strength can their's withstand,
A Soldier is a Devil—with Sword in hand.
Rejoyce ye Sparks, that walk about and huff
From *Will's* to *Tom's*, and so take Towns—and Snuff.
Ye now shall be employ'd, each have his Wench
And so perhaps ye may engage the *French*.
Rejoyce ye *Criticks*, who the Pit do Cram,
For ye shall have a glut of Plays—to damn.

Chapter One

1. The account given in this paragraph, except for the annual income of William Farquhar and the size of his family (see *DNB*), comes from manuscript material discovered by James Sutherland, and published as a letter, "New Light on George Farquhar," *Times Literary Supplement*, March 6, 1937, p. 171.

2. "The pliant Soul" is claimed as a work of the ten-year-old Farquhar in *The Works of the late Ingenious Mr. George Farquhar . . . . To which are added some Memoirs of the Author, never before Publish'd* (6th edition: London, 1728), sig. A2. The poem itself, like all of Farquhar's work quoted in this book (unless otherwise indicated) is quoted from *The Complete Works of George Farquhar*, ed. Charles Stonehill, 2 vols. (London, 1930). Italicized page numbers refer to

Volume II. For other biographical information in this and succeeding paragraphs, I am indebted to Willard Connely, *Young George Farquhar: The Restoration Drama at Twilight* (London, 1949).

3. Article on Farquhar (in alphabetical place) in David Erskine Baker, Isaac Reed, and Stephen Jones, *Biographia Dramatica; or a Companion to the Playhouse* . . . , 3 vols. (London, 1812). The anecdote about Farquhar's joke before his tutor is also from this article. The anecdote about Burnet's *History* and the bellows comes from W. R. Chetwood, *A General History of the Stage* (London, 1749), pp. 151–52.

4. Chetwood, p. 81.

5. *The Life of that Eminent Comedian Robert Wilks, Esq.* (London, 1733), p. 5. Theophilus Cibber, *et al., The Lives of the Poets of Great Britain and Ireland* (London, 1753), III, p. 125. Daniel O'Bryan, *Authentic Memoirs . . . . Of that most Celebrated Comedian, Mr. Robert Wilks* (London, 1732), p. 13.

6. O'Bryan, pp. 13–14.

7. For this information, and much other information about performances, I am indebted to *The London Stage, 1660–1800*, Part II (1700–1729), ed. Emmett L. Avery (Carbondale, Ill., 1960), and to the succeeding volumes of this invaluable series, edited 1729–1747 by Arthur Scouten (1961) and 1747–1776 by George Winchester Stone, Jr., (1962).

8. Thomas Wilkes's Life of Farquhar, prefaced to *The Works of George Farquhar,* 3 vols. (Dublin, 1775), p. v. Farquhar's letter to Mrs. Cockburn (*221*) seems to prove that *Love and a Bottle* had at least a third night.

9. "Playbill" (Boston edition), I, xii (December, 1964), p. 5.

10. *London Stage,* ed. Avery, part I, c. See pp. c-cii for authors' benefits.

11. Stonehill, p. xvii.

12. William Egerton [pseud.], *Faithful Memoirs of the Life . . . Of . . . Mrs. Anne Oldfield* (London, 1731), pp. 76–77.

13. Preface to *The Inconstant* (221). *A Comparison Between the Two Stages,* ed. S. B. Wells (Princeton, 1942), p. 32.

14. Richard Steele, Tatler 201.

15. Abel Boyer, *Achilles; or, Iphigenia In Aulis* (1700), sig. A3. John Cory, *A Cure for Jealousie* (1701), sig. A^{v}.

16. John Oldmixon, *An Essay on Criticism* (London, 1728), ed. R. J. Madden, Augustan Reprint Society, No. 107–8 (Los Angeles, 1964), p. 59.

17. *Memoirs Relating to the late Famous Mr. Tho. Brown. . . .* (London, 1704), pp. 1–2.

18. *Works* (1728), sig. A3^{v}.

19. *Memoirs . . . Tho. Brown,* p. 19.

20. Mrs. Mary Griffith Pix, *The Different Widows: or, Intrigue A-la-Mode* (1703), sig. A3.

21. Wilkes, I, ix.

22. See M. Dorothy George, *London Life in the XVIIIth Century* (London, 1925), pp. 163–65, and *passim.* It should be recalled that one could live, or rather subsist, very cheaply in the eighteenth century. For instance, Smollett's Roderick Random could rent a tiny room for two near St. Martin's Lane, where Farquhar was living in 1707, for two shillings a week; and could dine "most deliciously" for 2½d., "bread and small beer included" (Chap. xiii).

23. Wilkes, I, ix–x. Chetwood, p. 152.

24. Quoted by D. Schmid, *George Farquhar, Sein Leben und seine Original-Dramen,* Wiener Beiträge zur englischen Philologie, Band XVIII (Vienna and Leipzig, 1904), p. 245. Lord Orrery's testimonial is quoted by Sutherland, "New Light on George Farquhar."

25. Reported by Wilkes, I, xi–xii. O'Bryan, p. 25.

26. *Life of That Eminent Comedian Robert Wilks, Esq.,* p. 20.

27. Chetwood, p. 151.

28. *Works* (1728), sig. A3^{v}.

29. O'Bryan, p. 25.

30. Article on Farquhar in [William Oldys], *Biographia Britannica* (London, 1750), III, 1898. The *Biographia* is also the source of the false date for Farquhar's burial, an error occasioned by Oldys' having entrusted the research to a friend.

Chapter Two

1. Paul E. Parnell, "Equivocation in Cibber's *Love's Last Shift,*" *Studies in Philology,* LVII (1960), 519–34.

2. Adolphus Willam Ward, *A History of English Dramatic Literature to the Death of Queen Anne* (2nd edition: London, 1899), III, 482.

3. Cf. the comments of the Chevalier de Méré (1610–1685), an arbiter of manners: "Si quelqu'un me demandait en quoi consiste l'honnêteté, je dirais que ce n'est autre chose que d'exceller en tout ce qui regarde les agréments et la bienséance de la vie." Quoted by Adrien Cart and E. Labarère in their edition of Pierre Marivaux, *Le Jeu de l'Amour et du Hasard* (Paris, n.d.), p. 20.

4. For a full discussion, see John Harrington Smith, *The Gay Couple in Restoration Comedy* (Cambridge, Mass., 1948).

5. Although Stonehill's text is that of the Third Quarto (1701) at this point, Farquhar had revised this scene by the time of the Second

Quarto (January, 1700). The first Quarto (1699) has Sir Harry reacting with much more knightly fervor: "Redress your Wrongs! Instruct me, Madam: for all your Injuries ten-fold recoil'd upon me. I have abused Innocence, murder'd Honour, stabb'd it in the nicest part: A fair Lady's Fame.— Instruct me, Madam: For my Reason's fled, and hides its guilty Face, as conscious of its Master's Shame" (362). This earlier handling of the scene works for a simpler and easier reaction than the later; it makes its point, as Farquhar must have realized, only through sacrificing consistency of theme and characterization. Even at a time, 1700, when he was moving toward a use of melodrama for moral purposes, he recognized that to keep the melodrama here would falsify what he had been doing in the play, and removed it. See G. W. Whiting, "The Date of the Second Edition of *The Constant Couple*," *Modern Language Notes*, XLVII (1932), 147–48.

6. For newspaper accounts, and for a sense of English attitudes about the Jubilee, I am indebted to Richard Morton and William M. Peterson, "The Jubilee of 1700 and Farquhar's *The Constant Couple*," *Notes and Queries*, CC (1955), 521–25.

7. Article, "Jubilee," in [Daniel Defoe ?], *Dictionarium Sacrum seu Religiosum. A Dictionary of All Religions, Ancient and Modern* (London, 1704).

8. *Wit and Mirth: Or, Pills to Purge Melancholy*, ed. Thomas D'Urfey (1719–1720) (Facsimile reproduction of reprint, 1876: New York, 1959), V, 264–66.

9. *An Apology for the Life of Mr. Colley Cibber Written by Himself*, ed. Robert W. Lowe (London, 1889), II, 241.

10. For detailed discussion of farce and farceurs between the Restoration and the mid-eighteenth century, Leo Hughes, *A Century of English Farce* (Princeton, 1956), is extremely helpful.

Chapter Three

1. *A Short View of the Immorality and Profaneness of the English Stage, Together with the Sense of Antiquity upon this Argument* (London, 1698), pp. 155–56, sigs. L6, L6ᵛ; excerpted in *Critical Essays of the Seventeenth Century*, ed. J. E. Spingarn (Oxford, 1908), III, 263.

2. "Rules For Self-Examination, Extracted out of the Writings of an Eminent Divine, very necessary for Christians at all Times . . . ," (London, 1685), broadside.

3. Alexandre Beljame, *Men of Letters and the English Public in the Eighteenth Century* . . . , trans. E. O. Lorimer, ed. Bonamy Dobrée (London, 1948), pp. 230–43, brings up a number of these points. Also see Sister Rose Anthony, *The Jeremy Collier Stage Con-*

troversy, 1698–1726 (Milwaukee, 1937) and Joseph Wood Krutch, *Comedy and Conscience after the Restoration* (2nd printing: New York, 1949) for detailed discussion of the controversy.

4. Krutch, pp. 264–71. This bibliography, compiled by Gellert S. Alleman and Krutch, does not include tangential references like Farquhar's.

5. Quoted by Stonehill, p. 84.

6. *Short View*, p. 2, sig. B^{v}. (Not in Spingarn.)

7. Wilkes (I, x) claims that *The Twin-Rivals* ran thirteen nights and "met with good success." Since the latter contradicts Farquhar's own statement, and since Wilkes has the wrong year (1705), this testimony cannot be believed. Furthermore, Shadwell's *Lancashire Witches* was playing at Drury Lane on December 22, only eight days after *The Twin-Rivals'* opening on the 14th. (See *London Stage*, ed. Avery, I, 30.)

8. See Richard Hindry Barker, *Mr. Cibber of Drury Lane* (New York, 1939) for discussion of Cibber's notoriety as Richard III.

9. *King Lear*, rev. Nahum Tate (London, 1689), sigs. H2, D4. Connely, p. 193, also notes the closeness of Benjamin's speech to Edmund's.

10. The phrase, applied to the heroic play, comes from Arthur C. Kirsch, "The Significance of Dryden's 'Aureng-Zebe'," *ELH: A Journal of English Literary History*, XXIX (1962), 166.

11. Frederick Wood, "The Beginnings and Significance of Sentimental Comedy," *Anglia*, LV (1931), 370, remarks that "sentimental comedy" was "an attempt to write comedy by the methods of tragedy." This, although oversimplified, has a great deal of truth to it. Dennis complained that Steele's comic theories would better have suited happily ending tragedy; and E. N. Hooker (*The Critical Works of John Dennis*, II (Baltimore, 1943), p. 501) quotes Benjamin Victor as having bluntly said that "that part of Comedy . . . [seems] best which is nearest Tragedy."

12. John Harrington Smith, p. 203. Kaspar Spinner, *George Farquhar als Dramatiker* (*Swiss Studies in English*, XL, Bern, 1956) points out that in the earlier Farquhar plays each couple is made up of one sober and one "wild" member. *The Twin-Rivals*, which is more interested in the lovers' unity than in lovers' conflicts, alters the pattern. The villain Richmore's slander of Aurelia produces the one such conflict, and its resolution comes only when villainy is rendered impotent; the resolution cannot be generated from the lovers themselves.

13. Farquhar himself, since he was so friendly with Wilks, may have suggested casting Wilks and Jane Rogers, who had played gay

leads in his earlier comedies, as the sober couple. Such use of the audience's sense of actors' usual roles adds to the evidence favoring Farquhar's having deliberately recalled Cibber's Richard III.

14. (London, 1704), sig. a3v. For examples from contemporary criticism of tragedy that specifically called for such vicarious benevolence, see my "English Tragic Theory in the Late Seventeenth Century," *ELH: A Journal of English Literary History,* XXIX (1962), 306–23.

Chapter Four

1. Antoine Adam, *Romanciers du XVIIe Siècle* (Paris, 1958), p. 47.
2. *Scarron's City Romance, Made English* (London, 1671), pp. 45–46, sigs. D7–D7v.
3. Sir Paul Harvey, in Sir Paul Harvey and J. E. Heseltine, *The Oxford Companion to French Literature* (Oxford, 1959), writes in the article on the *Roman Bourgeois* that "All is told with simple realism (though without charm or gaiety), giving a picture of *bourgeois* life such as we find in a novel of Balzac [*sic*], but without the drama." And Adam, in his monumental *Histoire de la Littérature Française au XVIIe Siècle,* IV (Paris, 1954), 195, says that Furetière "n'atteint que la surface des choses. Il les décrit longuement, implacablement, comme pourrait le faire un myope. La réalité, avec ses arrière-plans, ses jeux complexes de forces, ses foyers d'activité secrets, lui échappe." Adam's assessment of Furetière recalls Dr. Johnson's of Fielding, and seems to me just as inadequate.
4. *City Romance,* p. 60, sig. E6v.
5. *City Romance,* p. 85, sig. G3.
6. This declaration may not be quite so open as it seems, however. "Et quorum pars magna fui" comes from the *Aeneid* II, 6, just before Aeneas tells Dido of the fall of Troy. In this small and pointedly unepical tale of Farquhar's, suggesting such a context smacks of deliberate mock-heroic, in harmony with the use of the names "Peregrine" and "Lord C——" to parody Farquhar's high patriotic dedication of *Love and a Bottle* to Peregrine, Lord Carmarthen. These may be private jokes to some extent, but they indicate something of Farquhar's attitude in writing.
7. "He found her in an Undress sitting on her Beds-feet in a very Melancholy posture; her Nightgown carelessly loose discovered her Snowy Breasts, which Agitated by the violence of her Sighs, heaved and fell with a most Languishing motion . . ." (*212*). This sort of romantic description can only be set within a context of pretense and cheat.

8. Arthur Colby Sprague, *Beaumont and Fletcher on the Restoration Stage* (Cambridge, Mass., 1926), p. 122.

9. See John Harold Wilson, *The Influence of Beaumont and Fletcher on Restoration Drama* (Columbus, 1928), pp. 10, 49, 143.

10. Although in the seventeenth century the joint authorship of *The Wild Goose-Chase* seems to have been widely accepted, modern scholarship attributes the play to Fletcher alone. See G. E. Bentley, *The Jacobean and Caroline Stage,* III (Oxford, 1956), pp. 426, 430.

11. Quotations from *The Wild Goose-Chase* come from Francis Beaumont and John Fletcher, *Works,* eds. Arnold Glover and A. R. Waller, IV (Cambridge, 1906). I have inserted page references to this edition after the act and scene references in the text of this chapter.

12. Sprague, p. 253.

13. Sir E. K. Chambers, *William Shakespeare, A Study of Facts and Problems* (Oxford, 1930), I, 83. Bentley, II (Oxford, 1941), pp. 499–506. John Genest, *Some Account of the English Stage, from the Restoration in 1660 to 1830* (Bath, 1832), III, 594–96.

14. Many of the characteristics that differentiate *The Inconstant* from *The Wild-Goose Chase* occur in Beaumont and Fletcher, but in their tragicomedies rather than their comedies—in particular, this is true of devices to hold the passions of the audience in suspense, of engaging their empathy. See Arthur Mizener, "The High Design of *A King and No King,*" *Modern Philology,* XXXVIII (1940), 133–54; and Eugene Waith, *The Pattern of Tragicomedy in Beaumont and Fletcher* (New Haven, 1952).

Chapter Five

1. Dennis, Preface to "The Court of Death," *Critical Works,* I, 42. John Dryden, *Essays,* ed. W. P Ker (Oxford, 1926), "Preface to *Sylvae,*" I, 267. If one looks in a seventeenth-century collection of critical opinions, like Thomas Pope Blount's *De Re Poetica* (London, 1694), he finds unanimity about the characteristics of the Pindaric ode: Blount, for instance, not only quotes Dryden (p. 66, sig. K^v) but also Rapin, who calls for "Nobleness, Elevation, and Transport" and Norris, who explains that the ode is at times to move peaceably and at times "like an impetuous Torrent, to *roul* on extravagantly, and carry all before it" (pp. 65, 67; sigs. K, K2). Example and precept were accessible in profusion for the new poet, so that someone like Farquhar must have had an absolutely clear idea of what he was doing and how he was to go about it, when working within a set genre.

For the relevant history of the Pindaric ode, see Carol Maddison,

Apollo and the Nine (London, 1960), which ends with Cowley; George N. Shuster, *The English Ode from Milton to Keats* (New York, 1940); and Norman MacLean, "From Action to Image" in *Critics and Criticism,* ed. R. S. Crane (Chicago, 1952), which discusses the Pindaric ode as part of its general discussion of the eighteenth-century lyric. MacLean discusses various critics of the ode, pp. 422–25.

2. "A Discourse on the Pindarique Ode," prefaced to *A Pindarique Ode, Humbly Offer'd to the Queen* (London, 1706).

3. *English Historical Documents 1660–1714,* ed. Andrew Browning (London, 1953), pp. 753–55. *The Glorious Life and Heroick Actions of . . . William III* (London, 1702), sigs. E12v–F.

4. Margaret Farquhar's undated letter has been reprinted by the Historical Manuscripts Commission, 15th Report, Appendix, Part IV, MSS Duke of Portland, Vol. IV: she writes Harley that the Duchess of Devonshire has been the Queen's intermediary in presenting her with ten guineas. G. M. Trevelyan, *The Peace and the Protestant Succession* (*England Under Queen Anne,* Vol. III) (London, 1934) mentions, p. 40 n., that Margaret Farquhar received three payments of £10 each from the secret service funds, but remains reticent about dates or possible reasons for the payments.

The career of the Earl of Peterborough can be followed in Colin Ballard, *The Great Earl of Peterborough* (London, 1929).

5. *Comparison Between the Two Stages,* p. 93.

6. *The Lover's Secretary . . . . Being a Collection of Billets Deux, Letters Amorous, Letters Tender, and Letters of Praise* (London, 1692), p. 30, sig. C3v.

7. John Stowe, *A Survey of the Cities of London and Westminster,* ed. and augm. John Strype, 6 bks. in 2 vols. (London, 1720), VI, 85. Hugh Phillips, *Mid-Georgian London* (London, 1964), p. 238.

8. Samuel Richardson, *Clarissa. Or, the History of a Young Lady* (6th ed.: London, 1768), I, xi.

9. Oldmixon, *Essay on Criticism,* p. 59.

10. [Abel Boyer], *The History of King William the Third,* III (London, 1703), 439, 451. Keith Feiling, *A History of the Tory Party 1640–1714* (Oxford, 1924) documents Tory attacks on the Dutch, pp. 337–40.

11. *English Historical Documents 1660–1714,* p. 134.

12. Gilbert Burnet, *History of His Own Time,* II (London, 1734), 134. Also see Ellen Douglass Leyburn, "Swift's View of the Dutch," *Publications of the Modern Language Association of America,* LXVI (1951), 734–45.

13. John Tutchin, *Selected Poems,* ed. Spiro Peterson, Augustan

Reprint Society, No. 110 (Los Angeles, 1964), pp. 5, 6. (The pages of the reprint are not numbered, so that each selection is separately paginated as in the original texts.)

14. Daniel Defoe, "The True Born *Englishman.* A Satyr" (London, 1701), in *Later Stuart Tracts,* ed. George A. Aitken (Westminster, 1903), p. 112.

15. See G. M. Trevelyan, *Blenheim* (*England Under Queen Anne,* Vol. I) (London, 1930), p. 420: "Whigs declared . . . that Rooke had no merit at all."

16. John Harold Wilson, *The Influence of Beaumont and Fletcher,* p. 19.

17. Molière, *Théâtre complet,* ed. Robert Jouanny (Paris, 1962), I, 365.

18. Dennis, *Critical Works,* I, 145.

19. Collier, *Short View,* p. 228, sig. Q2^{v}. In Spingarn, III, 288–89.

20. R. F. Jones, "The Background of the Attack on Science in the Age of Pope," in *Eighteenth-Century English Literature,* ed. James L. Clifford (New York, 1959), p. 69. This article, *passim,* connects scientific practicality with Protestantism, as does Jones's *Ancients and Moderns: a study of the background of the Battle of the Books* (*Washington University Studies in Language and Literature,* no. 6) (St. Louis, 1936), which has become the standard work on this subject.

21. Oldmixon, *Essay on Criticism,* p. 62; and see pp. 7 ff.

22. Dryden, Preface to *All for Love, Essays,* ed. Ker, I, 195.

23. John Tillotson, *Works* (10th ed.: London, 1735), sermon XXVIII, vol. I, 258.

24. Sir Roger L'Estrange, *Fables of Aesop And other Eminent Mythologists: with Morals and Reflections* (7th ed.: London, 1724), sigs. A3^{v}–A4. Since an engraving facing the first page of the life of Aesop in L'Estrange's edition shows Aesop holding a scroll marked "Utile dulci," one can guess where Farquhar learned about Aesop's motto.

25. *The Works of Sir William Temple, Bart.* (London, 1720), I, 247–48. Charles Gildon comes closer to Farquhar's position when he says that "regard must be had to the *Humour, Custom,* and *Inclination* of the Auditory; but an *English* Audience will never be pleas'd with a dry, Jejune, and formal Method that excludes Variety as the Religious observation of the Rules of *Aristotle* does." *Miscellaneous Letters and Essays, On several Subjects . . . . By several Gentlemen and Ladies* (London, 1694).

26. [Abel Boyer], *The English Theophrastus: or, the Manners of the Age* (London, 1702), ed. W. Earl Britton, The Augustan Reprint Society, Ser. I, No. 3 (Los Angeles, 1947), pp. 12–13. Boyer, who

accepts Farquhar's manner of reasoning, comes to conclusions as different from Farquhar's as those of André Dacier, who maintains the absolute jurisdiction of Aristotle in tragedy. Dacier wrote ten years before Farquhar, and Farquhar gives no indication of having read Dacier, but they are obviously familiar with the same body of argument. To read Farquhar, Boyer, and Dacier is to sustain one's faith in the intellectual coherence of the period, and to make one despair of establishing any satisfying logic of premises, argumentative techniques, and conclusions.

27. Lee Andrew Elioseff, *The Cultural Milieu of Addison's Literary Criticism* (Austin, Texas, 1963), pp. 137, 141. Elioseff's book is of extraordinary value in helping one comprehend the changes in critical attitudes and values in the early eighteenth century, and much of his work is tangential to the critical interests of the "Discourse."

Chapter Six

1. *Scarron's Comical Romance of a Company of Stage Players*, Part II, Chap. xiv, in *The Whole Comical Works of Monsr. Scarron*, trans. Thomas Brown, *et al.* (London, 1703), pp. 176–200. This is one of several editions of Sophia's story, "The Judge in her own Cause," that would have been available to Farquhar.

2. Two articles by Robert L. Hough in *Notes and Queries* discuss all these errors save the bumpkins' change of names: "An Error in 'The Recruiting Officer'" and "Farquhar: 'The Recruiting Officer'," in vols. CXCVIII (1953), 340–41, and CXCIX (1954), 474, respectively.

3. William Gaskill's otherwise excellent production of *The Recruiting Officer* at the National Theater in London (1963) tried to stress skeptical anti-heroic elements, even to the extent of minor tampering with Farquhar's text. One proof of Farquhar's deep militarism is that Gaskill's careful changes of stress and text seemed discordant and failed of their effect.

4. Farquhar's handling of this scene may be contrasted with that of Bertold Brecht, who adapted *The Recruiting Officer* in 1955 as *Pauken und Trompeten* (*Drums and Trumpets*). Brecht, who turns the play into a piece of pacifistic zealotry, ends the scene with Kite's herding the recruits into the barracks, in a rigid repetition of the action of confinement. Without Farquhar's rhetoric of good feelings, the only pleasure in the scene is cruel. A general comparison of *Pauken und Trompeten* with *The Recruiting Officer* illustrates much about Farquhar's methods; unfortunately, it is outside the scope of this study.

5. *Pills to Purge Melancholy*, V, 316–21.

6. I am indebted to Professor John Anson for pointing out to me the possibility of reading Viola's disguise as a central creative act.

Chapter Seven

1. Stonehill (xxvi) quotes an obituary for Bond appearing in *The Grand Magazine* at the time of Bond's death in late December, 1758; this may be the source for the *Gentleman's Magazine* obituary that I have quoted here. Harwood's *History and Antiquities* was published in Gloucester, in 1806; the references to Farquhar occur on p. 501.

2. Paul Mueschke and Jeanette Fleisher, "A Re-evaluation of Vanbrugh," *Publications of the Modern Language Association of America,* XLIX (Sept., 1934), 848–89, call attention to Vanbrugh's interest in "a new code of social values." They dwell—rather too much, I think—on Vanbrugh's social conscience, and make little distinction between his attitudes and those of Farquhar. As I have pointed out in discussing *The Twin-Rivals,* and point out again in this chapter, Farquhar was conscious of differences between himself and Vanbrugh; I have not emphasized, as Mueschke and Fleisher undoubtedly would, that the very forms of Farquhar's parodying Vanbrugh suggest a kinship between them. Etherege and Wycherley are so removed from Farquhar that he could not make his dramatic points precisely by parodying them.

3. My references to Vanbrugh come from *The Complete Works of Sir John Vanbrugh,* the plays edited by Bonamy Dobrée, 4 vols. (London, 1927). The seduction scene is IV. iii (Vol. I, pp. 68–69). The speech by Berinthia quoted below, beginning "Like Man and Wife, asunder" comes from II. i, 45.

4. Vanbrugh, I, 209.

5. This discovery and my examples are due to the researches of Martin A. Larson, "The Influence of Milton's Divorce Tracts on Farquhar's *Beaux' Stratagem,*" *Publication of the Modern Language Association of America,* XXXIX (1924), 174–78.

6. Connely, pp. 283–84.

7. William Burnaby, *The Ladies Visiting-Day* (1701) in *The Dramatic Works of William Burnaby* (London, 1931), p. 270.

8. Gellert Alleman, *Matrimonial Law and the Materials of Restoration Comedy* (Philadelphia, 1942), p. 112.

9. John Chamberlayne, *Magnae Britanniae Notitia: Or, the Present State of Great Britain* (London, 1718), part I, book iii, pp. 176–77. This standard handbook—the edition that I cite is the twenty-fifth after 1669—presents what most Englishmen would have thought the

salient points about women's legal rights. For a more detailed discussion, see *Baron and Feme. A Treatise of the Common Law Concerning Husbands and Wives* (London, 1700).

10. Vanburgh, I, 207; Sir John's " 'tis a Moot Point," I, 181.

11. John Locke, *Essays on the Law of Nature,* ed. and trans. W. von Leyden (corr. ed.: London, 1958), p. 111; pp. 49–50. The former reference is to Locke's text in von Leyden's translation; the latter to von Leyden's introduction.

12. Samuel Pufendorf, *Elementorum Jurisprudentiae Universalis Libri II* (Cambridge, 1672), p. 183.

13. Perhaps the association of "Boniface" with the Popes might have acted to denigrate the name with the Protestant English, and also to link the innkeeper with the Catholic Bellair and "Foigard."

14. It is significant that Gibbet (IV.i, *174*) speaks of the robbery in terms of an inverted patriotism, calling the thieves' depredations "a *Vigo* Business" in reference to Rooke's great naval victory of 1702. His earlier imposture as a captain is parodic in the same way.

15. George Cheyne, M.D., *The English Malady* (London, 1733), pp. 163, 180 81, xii.

16. Alleman, pp. 106–7.

17. Furthermore, as late as the end of the last scene (*187*), Archer is still referring to Cherry as "my Wench," in Mrs. Sullen's and Sir Charles' presence.

Chapter Eight

1. Connely reproduces the picture facing p. 225. The quotation from Jonson, italics mine, comes from "Horace, of the Art of Poetrie," *The Complete Poetry of Ben Jonson,* ed. William B. Hunter, Jr. (New York, 1963), p. 299.

2. Dryden, *Essays,* "Defence of the Epilogue," I, 172, 177.

3. Alexander Pope, "The First Epistle of the Second Book of *Horace,*" *Imitations of Horace,* ed. John Butt (2nd edition, corrected: London and New Haven, 1961), p. 219, lines 284–89.

4. Quoted by Schmidt, p. 369.

5. *Muses' Mercury* quoted by Connely, p. 304. "Something too low . . ." comes from a letter written to Mrs. Oldfield by "William Egerton," *Faithful Memoirs of . . . Mrs. Oldfield,* pp. 112–13; the comment has been lifted from Tatler 19, written in 1709, twenty-two years earlier than *Faithful Memoirs. Lives of the Poets,* III, 136.

6. *Boswell's Life of Johnson,* ed. R. W. Chapman (London, 1952), p. 1070.

7. "Life was . . . laughter" comes from Bonamy Dobrée, *Restora-*

tion Comedy 1660–1720 (Oxford, 1924), p. 167. H. T. E. Perry, *The Comic Spirit in Restoration Drama* (New Haven, 1925) measures Restoration comedy by Meredith's standards.

8. John Palmer, *The Comedy of Manners* (London, 1913), p. 268.

9. William Congreve, "Concerning Humour in Comedy," Spingarn, III, 248, 246.

10. Ben Jonson, Induction to *Every Man out of his Humour, Ben Jonson,* eds. C. H. Herford and Percy Simpson, III (Oxford, 1927), p. 432.

11. James D. Redwine, Jr., "Beyond Psychology: the Moral Basis of Jonson's Theory of Humour Characterization," *ELH: A Journal of English Literary History,* XXVIII (1961), 323.

12. Redwine, p. 326.

13. Maximillian E. Novak, *Defoe and the Nature of Man* (London, 1963).

14. Sheldon Sacks, *Fiction and the Shape of Belief* (Berkeley and Los Angeles, 1964), describes a related technique of Fielding's. In speaking of "situation characters," who are defined by a single trait for the benefit of a single situation, Sacks remarks: "When we reduce each of the situation characters to his limited component, their ethical characterization may seem oversimplified and shallow. . . . This does not derogate from Fielding's artistry, since it is by simplifying them, reducing them to a single function, yet presenting them in an animated, witty fashion that he is able to present a world in which value judgments are complicated indeed, where morality is never reduced to an aphorism. Each of them is simplified; what their interaction reveals is highly complex" (pp. 98–99). Farquhar's characters are no more reduced and simplified than is common in Restoration comedy —indeed, Fielding's simplifications may be an attempt to reproduce stage effects in novelistic terms—but the reliance on vividness and interaction marks an important area of similarity between the comic techniques of the two men.

15. This picaresque quality has been noted by J. Hamard, review of *George Farquhar als Dramatiker, Etudes Anglaises,* XII (1959), 67–68.

16. Dale Underwood, *Etherege and the Seventeenth-Century Comedy of Manners* (Yale Studies in English, 135) (New Haven, 1957), pp. 94–95.

17. My quotations from Congreve come from William Congreve, *Comedies,* ed. Bonamy Dobrée (London, 1925).

18. Hamard, p. 67, declares that "à Trinity College il s'emprégna de la philosophie de Locke, qui, avec lui, remplaça dans la comédie anglaise la vision pessimiste et hautaine de Hobbes." Within the con-

fines of a review, of course, Hamard cannot document this contention, so that one can hardly pass on its merits.

19. Connely, p. 316.

20. Louise Imogen Guiney, *A Little English Gallery* (New York, 1894), pp. 134–35.

Selected Bibliography

Primary Source

The Complete Works of George Farquhar. Ed. Charles Stonehill. 2 vols. London: Nonesuch Press, 1930. This is the only reasonably scholarly edition of Farquhar's works. Its discussions and annotations are occasionally misleading or inadequate—the last two hundred pages or so of the second volume have been left completely unannotated—but by and large they are helpful. The volumes are handsome and easy to read.

Secondary Sources

I have excluded eighteenth-century materials from this list, since they are all gathered in the footnotes to chapters 1 and 8.

ARCHER, WILLIAM, ed. *George Farquhar* (Mermaid series). London and New York: T. F. Unwin, 1906. Like Strauss's preface to his edition of selected works of Farquhar's (see below), Archer's preface is lively and intelligent. If it is not incisively analytical or free from certain Victorian bigotries, it is nevertheless sensitive to the importance and *esprit* of Farquhar's plays.

BERMAN, RONALD. "The Comedy of Reason," *Texas Studies in Literature and Language,* VII (1965), 161–68. Concentrates on the rational obsession with money in *The Beaux' Stratagem.* Berman concludes that the play is paradoxical: "The play has stated that nothing is durable except money, and we can see that money is not durable. It then offers the statement that nothing is necessary but passion, and we already have a sense of how far that is durable."

CONNELY, WILLARD. *Young George Farquhar: The Restoration Drama at Twilight.* London: Cassel, 1949. Connely's biography is useful as a source of information, all of which must, however, be carefully checked. Many of Connely's surmises and some of his "facts" are dubious or wrong. His criticism of Farquhar's work is negligible.

DOBRÉE, BONAMY. *Restoration Comedy 1660–1720.* Oxford Univ., 1924. Dobrée's discussion of Farquhar makes some interesting points, but is hardly penetrating; his criticism is too often impressionistic or arbitrary. His later remarks on Farquhar in *English Literature in the Early Eighteenth Century* (Oxford History of English Literature, VII [Oxford Univ., 1959]), pp. 223–34, are embarrassing—they misquote, misstate, and say little.

HELDT, W. "Fletcher's *Wild-Goose Chase* and Farquhar's *Inconstant,*" *Neophilogus,* III (1917), 144–48. Attributes the changes that Farquhar made to a desire for increased verisimilitude and for a Restoration tone of coarseness and contemporary allusion. Heldt does not distinguish Farquhar's basic intent from Fletcher's.

HOUGH, ROBERT L. "An Error in 'The Recruiting Officer'," and "Farquhar: 'The Recruiting Officer'," in *Notes and Queries,* CXCVIII (1953), 340–41, and CXCIX (1954), 474, respectively. These notes are summarized in Chapter 6.

JAMES, EUGENE NELSON. "The Burlesque of Restoration Comedy in *Love and a Bottle,*" *Studies in English Literature,* V (1965), 469–90. Advances the improbable thesis that the novice Farquhar satirized through statement and parody the mode of Restoration comedy in *Love and a Bottle.*

KAVANAGH, PETER. "George Farquhar," letter in *The Times Literary Supplement* (Feb. 10, 1945), p. 72. About Farquhar's having been disciplined while in college.

LARSON, MARTIN A. "The Influence of Milton's Divorce Tracts on Farquhar's *Beaux' Stratagem,*" *Publications of the Modern Language Association of America,* XXXIX (1924), 174–78. Straightforward presentation of parallels between Milton and Farquhar. See discussion in Chapter 7.

MORTON, RICHARD and WILLIAM M. PETERSON. "The Jubilee of 1700 and Farquhar's *The Constant Couple,*" *Notes and Queries,* CC (1955), 521–25. Morton and Peterson refer to Farquhar tangentially in their detailed account of English reactions to the Papal Jubilee of 1700.

NICOLL, ALLARDYCE. *A History of English Drama 1660–1900,* Vols I and II. Cambridge Univ., 1923 and 1925 (and subsequent revisions). The commentary on Farquhar is of necessity brief, and is also, I think, insensitive; but Nicoll is invaluable for providing a context of works within which Farquhar wrote.

PALMER, JOHN. *The Comedy of Manners.* London: G. Bell and Sons, 1913. This important and perceptive book operates on the thesis that the airy amorality of Restoration comedy marked a peak from which Vanbrugh and still more Farquhar sadly lapsed. If one disagrees with Palmer's bias, and denies his insistence that Farquhar was trying awkwardly to write like Congreve, one can still translate his keen perceptions about the plays into terms less dependent on a univocal system of dramatic values, and still find them illuminating.

PERRY, H. T. E. *The Comic Spirit in Restoration Drama*. New York: Russell and Russell, 1962. Perry chooses the same five dramatists to discuss as does Palmer: Etherege, Wycherley, Congreve, Vanbrugh, and Farquhar. His testing them by Meredith's theories of the comic, mixed with a modicum of historical criticism, produces a rather thin and platitudinous set of essays.

PYLE, FITZROY. "George Farquhar (1677–1707)," *Hermathena*, XCII (1958), 3–30. Wholly derivative, this general account is without interest.

ROSENFELD, SYBIL. "Notes on *The Recruiting Officer*," *Theatre Notebook*, XVIII (Winter, 1963/4), 47–48. Miss Rosenfeld's brief popular article talks about the original casting of *The Recruiting Officer*, and Farquhar's exploitation of the known talents of the Drury Lane company.

ROTHSTEIN, ERIC. "Farquhar's *Twin-Rivals* and the Reform of Comedy," *Publications of the Modern Language Association of America*, LXXIX (March, 1964), 33–41. The substance of this article forms Chapter 3 of this book. The article—which has a few footnotes of interest to the scholar, perhaps, that are not in this book—is marred by somewhat heavy-handed simplification of the ethos of Farquhar's three early plays.

SCHMID, D. *George Farquhar, Sein Leben und Seine Original-Dramen*. Wiener Beiträge zur Englischen Philologie, XVIII. Vienna and Leipzig, 1904. A book of great interest when first written, Schmid's critical biography now seems outdated. Most of the analyses of plays consist of plot summary.

SPINNER, KASPAR. *George Farquhar als Dramatiker. Swiss Studies in English*, XL (Bern, 1956). At the time of this writing, Spinner's is the only critical book about Farquhar available. Much of the book is deadwood, because of Spinner's urge to categorize and arrange literary techniques whether the categories and arrangements serve a further purpose or not. Some individual critical comments are acute. See the review of this book by J. Hamard, *Etudes Anglaises*, XII (1959), 67–68.

SPRAGUE, ARTHUR COLBY. *Beaumont and Fletcher on the Restoration Stage*. Cambridge, Mass.: 1926. Sprague not only provides a context for Farquhar's adaptation of *The Wild-Goose Chase* but offers a detailed comparison of the two plays. His discussion is vitiated by his assumption (see Heldt above) that Farquhar and Fletcher wrote with similar dramatic intentions.

STRAUSS, LOUIS A., ed. *A Discourse upon Comedy, The Recruiting Officer, and The Beaux Stratagem.* Boston and London: D. C. Heath & Co. 1914. Strauss' long preface—fifty pages—stands as the best single essay on Farquhar, if one takes into account the biases of the age in which it was written.

SUTHERLAND, JAMES. "New Light on George Farquhar," letter in *Times Literary Supplement* (March 6, 1937), p. 371. This letter publishes important manuscript material, including petitions by Margaret Farquhar making certain biographical claims about her husband.

WHITING, G. W. "The Date of the Second Edition of *The Constant Couple,*" *Modern Language Notes,* XLVII (1932), 147–48. Demonstrates that Farquhar's revision of the last act of *The Constant Couple* was incorporated into the playing text soon after the original production.

Index